Fred,

With sincere best wishes.
Look forward to our paths crossing again.

Glenn Roy

Entrepreneur
—— OR ——
Employee?

*Should You Get Out
Or Stay In Your Current Job?*

By
Ken Chane and Glenn Poy

First Edition

Copyright © 1997 by Ken Chane and Glenn Poy
All rights reserved
Including the right of reproduction
in whole or in part in any form.

The Vanalden Press
9755 Independence Avenue
Chatsworth, CA 91311

Manufactured in the United States of America

Library of Congress Cataloging-in-Publication Data
Library of Congress Catalog Card Number: 96-90996

Chane, Ken and Poy, Glenn
    Entrepreneur or Employee? Should You Get Out Or Stay In Your Current Job?
    ISBN 1-890147-04-4
    1. Small Business. 2. Career Management
1. Title

*To the dispirited employee
who experiences the futility and loss of control
caused by turmoil in the workplace…
There is hope!*

The Two Authors Wish To Thank

Robert Mischel our "matchmaker" and good friend. Bob is responsible for introducing us to one another.

Our beta readers for their critique of our original text, and their excellent recommendations for improvement:

Mary Akpovi, Encino, California
Holly Blefgen, Campbellcroft, Ontario, Canada
Peter Chane, Seattle, Washington
Howard Hatoff, Philadelphia, Pennsylvania
Gregory Hocking, Markham, Ontario, Canada
Angela Matthews, Richmond Hill, Ontario, Canada
Robert Mischel, Agoura Hills, California
Janice Rooney, Toronto, Ontario, Canada
Lynn Shook, Thousand Oaks, California

Jan Kingaard of The Kingaard Organization International, whose knowledge of the book industry, editing proficiency, organizational skills and marketing acumen were instrumental to our book's success.

Peggy J. Rogers of Rogers Design Group, who did a superb job on the design of our cover and the layout of our book.

Joanne Gillespie, whose advice on trademarks and copyright proved invaluable.

Todd Tedesco, whose illustrations depict the major themes of our book.

The hundreds of people we interviewed extemporaneously at supermarket checkouts, in the aisles of bookstores, at trade shows, and at business meetings throughout the United States. Several with whom we spoke had been laid off as a result of downsizing or corporate buyouts, knew someone who was terminated, or were fearful that it would eventually happen to them. Others were looking seriously at making a career change. Still others were thinking about owning their own businesses. All offered encouragement to us, for which we thank them.

PERSONAL THANKS FROM KEN CHANE

To Sandy Chane, my cheerleader, my confidante, my best friend and my dear wife.

To Andrew Chane without whom I would not have had the time and piece of mind to complete this project.

To Peter Chane for his insightful thinking, refreshing analysis and counsel.

To Larry Chane and Abby Feinstein for their compassion and affection.

To Marvin Chane for his years of support and encouragement. No one could ask for a better friend and brother.

To Glenn Poy with whom I have had the good fortune to collaborate. He is a joy to work with and a superb complement to me.

PERSONAL THANKS FROM GLENN POY

To Milly Poy, my mother, whose never-ending encouragement has taught me patience, wisdom and being prepared for whatever opportunities life presents us.

To Bill Poy, my father, whose courage and determination saw daunting challenges as minor obstacles to reaching his dreams.

To Mel, Marty and Caroline Poy, for their constant love and support.

To Lynn Shook, whose friendship and counsel I hold with utmost respect and appreciation.

To Ken Chane, whose vision made this book a reality. His leadership and constant energy make our collaboration a truly great honor and privilege.

SPECIAL ACKNOWLEDGEMENT

Over the twelve years that we have been researching this subject, several publications have done a superb job and provided a great service to their readers in documenting the changes in corporate America and the resulting dislocation of managers and workers.

Early in 1996, *The New York Times* presented a series of seven front page articles on downsizing and its effect on individuals, families, companies and communities. We recognize the *Times* for humanizing the trauma of employee terminations and economic uncertainty.

Over a long period, *The Wall Street Journal* has consistently done an excellent job of reporting on every aspect of corporate behavior as it relates to the treatment of employees. In addition, their continuing feature entitled *"Enterprise"* is recommended reading for all would-be entrepreneurs.

Success, *Entrepreneur* and *Inc.* magazines have nurtured the entrepreneurial spirit by presenting case histories and future opportunities, and stories of both business successes and failures. We salute them also.

In this book, we have provided solutions to help managers and workers face the challenges presented by these outstanding publications.

NOTICES

As a general note to readers, this book is not specific to gender, age, career stage or capabilities. We will, throughout the book, use "he/him" purely for writing ease and convenience, and the term is meant to cover "she/her."

The information, suggestions and recommendations contained in this book are not substitutes for specific legal and financial advice that may be necessary given the individual needs of the reader. We highly recommend that you consult with your attorney, accountant and/or financial advisor where necessary.

Although the authors and publisher have exhaustively researched all sources to ensure the accuracy and completeness of the information contained in this book, we assume no responsibility for errors, inaccuracies, omissions or any other inconsistency herein.

The use of company or product names in the book should not be considered endorsements of the companies or products.

While based on fact, the names of people used in our examples have been changed to maintain their anonymity.

Self-Engineering, *TypeE^N* and *Type E^M* are trademarks of the authors of this book, Ken Chane and Glenn Poy.

Table Of Contents

Why We Wrote This Book
Why has it become so important for you to take more control of your career? The authors tell you about their personal experiences which led to writing this book. *1*

Chapter 1 - Getting Started: How To Make This Book Work For You
How can you make your career decision easier? Here is a straight-forward approach, and a suggested set of tools you should have available to get the most out of this book. *15*

Chapter 2 - Get To Know Yourself
How do you assess your skills, capabilities and career tendencies? As a starting point, you'll complete nine exercises, and arrive at a personal profile that summarizes who you are and what makes you tick. *23*

Foreword to Chapters 3 And Chapter 4 - Getting Out Or Staying In: A Look at Both Sides ... Are You A *Type E^N* Or A *Type E^M*?
You'll find out if you have a *Type E^N* (entrepreneur) or *Type E^M* (employee) mindset, what the differences are, and how you can avoid dangerous and costly cross-over mistakes. *41*

Chapter 3 - Staying In: A Fresh Look At Being Employed
What are the factors that make a strong and satisfied employee? You'll understand the major elements that present employees with four basic options to stay employed. You'll also develop a plan of action to become a re-energized employee. *47*

Chapter 4 - Getting Out: Gaining Control Of Your Destiny
What are the signals that lead to termination, and why do people leave their jobs voluntarily? You'll see if you are ready to face the realities of becoming your own boss. You'll find out what it takes, and whether you are prepared to give it a try. *65*

Chapter 5 - Getting Fired: The ABCs Of Good Preparation
If you are thinking about starting your own business, what should you know about your current employer, potential competitors and the industry you are entering? This chapter offers sources of information, and tips on getting your financial house in order. It will help you to be better prepared for whatever comes next. *87*

Chapter 6 - Getting Fired: What If It Happens Before You're Ready?
How do you spot the danger signals to know your job is coming to an end? You'll learn what you're entitled to, whether you can get a better severance package once you've been given your notice and offered a settlement, and when it pays to see a lawyer. *117*

Chapter 7 - The Day After: Finding Yourself In Transition
Are your feelings of stress, tension and depression normal compared to others who experience job loss? The Do's and Don'ts in this chapter will help you pick yourself up and get started again. If you are over 55 or forced into retirement, there are steps to help you too. *145*

Chapter 8 - Career Options You Didn't Know You Had
With change and uncertainty in the business environment, will your job disappear? You will find a list of innovative career options and jobs that will become increasingly important in the Information Age. *159*

Chapter 9 - On Your Own: Navigating The Minefields
What are the basic considerations to help you face the realities of being in business for yourself? Where will the funds come from? How do you deal with bankers? You'll get an inside look at home-based businesses, family businesses and partnerships. You'll learn about the myths, common pitfalls and scams you may encounter in starting or buying your own business... *187*

Chapter 10 - Personal Stuff: The Spouse, The Kids, The Mortgage
What do you really need to know about your finances and credit worthiness before you make a decision? How can your spouse and children add confidence to your decision? What do you tell your friends and neighbors? *233*

Chapter 11 - Making The Decision
Do you have the right tools and information to help you make the *Entrepreneur or Employee* decision? You'll know whether to leave the corporate world and start your own business or to stay employed. You'll also know what to do next if you're not quite ready to decide. *255*

Chapter 12 - Back In Control Again
With a clear view of your career or business direction, you've gained peace of mind in your career and life again. You, not others, have made the decision…and that puts you back in control. *267*

Additional Resources/Recommended Reading. *277*

About the Authors. *279*

How to Reach the Authors. *281*

Quantity Purchases and Special Programs. *282*

Index. *283*

Registration Form

Order Form

Why We Wrote This Book

We worked in the corporate world for more than twenty years and enjoyed the perks, prestige, and challenges that went along with management positions. To colleagues, subordinates, and friends, it probably looked like we had it made. We thought so, too.

However, one minute we were on the inside overseeing people and projects, the next minute we were on the outside looking for opportunities. What happened to us could happen to you — both the bad and the good. So take note, and keep reading. We have collected the insights and wisdom our experiences gave us into a practical approach to save you some time, money and aggravation. You can read our personal stories at the end of this section to see what motivated us to create this road map for you.

Making the right moves at the right time has been the signature of the "successful" or "lucky" people we read about or see on television. For decades, we've been told that a good education, hard work and loyalty would reward us with a lifetime job and a good retirement.

Such expectations and any complacency are soon shattered by news headlines: "County Payrolls Slashed," "Only Three Major U.S. Airlines Likely to Survive," "Permanent Job Loss Edges Out Non-Technical Workers," "Peterson Publishing Says Yes To Buyout," "Urethane Tech Lays Off 11% Of Workforce," "Job-Stress On The Upswing With Downsizing." A *Wall Street Journal* article on increased merger activity suggests that "issues of job security and stagnating wages will combine to victimize American workers across the board." The flat organizational structure adopted by many companies has done away with millions of mid-level jobs and all but closed off opportunities for advancement in the traditional sense. Many managers will never make a vertical move again.

2 Entrepreneur Or Employee?

The bottom line is this: A new world of work with new requirements and rewards awaits a new breed of manager.

This certainly contributes to heightened worker insecurity and restrains overall wage growth. For long-term employees to be told that they "don't have the skills that fit with where the company is going" is devastating. For middle managers who are neither part of the product manufacturing process, nor part of a company's key decision-making circle, what is the answer? James Champy, author of *Reeingineering Management*, wrote that "middle managers serve the purpose of relaying information up and down — orders down, numbers up. But with the information technologies and more efficient forms of work, their purpose dwindles. Industries have incentive to shed 'information relayers' and make those who remain do more 'value-added work,' that is, something customers will actually pay for."

With change difficult to predict — but sure to continue — it is important to think of yourself as a package of marketable skills rather than a title. Why? Skills are transferable. If need be, you should be able to repackage yourself to take advantage of a range of new opportunities. The skills that you've used for a number of years might be updated and adapted to a new career opportunity that comes with the changing workplace. For example, the technical knowledge and people skills valued in a maternity ward nurse can build a bridge to a new career in selling equipment and training programs for nursing mothers.

The U. S. Bureau of Labor Statistics estimates that most of us will change jobs as many as seven times over the course of our careers, by choice or by chance. Rather than follow a prescribed path, you're likely to find yourself taking part in a number of ad hoc teams created for specific purposes; for example, to develop a software application, design an advertising campaign, market a new financial service or find a cure for a disease.

As companies continue to downsize and outsource more work, prepare yourself for a future that may include consulting, temping, running your own business, returning to college, making the transition to another career, or all of the above.

We want you to recognize four essential truths:
- You have options.
- How you spend your time is up to you.
- Compensation comes in many negotiable forms.
- Nothing lasts forever.

Work is important to us for tangible and intangible reasons. There are monetary and psychic rewards for physical or mental activity undertaken to achieve a purpose. Over a lifetime, working Americans will spend nearly one-third of their waking hours at their jobs, so it's time you take charge. Surveys show that people who are working and active and energized by their jobs report more positive things about themselves.[1] There's evidence that underemployment, or working at a job below the level of a person's skills and ability, may have the same adverse effects on people's health as unemployment. Nationwide, 17.4 million people were laid off between 1991 and 1995, the Labor Department reports. So, you need to be alert to the dynamics of the workplace.

Companies are continuing to "downsize," "rightsize," "restructure," or any of the other euphemisms for "you're-out-of-a-job." Whether you quit or are laid off, phased out, or fired, you're out of a paycheck, have no place to go every day, and lose part of your identity. Traditional career paths for middle managers are narrowing or ending abruptly. So where does that leave you?

If you are like most employees, you have thought about leaving your current job. Would someone else pay more for what you do? Is there greater opportunity for advancement elsewhere? Is it time to change to something you really like doing? Should you leave before they ask you to?

[1]*David Dooley, psychologist, University of California, Irvine's School of Social Ecology who has researched the job/health connection; The Orange County Register "Focus On Labor," Monday, September 2, 1996, News p.14.*

Many people sit on the fence doing nothing about their feelings and their thoughts. Each day they go to work and routinely face the drudgery of their job, doing something they really don't want to do for the rest of their lives. What holds them back from changing to something more fulfilling? A nagging feeling of the unknown: What about income, security, family, skills, and a whole range of other considerations? This group wonders "What if I don't like the new job any better than this one?" "What is it like to work in a different industry?" "Where do I begin to get the skills for a better position?" "Should I follow these strong feelings to do something on my own and to scratch my entrepreneurial itch?"

The difference between those who make the right choice in career and business and those who regret their decision is the ability to balance an objective view of themselves with a bit of intuition. This book provides the framework for helping you make career and business decisions you can live and grow with into the 21st century.

Until now, employers and personnel departments held all the playing cards. They have a wealth of reference manuals, seminars, books, corporate policies and lawyers. "Captains of industry" hire high-priced advisors to negotiate lucrative contracts or exit agreements.

Entrepreneur or Employee? is for those of you who cannot afford, don't have access to, or don't need that kind of assistance. If you are already an "orphan of industry," or someone who wants to be prepared for any opportunity or crises, this book is for you. In the twelve chapters that follow, you'll find the information you need to gain perspective and begin to think strategically, not reactively, about staying employed or going out on your own. You will be able to position yourself to take full advantage of current and future career opportunities.

In a large company, no one is indispensable. An employee may be a key employee one quarter and redundant or unnecessary the next. Even in Japan where companies and workers have lived with the philosophy of lifetime employment, work now depends less on seniority and more on performance and productivity. Add to these changes, the fact that increasing numbers of employees are putting family or quality of life issues before corporate loyalty or obedience. Two-thirds of American working men and women would take a pay cut or reduce their hours for more family or personal time, according to a poll by Robert Half International Inc.

Three key factors account for the volatility of our business climate. One is globalization — America now competes with companies and products on a world-wide basis. Second is consolidation — making companies more efficient through downsizing, mergers and acquisitions. And third is technology — the application of computer, communication and work automation technologies to squeeze the last bit of productivity out of company resources. Waves of large layoffs will continue as a normal part of business. Corporate employers seem willing to do whatever it takes to improve the bottom line in the short term to satisfy investors or creditors. Cutting employees and the costs associated with their salaries and wages continues to be one means of improving corporate bottom lines.

What is evident is the growing lack of paternalism on the part of corporations. When the company does well, it is the top brass who profit from the bonuses. And when profitability wanes, it is the employees who are the victims. Just remember, the top guys in the company have golden parachutes, while most companies' employees are hobbled by tarnished handcuffs.

What are you doing about your future?
- Do you dream about having another job or owning your own business?
- Are you uncertain about the future of your job?
- Do you wonder how your company's merger will affect you?
- Are you bored?
- Have you reached the top of the pay scale for your position?
- Do you think your skills are unappreciated or underutilized?

- Are you terrified by all the talk about downsizing and bankruptcies?
- Do you know how to get a better severance package?

We are not going to help you write your resume, find a particular job, or create a business plan for a new venture. Those topics are thoroughly covered in other publications. This book focuses on the core issues surrounding your employment and employability, and the options and choices that we can help you create for yourself. We wrote it as a result of not finding a resource to help us face the dilemma of *Entrepreneur or Employee?* that you are going through right now.

The defining proposition for *Entrepreneur or Employee?* is that we've "been there, done that," and succeeded. If you decide to stay in your present job, then this book performs a great service by helping you optimize your opportunities right where you are. If you decide to pursue a job in another company or start a business of your own, then you will clarify what you are looking for and know how to avoid feeling trapped again. We've succeeded in our mission if you honestly evaluate your status quo and take action to control your career within or outside of the corporate world.

Our very best wishes for your success,

Ken Chane   Glenn Poy

About the Authors

How we made the transition in our careers and lives may help you in viewing your situation. Over the course of this book, we will offer examples from others' as well as our own experiences. We hope they will be helpful to you as you face this life-changing decision.

Ken Chane
The Journey from Corporate Refugee to Entrepreneur

What an ideal situation I had. Although they didn't have a name for what I was doing in 1981, today they call it "intrapreneuring." I was recruited by one of the largest consumer food companies in the United States to develop an entirely new business for them. Based on my extensive background in retail management, I was given wide latitude and a mandate that was exciting, challenging and all-encompassing. Publicity in *The Wall Street Journal* and *Advertising Age* suddenly gave impetus to the company's stock price, which had previously not appreciated significantly over a long period of time. I had become the company's fair-haired boy. It was an exciting and stimulating time for the company and for me.

Then, came the day that all of us "corporate warriors" dread. The company was sold to an international conglomerate. After an initial meeting among top executives dealing mainly with legal issues, I was no longer invited to any of the numerous reorganization meetings that were held with the other vice presidents. Most executives acted as if I didn't exist. Talk about signals and vibes!

The acquiring company simply was not interested in operating a retail business, so the entire division that I headed was closed. It was one of many to be shut down or sold off. I soon became aware that once you become expendable to a large corporation, feelings don't really count. Many people were going to lose their jobs. The company showed little concern about the disruption it would cause in the lives of the soon-to-be terminated employees. Big companies go on and on — it's the employees that come and go.

I didn't see my own termination coming until almost the very last minute. It was only after the fact that I was able to piece together the rationale behind the decision to force me out. In comparison to my peers, I was considered an overpaid resource. There was no longer any place for my special talent and expertise. A clash in work style was apparent. I was a results-oriented, get-it-done kind of guy working among analysts. In my fifties, my tenure was subject to more regulatory scrutiny with each passing year. Sometimes it's ethnicity, or gender, or religion, or even lifestyle that sabotages a working relationship. Whatever the reason in my case, I knew I wasn't part of the culture of the new company.

From my experience, you may glean some insight into why and how terminations occur, even at a senior level. Some companies handle these matters better than others through good communications, more empathy, and a better understanding of each of the employees' unique problems. In my case, my employer just "left me hanging," with no discussion about my future with the company.

Shortly after my final day, bitterness began to well inside of me. Some of my subordinates received a better exit deal than I, taking into consideration my position and the fact that I relocated to accept the job in the first place. Once the dust settled, I realized that I had not prepared myself properly for leaving. If only I had had this book then! All's not lost. Hopefully, my experience will now benefit you.

"Big companies don't like bad publicity, and will do everything to prevent it," I said to myself. Recognizing this, I wrote a letter to the new CEO of the company detailing my performance and the promises made to me during my recruitment to and tenure with the company. As a result, I received a revised severance package which provided for extended salary continuation and other items very beneficial to me. The moral of the story: Ask and you shall receive ... just maybe!

After my termination, I decided not to ask my family to relocate again. Throughout my twenty-five year corporate career with numerous moves from one employment opportunity to the next, my family had always been in my corner. I felt I owed it to them to find work in the Los Angeles area where we lived.

As I earnestly began to look for a suitable situation, I found that my job prospects were rather slim. It was an agonizing period of my life. A place to work was gone. A steady income was gone. Some of my self-esteem was gone. My savings were being eroded. Stress and tension were high. What choices did I have?

Plan A: I pursued my "entrepreneurial itch" and became involved in some business ventures with friends and associates. I made some bad decisions. Through this process, I learned some important lessons about myself. Number one, partnerships were not for me; and number two, I'm a leader, not a follower. Plan A didn't work. On to plan B.

I started looking for businesses that were for sale. I examined dozens of them, some to the due diligence phase. During the process, I learned a lot about my strengths and weaknesses. One business relied heavily on computer operators who developed technical manuals. Not for me! I wasn't a technical kind of guy; I'd be lost. And, I had no knowledge whatsoever of the aerospace industry that this business served. Another company I looked at made miniature furniture and food for the hobby industry. In this arts and crafts type of business, I would have to depend on dozens of skilled laborers and others to develop new products. It was another poor fit for me.

A process of elimination led me to the mail order marketing company that I eventually purchased. I came to grips with what I was good at, and what I was comfortable with. Eight years later, I'm still confident that I made the right decision.

I share my story to help you appreciate the following:
- Sudden termination can happen to you.
- Getting to know yourself is the key to your future.
- Planning ahead reduces missteps.
- Being prepared is confidence boosting.

Glenn Poy
Finding What You're Looking For in Your Own Backyard

Having gone to school in Toronto, Canada, I had prepared for college by taking all those studies in science and math that Asian kids "were supposed to," so I could be an engineer, doctor or research scientist. My exposure to business in high school was limited to accounting and economics courses. Dealings with money always made clear sense to me. By the time high school was over, I was awarded scholarships for studies in engineering and business. I chose accounting because I thought that was what business was all about.

During my first few years in the profession, I discovered that being good at something didn't always mean that you enjoyed it, but it certainly made it harder to leave. While I was not satisfied with what I was doing, my friends and colleagues advised me to stay in the comfortable, stable world of accounting. Nonetheless, I wanted something else.

I knew there was more to business than number crunching. Even before completing my degree in accounting and finance, I knew my heart was not in it as a lifetime career. Deep inside, I knew that rolling up my sleeves, digging in, and taking a more pro-active role with people was much more my style.

Some people accused me of being a dreamer, because I envisioned forming a core of consulting experts — specialists in different disciplines — who would travel around the world as trouble-shooters for businesses. These experts would detect and dissolve problems, monitor businesses until they were on the right track, and then move on. A long-time friend and banking executive observed that I seemed to have all the characteristics of a risk-taker in business. Although very skeptical, he told me to follow my heart.

My mother mused that I had nomadic tendencies given my willingness to pack up and move wherever and whenever a business opportunity called. Parents always seem to know what's best for us. My mother said, "How many more times are you going to analyze this thing? You can't listen to everyone else. Accounting and money aren't what life is all about. Get out there and do what you love. Take the chance. Do it or you'll always regret that you didn't at least try!" She was right!

I left the world of accounting to join a company that managed tennis programs and projects at some of the most prestigious hotels and resorts. Marrying my financial management experience with a coaching background in tennis, I was off troubleshooting inventory management problems at hotel sports shops, and managing sports concessions and tennis programs in exotic locations and cultures throughout the world. Being flexible and able to adapt to different business and social situations made this an exciting experience for me.

In fact, this mix of tennis and business experience landed me a position in finance with a major Canadian automotive manufacturer. The company liked my varied background. I became involved with a core of engineers, marketers and business people to model and manage a diverse portfolio of businesses from Canada to Europe, covering real estate to automotive manufacturing to new technologies. I was in my element.

Then I was assigned to the United States to look at merging a traditional engineering business with an industrial design firm for new product development. One thing led to another. I helped structure a successful company buyout with a world renown European automotive company that took over a year to complete. All this time, I knew that I had also written myself out of a job. Yet, I wanted to believe that as a loyal company servant, my job and future with the company would be secure. In the end, the reality of the last day at work still came as a shock to me.

My heart knew that it was time for me to move on and pursue what I do best and enjoy most. I realized that I wasn't the cut-throat, walk-all-over-people type that personified the late '80s style of corporate management. Family and friends provided much advice, support and admonitions to spur me on. The most encouraging was this challenge from a friend in a major management consulting firm, "You don't have a snowball's chance in hell, Glenn." That gave me the final nudge.

I finally started my own management consulting practice. From my earliest recollections, I have always looked at opportunities and prepared for contingencies. In college, I took a double major just in case one didn't meet my expectations. I tried out for several sports just in case I didn't excel in one. Contingency planning was a big part of what I did as a professional sports coach, a business strategist, and a corporate manager. It is my way of keeping a foot in one door while opening a second, and moving swiftly when the time is right. It was my turn to formally use this talent on my own behalf.

I'm grateful that my background in finance allows me to see businesses more clearly, creating opportunities for my clients and for me. I study and develop models used by sports coaches and the business world as a means of applying strategy and getting management teams to work effectively together. Understanding the playing field, the competition, and the game you are playing are fundamental in sports and business. I help build and motivate strong management teams by getting them to execute the fundamentals essential to their business success. I teach them how to apply their core competencies in a continually changing marketplace.

I remember my father saying, "If you can keep building on your strengths while you take care of the weaknesses in your game, you can only become a better player." And that is a truism, even for business success.

If you've spent restless nights with career change decisions, here are some thoughts that may be helpful to you:
- Being good at something doesn't mean that you'll be satisfied doing it.
- Know yourself — both your strengths and weaknesses.
- As in sports, play your strengths <u>and</u> shore up your weaknesses.
- Build on your fundamental skills and strengths.
- Be open to changes that capitalize on your fundamental skills and strengths.
- Link your base of skills to your inclinations and what your heart is telling you.

Today's Business Environment is Marked
with Downsizing, Fear, Uncertainty, and Change

Chapter 1

GETTING STARTED:
How To Make This Book Work For You

Welcome to Ken Chane's and Glenn Poy's how-to book. Our primary goal in writing this book is to engage you, the reader, in a practical approach to planning your future.

Who will use this book? Those who know everything there is to know about careers, but want to be sure they're up to date. Those who know nothing about job-hunting, and want to be taught everything. Those who often wonder about leaving their current jobs, and are held back from making a decision by the nagging feeling of uncertainty about money, security, family, or their own capability. Those whose jobs are, or might be, impacted by downsizing, and who wish to regain control over their careers. We help you to understand your choices, and prepare for your next move.

Through this book, we will help you organize your thoughts and uncover the options that are appropriate to your circumstances, and help you answer the most important question on your mind: Is leaving or staying in your current job is the right decision for you? We will help you through a number of considerations that will challenge your thinking and choices, ultimately enabling you to live happily with your decision.

Some people work for a corporation because they believe that there are more opportunities with a big company than a small one. Is this true where you work? Perhaps you chose a company or career because it was "prestigious" or "made your parents happy." Or, you were recruited right out of school and now the benefits and salary are so good you don't feel you can leave even though you dread going to work everyday. Another scenario may be that you like your job and would like to keep it. Even if you plan to remain where you are, you will function much better if you know what your skills and strengths are, and where you like to use them.

Many of us think that leaving the corporate world requires financial security. We often read of executives who have been given golden handshakes, and think to ourselves, "If I had his money, I could surely start a business on my own." Certainly there are considerations other than money that impact this decision. But, if money is your main or only consideration, you may find yourself going through this very exercise of deciding whether to stay or leave your job again.

In the 1980s, if a company were in trouble, it would generally try to muddle through. Back then, a company in trouble usually gave plenty of warning signs before it started laying people off; you could see it coming. Today, it cuts its losses as fast as it can, even if it means cutting employees and staff arbitrarily. Now, layoffs occur with absolutely no warning.

The time to think about your next job is the day you start your present one. As we have seen, job security has become a fleeting thing. Career planning is no longer an optional exercise. It is an essential survival skill.

We will help you to better understand both your situation and yourself. In reading through the book, we hope you will take the time to honestly understand your desires, and your capabilities and limitations. We will help you to be comfortable with your decision to stay in or leave the corporate world. A large part of your decision will be based on whether you have the tendencies of a successful employee, or whether your entrepreneurial tendencies point you in the direction of a business of your own. We will help you evaluate and understand these tendencies. You will see a number of options appropriate to your circumstances. Throughout the book, the most important point to remember is that you know yourself better than anyone else.

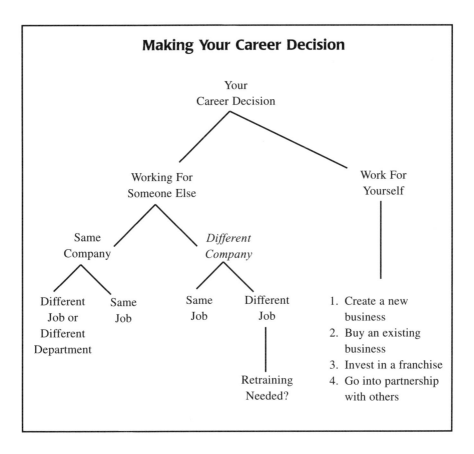

A Word About Decision-Making in General

Generally, decision-making is not complicated when you have the right tools. You probably already have the most important ones to accomplish this.

There have been critical points in your life at which you've had to make important decisions. What did you do to arrive at a decision? Who did you discuss it with? What was the result? If you had to make the decisions again armed with what you now know, would your decisions have been the same? Many, if not all, of your decisions are based on an intuitive decision-making process you follow, and on what you've learned from your past experiences.

There are some basic elements that help you make good decisions:

1) Start by clearly identifying the decision you are making (e.g., Should you buy a house? Should you take the trip? Do you want to get married? Should you go back to school?). The clearer you can identify the decision to be made, the more confident your answer will be. If the decision is a difficult or complex one, you should break it into smaller decisions that are more manageable, and that you can more effectively address.

2) What is the range of possible choices or options for the decision? Each option can be analyzed using a two-column approach – listing the pluses in one column and the minuses in the second column. In the plus column, jot down the positive benefits that you would receive as a result of choosing this option. In the minus column, think of the negative features that would cause you to abandon this option altogether.

This will help you look at the decision and the options objectively from all sides, to determine the facts for and against each of the available options. It will also identify the worst-case scenario – the decision outcome with the highest risk or the least desirable result.

3) What are the factors and/or criteria that will contribute to a good decision? For example, if you are deciding on whether to buy a house or not, budget and family needs would be two important criteria to help you make the decision. You might consider what you can afford, where you will put the furniture you already have and what additional furniture you'll have to buy, whether there is a playroom, or how convenient shopping, schools and public transportation are. There are different factors in every decision that will keep you focused and give you comfort and confidence that your decision will be a good one.

4) What is your decision-making style? Are you an analytical or methodical person who gathers information before making any decision? Or are you an emotional or impulsive person who relies on "gut feelings" to make decisions? While there is no best way or right or wrong way to make decisions, consider the nature, importance and urgency of the decision. The more difficult or complex the decision, the more you'll have to separate emotion and wishful thinking from the hard facts.

5) Do you have enough information to make the decision? Given the information you have and what you already know from past experiences, what additional information do you need to make a good decision?

6) Can you validate your decision with an objective third party? For example, do you know anyone who has succeeded by following the same path you're about to take? This can certainly give you more confidence in the decision you are making.

In this book, we will guide you through a practical approach to face the *Entrepreneur or Employee?* decision. We'll help you arrive at appropriate options given your circumstances, and to answer the question, "Should you get out or stay in your current job?"

How Do I Get Started?

Many of us are afraid of gaining insight into our deepest desires as they may point us to a place different from what we originally thought. No doubt the thought of leaving the corporate world can leave you with feelings of anxiety and uncertainty. To alleviate those feelings, you will take an objective view of your financial, psychological and personal skills. We will help you constructively deal with the risks and realities of getting out or staying in your corporate job.

Our aim is to help you with a framework for choosing what is best for you. Are you more suited for the corporate world governed by others, or a business world in which you have all the responsibilities? In a later chapter, we will expose some very serious misconceptions people have about entrepreneurship, many of which have resulted from the proliferation of publications, seminars, and offerings aimed at the entrepreneurial spirit that exists in all of us. In this book, you'll discover your strengths and weaknesses, your comfort zone and your options. You'll gain greater confidence to arrive at the right decision and act accordingly.

Along the way, we'll offer some of our thoughts and hindsights so that you will benefit from our experience and avoid some of the pitfalls that others have encountered in their personal decision-making process.

In some parts of the book, we want you to go through the exercises, answering the questions, making lists and taking notes. In other parts, the information is presented in such a way that gives you the steps we want you to follow. In other parts, we simply provide sources of information to point you in the right direction. What we're doing is leading you through the same decision-making process that we went through in answering the *Entrepreneur or Employee?* question.

Starting Your Plan

Important decisions should not be made impulsively. As you read this book, your deeply rooted thoughts should start popping to the surface. This should be a period of great discovery. We recommend that you highlight key thoughts that are helpful to you, and write notes in the margins of the pages. As well, you'll find it very helpful to have a notebook and pen handy for any additional ideas you want to capture. You will want to write in your own words, and date your notes to help you think about the progress you've made. In this way, your thoughts will be very fresh and they will make a lot of sense when you go back and read them over at a later date. Using a notebook will help you avoid keeping track of loose pieces of paper or restaurant napkins that ultimately disappear.

This is the beginning of a plan you're building for yourself, complete with assumptions and declarations "you to you."

Chapter 2 will lead you through a self assessment of your work habits, your likes and dislikes, your willingness to take business risks, among other topics. These exercises will identify whether you have the characteristics of an entrepreneur or an employee. You may find the details a bit tedious, but we encourage you to take the time to go through it carefully and thoroughly.

As a planning note, allocate time to read the book with care. It took us a long time to refine the elements and the framework, and to face all the issues ourselves. We don't expect that you will complete any one of Chapters 2 through 4 in just one sitting. By going through these chapters methodically, you will avoid feeling rushed, frustrated or discouraged. This will be quite helpful as you work through this important decision about your future.

Once you get to the end of Chapter 4, you'll find the remainder of the book much easier to read and work through. Chapters 5 to 12 will build on the foundation that you develop in the first four chapters, so please schedule enough time to work through the chapters.

This is your personal exercise, so let the "real" you come out. Allow yourself to be creative. Each of us experiences flashes of brilliance which we think we will remember, only to forget as quickly as the next thought arrives. You'll want to make note of your breakthrough ideas in order to follow up on them later.

Chapter 1 Checkpoint

This book is a working tool to help you organize your thoughts, options, choices in getting out or staying in your corporate job.

✐ Keep a notepad or notebook, and a highlighter or pen nearby to note interesting passages and capture your thoughts and answers.

✐ Find a quiet and comfortable place to read and work through this book. We found that our most productive work and reflection was done alone in a quiet place at home, on a patio, or in a park.

You're now ready to begin your journey through this book with us.

Chapter 2

GET TO KNOW YOURSELF

After reading a film critic's review of a movie that I saw recently, I wondered if we had seen the same film. Each time I read a critic's review of a movie, I get a better appreciation for why he or she is called a critic. Every voice inflection, body movement, eye contact, every half smile and casual glance is dissected by the critic. These points are then followed by an insightful analysis of character development and dialogue, and why they make the film a success or a flop.

How do the critics do it? Experience and training play a major role in their insight. However, I suspect that the high caliber of their work is a combination of their laser beam-like intensity, and professional objectivity.

As you ponder your career decision, take a lesson from the film critic. Scrupulously review and analyze your characteristics to identify your strengths and weaknesses. If you can apply the same vigor in observation and analysis of others to yourself, you'll take a major step forward in directing your decision-making process.

One of the keys to forecasting the future of a business is to identify what it is good at doing. Are its products well made? Does the company have a wealth of usable technology? Perhaps it has a super sales team that sells like there's no tomorrow and offers excellent after-sales service and support. A similar analysis can be applied to individuals as well. Perhaps Mary was promoted because she has a sound grasp of the finances of the company and is an excellent negotiator with suppliers. Maybe the business is successful because of Frank's exceptional management of the warehouse crew, and his "just in time" inventory method keeps stock at the most efficient levels.

What is your core competency? What do you do best? Where can you do it best? Think about it. Are your aptitudes and skills being used in your current job? Do you like the talents your job demands? How long has it been since you exercised your unique gifts? Many of us dream of one day finding the job, career or work environment that is specifically suited to our capabilities. In the next few chapters, we're going to help you find the path that will support you economically and emotionally.

Some of us take a number of years of working for different companies before deciding what our purpose in life is. The most difficult part is to be perfectly honest and candid with ourselves. Just as children are told not to cry, adults are taught to suppress "fanciful," "unrealistic," and "unconventional" desires.

A good example of this is revealed in interviews of famous actors. Invariably, their families frowned upon their choice of careers. You know the reaction. "When are you going to get a real job?" "You can't make a living playing, pretending to be someone else." We're fortunate that these accomplished actors listened to themselves, knew what they wanted, knew what they were capable of, and pursued a career that satisfied their needs and desires.

How did you get where you are? Have you worked for the same company since you left school? Did you get the job to work with a friend, or to pay off your student loan, and just stayed? Was your industry "the place to be," so you went along for the ride? Is the work satisfying now? Think of three reasons why or why not.

If you're unhappy at what you do, why aren't you doing something else? Are you so discouraged about your prospects for finding satisfaction in the workplace that you would rather do nothing and stay where you are? Have you lost your verve for job hunting because your skills need updating? Do you fear competing with youths whose skills and salary expectations make them more marketable than you? Maybe you are afraid that you won't find a position that pays the salary you've been accustomed to, or that challenges your complete base of skills. Is your heart tugging at you to be in business for yourself, while your mind is going through the motions of finding a new job working for someone else?

The hardest part is knowing where to start to get yourself motivated to look seriously at what you want to do — not "should" do. How do you get in touch with feelings and interests buried long ago under responsibilities and convenience?

It's not easy, and it doesn't happen all at once. We took long and circuitous routes to arrive at our decisions about getting out or staying in our corporate jobs. In fact, our journeys took a number of years. We're going to show you some shortcuts.

Taking Your Own Temperature

To begin, you must critique yourself like never before. This is what we call *taking your own temperature*. The purpose is to develop a point of reference you can use to prepare you for your decision. This is a good time to begin making entries in your notebook.

The first step in evaluating yourself has three components: Broadly define (1) your job likes and dislikes, (2) your career likes and dislikes, and (3) your range of skills. How do your answers relate to the list of positions you've had? What does this say about you? How does your job history define you? What can you learn from the career moves you've made?

The objective is to point out those facets of your working life that you want to hold on to, and those you might want to change. In coaching terms, this is an opportunity to build on your strengths and shore up your weaknesses.

Nine Lists to Assess Who You Are

As you make the following nine lists in your notebook, be sure the answers are your true beliefs, not someone else's expectations. You know yourself better than anyone else does. There are no "wrong" or "right" answers. No one else will be reviewing what you write down unless you choose to share your thoughts.

We might mention that these lists don't all have to be made at one time. In fact, you may want to schedule enough time to think and reflect on one group at a time. For those of you who know yourselves quite well, it may only take a week to complete the lists. For those who struggle to articulate your true feelings and perceptions, this may take two or three weeks. Because we're talking about your innermost thoughts, try to go through this process in a quiet space and during a quiet time. If you can't find tranquillity at home because of the kids or other distractions, do your serious thinking in your car, while taking long walks, or at the library. Find a regular place or time to commit to studying this major decision you're about to make. By making and keeping appointments with yourself, you acknowledge and attach importance to this task and your future.

List #1 - What I Like Least

What are some of the responsibilities in your everyday business or work routine that you leave until last to look at or carry out? Some salesmen love to sell, but detest writing up the orders. Some marketing people love to devise strategies and come up with great ideas, but hate to deal with the statistics and finances. Some warehouse people like to get product inventory organized and shipped out quickly, but hate the minutiae involved with inventory reconciliation.

List those things that you don't like to do. We usually acknowledge them in our thoughts. Now we're asking you to commit them to paper. A good place to start is to think about your normal work week. What projects do you do last? They are the ones you probably hold the least passion for.

List #2 - Things I Find Difficult To Do or Do Not Possess the Skills For

For your second list, identify those functions which are part of your current job that you don't do as well as you think is necessary. Maybe your mathematical skills are not as strong as your coworker's. Maybe you don't like to deal with customers on a one-to-one basis because you're a shy person. Or, perhaps you don't like to write reports. Is it because your writing skills are deficient, your vocabulary limited, or you can't get to the point?

Many people find it difficult to describe in detail the job responsibilities they find easy or enjoy, but have little problem describing things they don't like or can't do. This exercise helps you become aware of your level of competence in various areas.

List #3 - Where My Interests Lie

We're now crossing that fine line between work and personal interests. Stephen Covey says in his book *The 7 Habits of Highly Effective People*, "Success is being the same person in all aspects of your life." How many of us actually experience this? Some people are brought up to believe that enjoying work (or doing things that might be considered leisure activities) is inappropriate. Nonetheless, thousands of people have turned their interests into viable businesses, and become more confident and happy people.

Let's focus on those areas in which you have a great deal of professional and personal interest. Are you particularly fascinated by motors and devices? Do you like to tinker and take things apart? Do you have expertise in Middle East cooking? Are you an artist? Are you fascinated with computers and various software packages? Even though your passion for French literature may not appear applicable to the workplace, list it anyhow. Do not censor your answers during this exercise. Allow your thoughts to flow freely. Remove all boundaries from your thinking.

List #4 - What Turns Me On

In lists one and two, you wrote down things that turn you off or discourage you. Now do the opposite. What really turns you on? What gets your adrenaline flowing? What projects get you to work early? What projects or activities motivate you so much that you want to take them home with you?

When you have finished this exercise, you will have four lists. These aren't set in stone; they're just thought stimulators. As we progress through the chapters, you'll probably want to change what you've written, add new items, and perhaps even move items from one list to another.

Before going any further, go back over the four lists and rank each entry on each list from the most important to you to the least significant. For example, the one aspect I least enjoy is disciplining an employee. My second least favorite thing is preparing for weekly status meetings. You get the idea. Don't be too hasty in eliminating items from your list. As you'll see later, people create unique businesses from what appear to be disjointed or frivolous interests.

If you're having trouble working up these lists, here is an interesting way to undo writer's block. Sit down with the classified advertisement section from a major metropolitan area newspaper. Study the Help Wanted and Business Opportunity sections. Move your finger down the columns, looking only at the first word – Accountant, Beautician, etc. What catches your eye? What classifications and descriptions interest you? If you hesitate over the call for circus acrobats, thinking, "Gee, I always wondered what it would be like to do that," make a note of your interest. What appeals to you? The physical nature of the job? Discipline? Risk? Applause? Costumes and pageantry?

A second approach with the classified ads is to write every job title in either a "like" or "dislike" column. Don't list the job title in the "dislike" column just because others may think it silly or ordinary.

A third technique for getting in touch with your true interests is to browse the employment display ads over the next few weeks. Cut out career ads that appeal to you. Don't be limited by geography, educational or other requirements. Your objective is to take a fresh look at all the options currently available. Then sit down with the ads in front of you, and make sure that the words or phrases that attracted you to the position are included on one of the lists that you've prepared.

By taking an overview of the ads you've selected, see if you can define the common themes or elements among them. If this is a difficult exercise for you, try to write a summary of your ideal job description, including a job title based on the display ads you've collected. The easier this becomes for you, the more comfortable you'll feel about where you're headed.

List #5 - Getting Feedback From Others

It is important for you to develop this list with someone who knows you rather well — a spouse, a best friend, a parent, or a business associate. Work with someone with whom you won't feel defensive, and whose comments and opinions you respect and will accept at face value. For ease and convenience of writing only, we'll use the pronouns he/him to help you through this exercise. Please substitute she/her should it apply to your situation.

Have your friend tell you:
- What he thinks you're good at
- What you're not so good at
- What he thinks your interests are

This can be very insightful and rewarding if you don't attempt to edit or refute his remarks. Just listen without interrupting. A good point to remember is that while your friend may not be accurate in his evaluation or impressions of you, his perceptions of you have developed over a period of time by the signals you've been giving out. Another point to consider is that friends can sometimes be brutally honest. With this in mind, make certain that both you and your friend take this exercise seriously and without fear of ridicule.

List #6 - Why Do I Want to Stay in the Corporate World?

What appeals to you about working for a corporation? Think in terms of the tangible benefits surrounding people, places, things; and the intangible rewards of feelings, image and beliefs.

Reflect on what brought you through the doors to begin with, and what's holding you there. How has the environment changed? How have you changed? What does the future look like in your industry, company, department, job?

What would you change about your workplace? What would you change about your position — your duties, responsibilities, pay, benefits, rewards, the people you work with? How are your feelings of self-worth tied to the job? Is there a connection between your professional and personal lives?

List #7 - Why Am I Interested in Leaving the Corporate World?

For this list, give all the reasons that prompt you to think about leaving your corporate job. Is it simply because you don't like your current boss, or are you driving too far to work every day? These certainly are reasons that come to mind, and may be strong motivators to create a new life or lifestyle. Jot down all the things that bother you about your job. Nothing is too petty or too common. Let your thoughts flow and list whatever comes to mind. Just let your complaints roll.

Your education, training or previous experience may or may not provide real clues to the answers you are looking for. For one reason or another professional burnout often accounts for a number of career changes. We know of several individuals who gave up successful law practices to open restaurants. Numerous CEOs who headed some of the most prestigious companies in America are involved in businesses far removed from their initial training and education. Ken Chane is a professionally trained pharmacist who hasn't practiced in many years. Still others have applied their skills and talents to creative pursuits. Glenn Poy applies his business and sports coaching backgrounds to assist businesses in implementing strategy and performance management systems. Many successful people took an indirect route to their eventual good fortune.

And, it can happen to you too. The important point here is that you listen to that inner self of yours. What is it saying to you? What do you think you're capable of? And why do you think so?

Is your pride or ego interfering with your answers? Are you unduly influenced by "the neighbors will think I'm nuts" syndrome? For this exercise, forget what your neighbors, friends or family think about what could be a radical change in your life and your career. As you did on the previous lists, rank the items on your lists of reasons for staying in or leaving the corporate world (Lists 6 and 7) from most convincing to least convincing in your heart and mind.

List #8 - Do I Willingly Take Risks?

Are you a risk-taker? Do you know what risk-taking is? Your point of reference may be your father. If your dad was always a loyal company employee and had a tranquil life, then you may find it difficult to see an alternative way of living. You may look upon entrepreneurship – using your house as collateral for a business loan, and "meeting a payroll" – with great trepidation. Who told you that you had to work for the same company or in the same industry all your life? You're not alone. Many people are indoctrinated in these myths.

Let's take a look at risk-taking. For this discussion, we'll define it as the willingness to take an action that exposes you to financial, emotional or physical harm if the right result doesn't occur. Examples might include investing in the stock market, exceeding the speed limit, or making a bet at the race track.

In this section, you'll find out whether you are willing and able to put your money where your mouth is. In List 8, note examples of risk-taking, and check which ones do or don't apply to you.

List #9 - Why Do I Want a Business of My Own?

Here are pertinent questions: Why do you want a business of your own? What is your motivation? Is it that you can't find a suitable position, and are, "buying" a job for yourself? Will your decision to leave the corporate world be a rational decision made with your head, or an emotional decision made with your heart?

Make a list of your reasons for wanting to buy or invest in a business of your own. Try to get to the heart of the issue. Think of your skills, your attitude, your financial motivation, the expertise you have, how well you work with, manage and lead others, along with other reasons that come to mind.

As before, rank your list of reasons from those which are strongest in your mind, to those which are more emotional.

You should now have made these lists:
1) What I Like Least
2) Things I Find Difficult to Do or Do Not Possess the Skills For
3) Where My Interests Lie
4) What Turns Me On
5) Getting Feedback From Others
6) Why Do I Want To Stay In the Corporate World?
7) Why Am I Interested in Leaving the Corporate World?
8) Do I Willingly Take Risks?
9) Why Do I Want a Business of My Own?

Now, review the lists. Start fine tuning them by going over them until they truly express how you feel about the issues. Think about how workable your answers are, and how compatible they are with you and your capabilities and passions. This is a good time to have someone who knows you well act as your sounding board and give you feedback.

Your Personal Profile Should Be Getting Clearer

Once you've gotten some input, take your lists and use the information to write a summary that accurately profiles you. This process may take several attempts, so just start writing and see what comes out. While you don't want to write a novel or autobiography, a paragraph would probably be too short to give a clear reading on who you are.

This self-appraisal will produce a picture that may surprise you. Take a copy of your most recent resume and compare it to the lists you've prepared, and to the summary profile you've created. Ask yourself if your resume and experience are consistent with your lists. Try to see which specific elements from your lists can be related to the elements in your resume. Are you surprised at how consistent or inconsistent your experience has been relative to the opinions you've expressed?

Now compare the classified advertisements you've collected to the lists you've prepared. Ask yourself if the ads you've collected are consistent with your lists. Again, try to see which specific elements from your lists can be related to elements in the job ads. Are you surprised at the consistency or inconsistency of your lists with the ads?

Here are some examples:

1) If your "Where My Interests Lie" and "What Turns Me On" lists show a clear set of interests and areas that excite you, look for a variety of jobs that might offer these elements. Don't just look at the positions that you've been in before. One reason that you might be interested in the job ads is that you're unhappy with the very job you're in. Does it justify looking for the same or similar job again?

2) You might be attracted to an ad that calls for many items you've included on your "What I Like Least" or "Things I Find Difficult to Do or Do Not Possess the Skills For" lists. For example, you may detest writing up orders or designing computer databases. So don't kid yourself; consider improving these weak skills or know that this is not the job for you.

3) Make sure your resume highlights those elements of your skills and capabilities that reflect where your interests lie and what turns you on. Then look at how these can be transferable to other companies or industries. Look at how the things you like least or find difficult to do can be shown in a positive light. Does your current job or company fulfill your needs?

4) Are you finding many of the ads restrictive or confining? Are the reasons that you dislike them on your lists for "Why Am I Interested in Leaving the Corporate World?" or "Why Do I Want A Business Of My Own?"

5) Do the comments from your "Getting Feedback From Others" sessions confirm what you have discovered about yourself in your lists?

> **DID YOU FIND ANYTHING SURPRISING?**
>
> One individual liked marketing, and wanted to develop a mail order business around his great interest in horses. However, he had an aversion to borrowing money from family, friends, and even the bank. Funds were needed to start the business and to produce personal income until the business could support itself. This could have taken two to three years. The person was unwilling to put himself at such great financial risk, so he begrudgingly stayed in his job.
>
> Another case involved a Certified Public Accountant with a large accounting firm. After several years of practicing in his profession, he became bored doing other people's financial statements, and disliked the minutiae involved in accounting. After some introspection, he sold his practice and became a part owner of one of his manufacturing clients.

Having a Problem Working Through These Lists?

You might find that you still need a little more time to complete the lists, or to make changes to them. People will have different degrees of comfort in learning about themselves.

If you are comfortable about what you've written down, and you are confident about where you're headed, you're ready to finalize a summary paragraph about yourself. This is similar to the two minute exercise, "Tell me about yourself," that many public speakers, networkers or interviewers are familiar with. The paragraph you write is a short summary of who you are, what your career aspirations and passions are, and what capabilities and strengths define you.

1) If you haven't done your lists, or feel you've got it all in your head, please do take the time to write them down on paper. Demonstrate to yourself that you are serious and committed to making this important decision.

2) If you are struggling a bit with the lists, you probably aren't the only one in this situation. Give yourself a realistic period of time, perhaps one week, in order to give more serious thought to completing the lists. At that time, if you're not satisfied that the lists have captured who you are, set another date by which you will have added to or refined the lists. The point is to make sure you're committing some time to an exercise that is very beneficial to you.

Creating the lists is important. You'll find it helpful to refer to them throughout your career. In fact, they will help you when you network with professional and social groups, or if you are preparing a resume, because they give you greater awareness of who you are and what you're capable of doing.

You Must Shake the Influences of Your Past

In doing the exercises in this chapter, keep in mind that consciously or subconsciously, your family orientation may have a large impact on your thinking. For instance, if your father worked in a manufacturing plant and relied on company benefits for his security, you may not have been exposed to ways of providing for your own welfare. As a child, you may have heard derogatory talk about "the awful company," which tainted your opinion about employers in general. If no one in your family has ever started or operated a business, the thought of borrowing funds to start a business may be foreign to you.

On another note, if you received your college degree and education as a chemical engineer, you may only see a future in research and manufacturing related to formulating chemical compounds or drugs. Or, if you've got an accounting education, the security aspects of a career in corporate finance or financial reporting may be paramount.

Whether you acknowledge it or not, your family's and your own experiences and attitudes have quite an effect on your thinking and decision-making. Try to cast aside these ingrained prejudices and take stock of your own inner thoughts, likes and passions. Step out of any of the boundaries which may have been created *for you* or *by you*. At this point, try not to think about having to please your friends, mother or father. If the thought, "My God, what would they think of me wanting to leave my job to start a graphics design business?" is in your mind, keep at this exercise until you value your own opinions more than you fear those of others.

Some people are frustrated by doing something that they are uncomfortable with at an early age. Some will take the bull by the horns late in their career. There is really no good time or bad time. It's what makes sense for you in your situation. Perhaps all you needed this book for was to help you to come to grips with that person that nobody else knows.

Chapter 2 Checkpoint

By taking your own temperature, you have a point of reference from which to prepare for your decision.

✎ Your personal profile helps you to describe who you are, what your career aspirations and passions are, and where your capabilities and strengths lie.

✎ Your attitude, upbringing and past experiences significantly influence your career and life decisions, and can prejudice your thinking. Now is the time to step beyond your self-imposed boundaries.

Your inner thoughts, passions and weaknesses are the first step in understanding whether you should work for someone else or for yourself.

Taking Your Own Temperature

List #1: What I Like Least

1. Writing up orders
2. Analyzing sales statistics
3. Dealing with returned goods
4. Disciplining staff
5. Meetings with my boss
6. Taking orders from my boss

List #2: Things I Find Difficult To Do Or Do Not Possess the Skills For

1. Following up with sales staff to make sure they're selling
2. Identifying new customers
3. Calling on new customers
4. Presenting to large audiences
5. Fixing broken machines

List #3: Where My Interests Lie

1. Like to work with computers
2. Enjoy learning new languages
3. Like to solve problems as a member of a team
4. Like to run with a project from begining to end

List #4: What Turns Me On

1. Meeting tight deadlines
2. Finding sources of capital
3. Reading about new technologies
4. Knowing where the competition fails
5. Understanding how to beat competition
6. Being hands-on in all aspects of a project or business

List #5: Getting Feedback From Others

What I'm good at ...
1. _____
2. _____

What I'm not good at ...
1. _____
2. _____

Where my interests lie ...
1. _____
2. _____

List #6: Why Do I Want To Stay in the Corporate World?

1. Steady paycheck
2. Enjoy working on teams
3. Develop work-related friendships
4. Build a corporate career
5. Like a more predictable work environment
6. I don't like making big decisions on my own

List #7: Why Am I Interested in Leaving the Corporate World?

1. Independence
2. I have know-how for a product
3. I love to sell
4. I know how to raise money
5. I understand how to beat the competition
6. I'm a very organized individual

List #8: Do I Willingly Take Risks?

1. Like to dabble in stock market
2. Don't get sensitive about losing money
3. I love bunjee jumping
4. Comfortable with dealing with money
5. I date often and love being a ham in the crowd

List #9: Why Do I Want A Business of My Own?

1. Have run a business
2. Like calling the shots
3. Know how to read P&L
4. Managing cash flow is a talent I have
5. Have a great product to sell
6. My brother has a business
7. People say I'd be good at running a business

Get To Know Yourself 39

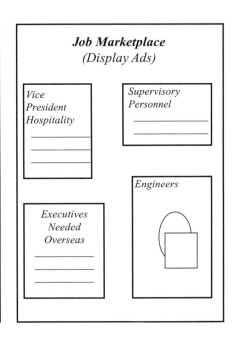

My Resume
Accomplishments
_____
_____
Career Experience
_____
_____
_____

How consistent are your most recent resume and the ads you've collected with the elements you've noted on your lists?

The more consistent they are, the more likely it will be that you understand who you are and what makes you tick.

If this is the case, you're ready to move on.

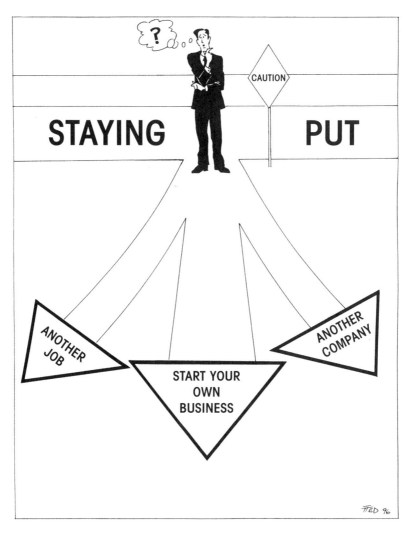

Gaining Control of Our Lives Requires a Cautionary Look at the Available Options

Foreword To Chapters 3 And 4

GETTING OUT OR STAYING IN:
A Look At Both Sides ...
Are You a *Type E^N* Or a *Type E^M*?

Because very few people like change, there will be a part of you pulling one way, to stay put. By doing nothing, no changes are involved; no discomfort or disruption of the status quo. Another tug will be in the direction of changing jobs. Is this the energizing force you need? Then there's also the temptation to strike out on you own. What is your destiny?

In life, we seek and place a high value on an overall sense of control over three important aspects of our lives — our self, our career, and our income. Having completed Chapter 2, you should be fairly comfortable with the discoveries you've made about yourself by doing the exercises. Your written answers give you a good sense of who you are and where you are headed. Now what? Let's start forming some conclusions about whether you want to work for someone else or for yourself.

You've Reached the Fork in the Road

One of the reasons you are reading this book may be that the thought of leaving the corporate world intrigues or excites you. You truly want

to find out if it is an appropriate option for you. Let's outline the choices available. You can:
- Do nothing and stay where you are.
- Stay with your present company and join another department.
- Leave your present company and join another.
- Leave your present company and start your own business.
- "Sit tight," but begin preparing a plan for your next move.

At this point in your decision-making process, you've come to grips with your feelings, strengths and weaknesses. You've reached that fork in the road that represents a fundamental — and life changing — point of departure for your career and your life. One branch of the road leads you away from the corporate world toward your own business, and the other branch keeps you in the corporate world in a steady employment situation. There is no universal right or wrong answer about which branch to follow. But you'll find that there is a right path for your unique needs and tendencies.

In the next two chapters, we're going to give you some perspectives on being an employee in the corporate world, and also on being an entrepreneur with your own enterprise. We'll delve into some of the myths, uncertainties, and unknowns about these different paths. You'll always find both advantages and challenges to being in either of these situations. In many cases, individuals will find that the advantages of being employed outweigh the alternatives. These people will remain employed with one or more companies for the balance of their careers. In other cases, the advantages of running their own company lure people away from their employers to become self-employed.

Are You a *Type E^N* or a *Type E^M*?

We use the terms *Type E^N* and *Type E^M* as a means to identify individuals with entrepreneurial or employee attributes. The following provides a brief definition of the terms.

Type E^N: The Entrepreneur Mindset

Type E^N individuals have the characteristics, traits and attributes of an entrepreneur. They are likely to take risks, to start businesses on their own, or to be happy in an entrepreneurial environment. They show strong leadership traits and tend to be tenacious and achievement-oriented, with a strong desire to succeed even in the face of several failures, ambiguity and uncertainty. They will not take "no" for an answer. *Type E^N* individuals are usually the ones who started lemonade stands, cut the neighbors' lawns, or worked at a part-time job after school or on weekends, as kids.

Type E^M: The Employee Mindset

Type E^M individuals have the characteristics, traits and attributes of an employee. They are likely to be strong and loyal employees who enjoy a career in the corporate world, and are happy to be employees of a company. They want to build a traditional career, like to work regularly with a work team or group, and enjoy the camaraderie and friendship of co-workers, managers and assistants. They tend to like a structured set of responsibilities in secure and predictable surroundings.

"Cross-Over" Mistakes

Each individual type has its own strengths and challenges. "Cross-over" mistakes are often made when one type crosses over and tries to be the other type. That is, a strong entrepreneurial type will generally be frustrated in a more rigid and bureaucratic employee environment. Similarly, a typical employee type will experience great discomfort and anxiety in making all of the decisions alone in an entrepreneurial venture, and be unprepared to operate a business of his own.

Our research found a number of common examples in which people were drawn into cross-over mistakes, illustrating the adage of "trying to fit a square peg into a round hole."

Type E^M individuals sometimes act against their better judgment to take part in an entrepreneurial venture.
- They are drawn by the lure of a "quick buck."
- They are eager to participate in a ground floor opportunity.
- They don't want to miss a once-in-a-lifetime investment opportunity.
- They are impatient with their inability to quickly secure employment after being fired.
- They fall victim to the financial pressures brought on by the loss of a steady paycheck.

In most cases, *Type E^M* individuals who make the crossover mistake quickly discover their error. Apprehension and anxiety build as they lose the comfort of a support system, a steady paycheck and the personal relationships that a corporate environment offers. CAUTION: Don't be drawn into a world you may not belong in.

Type E^N individuals, on the other hand, may be wooed by established companies offering them creative and operational autonomy and clout.
- They are promised a new title, new office, attractive management perks, or relocation to a more desirable location.
- They crave the publicity and perceived power that large companies confer.
- They thrive on recognition from their company, business associates, family and friends.
- Their ego is massaged by the promise of additional staff and resources, or "carte blanche" on a new company project.

Type E^N individuals who make the crossover mistake quickly lose their enthusiasm. Their non-conformist ways are not compatible with corporate structure, no matter how hard they try. They resent the loss of control, the lack of independence, and the loss of ability to make decisions on their own. **CAUTION: The innate yearning to "do your own thing" can be suppressed, but never extinguished.**

By understanding your *Type E^N* or *Type E^M* tendencies, strengths and weaknesses, you will be more confident in your decision about getting out of the corporate world, or staying in. You'll be more focused on the key aspects that make each type successful.

The following two chapters will help you identify and understand your *Type E^N* or *Type E^M* tendencies, and focus on the key aspects that make each type successful.

Checkpoint

✏ Each of us has *Type E^N* or *Type E^M* tendencies, which bring with them a unique set of strengths and challenges.

✏ There are many examples of "cross-over" mistakes which occur when one type tries to be the other type. This highlights the adage of "trying to fit a square peg into a round hole."

Chapter 3

STAYING IN:
A Fresh Look At Being Employed

There are many positive aspects of working for someone else. The safety and warmth of the corporate womb is accompanied by a steady paycheck, health care benefits and hospitalization, holidays and vacations, company paid professional development, a subsidized company cafeteria, and the opportunity to purchase the company's stock at a favorable price. Generally speaking, most managers are treated quite well by the company they work for.

As an employee, you may have the good fortune of developing some long-lasting friendships with your co-workers and staff, sharing company outings, celebrating birthdays, promotions and other events. Many employees derive a lot of pleasure from the people they meet on the job and look forward to socializing outside of work. After all, when you spend eight to twelve hours seeing the same people every day, you develop social bonds. If nothing else, employees usually find a confidante with whom to share the latest company scuttlebutt by the water cooler or over a sandwich at lunch time. Workplace friendships are quite an important benefit of being employed in a company.

Feeling connected with others flows to your professional relationships as well. Many individuals are accustomed to working with a product development group, being on a sales or marketing team, or collaborating with a group of managers or staff. Working with a team of competent people who contribute ideas, share the workload, and bring synergy to the workplace is quite a satisfying experience. One of the benefits of working as an employee in a company environment is the many opportunities to interact with others to solve problems. This is also the case when developing and introducing a product to market, opening a new division, or planning a corporate conference.

Are You a *Type E*^{M} **Individual?**

Most people have always been employed by others, and have never given much thought to whether or not they are the "employee type." In the previous chapter, you wrote down your likes and dislikes, passions and priorities. Now, you're going to delve a little deeper into your preferences and points of view to bring your career aspirations into clearer focus. Let's see if you fit the profile of the *Type E*^{M} individual, the strong and loyal company employee:

	Agree	*Disagree*
1. Being in charge of a business (including its financing, business development, product, human resources and service quality), does not appeal to you because of the risks involved.	☐	☐
2. You would rather receive a regular paycheck and paid holidays and vacations, employee perks and health care benefits, than be the one solely responsible for your own livelihood and that of others.	☐	☐
3. Advancing up the corporate ladder, and receiving recognition from managers and peers, is important to you. Being part of a work team or group makes you more comfortable and confident.	☐	☐
5. Taking complete responsibility for the success or failure of a project, a product launch, or a business unit is not attracticw to you.	☐	☐
6. Having the camaraderie and friendship of fellow employees is important to you.	☐	☐

7. Company perks — transportation, subsidized company cafeteria, performance bonuses, and stock options are important to you.
8. You are more likely to participate in professional development programs that are paid for by your employer than those you have to pay for yourself.
9. You believe that you can best advance your career in the structured environment of a company rather than the uncertain world of self-employment.
10. You would prefer to work with someone else who will take the risk to finance the business, while you offer your special skills to make his or her business successful.

If you agree with six or more of the above statements, you have more tendencies of a *Type E^M (employee)* than of a *Type E^N (entrepreneur)*. Type E^M individuals tend to be strong and loyal employees who enjoy being part of a bigger company team, and making a contribution with their specialized area of expertise. *Type E^M* individuals are driven by a defined scope of work and set of responsibilities, the supervision of others, and having the guidance of managers as a regular part of their duties and work environment.

Do You Enjoy Your Job and Where You Work?

Workplace surveys indicate that there's more to a job than financial compensation. Key factors to career satisfaction are feeling that you are fully employed based on your education and skills, that you have a good chance to move up in your job and achieve your career goals, and that you are doing meaningful work. A *Fortune* magazine article reported that "the 1993 class at Harvard Business School ranked salary seventh among the reasons for the career choices that they made. Leading the list were job content and level of responsibility, with company culture and the caliber of colleagues close behind."

To get a good idea of the factors which influence your enjoyment or displeasure at work, let's look at several factors that affect your productivity and happiness. How do the following aspects of your job affect your satisfaction with your current employment? Note the reasons you do not enjoy being an employee of an organization. This will give you one or more parameters to consider before you strike out on your search for a new job or business

Job Content:

Agree Disagree

1. *You clearly understand the set of responsibilities that you are being employed to carry out.* ☐ ☐
2. *Your set of responsibilities are a good match for your skills, capabilities, and experience.* ☐ ☐
3. *Your set of responsibilities are a good match for your education, interests, and future happiness.* ☐ ☐
4. *Your set of responsibilities provide you with the challenge, level of variety (or routine) that you seek.* ☐ ☐
5. *Your job gives you good opportunities for further development of your skills and capabilities.* ☐ ☐

Job Responsibility

Agree Disagree

1. You have an appropriate range of control over the quality and outcomes of your duties. ☐ ☐
2. You can control the pace of work and deadlines in completing your responsibilities. ☐ ☐
3. You receive feedback that fairly reflects your efforts and achieved outcomes in your work. ☐ ☐
4. You have reasonable freedom and autonomy in controlling how your responsibilities are carried out. ☐ ☐
5. You have a clear understanding of where your efforts fit in the big picture within your organization. ☐ ☐

6. You are well respected and would be a strong candidate to replace your boss should he leave the company.
7. Your working hours are reasonable.
8. Your job provides reasonable opportunities for advancement and promotion.

Does your current job provide many of the factors listed above in Job Content and Responsibility? If so, your job is a good fit with your capabilities and the degree of responsibility with which you are comfortable. If you disagree with six or more of the factors, go back to the lists you created in Chapter 2. Check whether the set of duties and responsibilities you are employed to carry out is consistent with who you are and what you want to do with your life.

Note that many of the items defining your happiness at work are impacted by the culture of the organization you work for. Within your company, "how we work around here" will influence:

1) The type of relationships you develop with your co-workers.

2) How participative or collaborative the work environment is (i.e., whether projects are generally task-driven or team-driven).

3) The extent to which your managers take time to develop your management skills, and encourage continuous education.

4) The extent to which your company employs new technologies in the workplace.

5) The extent to which your company emphasizes product development and fosters innovation as a clear market advantage over its competitors.

6) Whether your company provides opportunities for self-directed teams and project assignments, or tightly defines your responsibilities and structures procedures.

7) The degree of personal control you have over the approaches, results and measurement of the work that you do.

Given the above, it would not be surprising that two people who have similar responsibilities in different companies show different degrees of enjoyment in their work. This is due in large part to the work environment they are in. If your work style and your work environment are well matched, you have a better chance of finding satisfaction as an employee of a company.

When you understand the elements of job content, responsibility, and company culture as they relate to your career satisfaction, some preliminary considerations about whether or not you belong in your current job or company are brought to light.

A job can be a means to an end if you take a long-term view. As an example, a *Fortune* magazine article, "Kissing Off Corporate America," noted a shift from MBAs (Masters of Business Administration) joining large manufacturers to MBAs going into consulting and investment banking fields when they enter the job market. By gaining experience in business finance early in their careers, these managers are getting valuable training in the business world at large that they can leverage as entrepreneurs when they are ready.

Many people who have a college education psychologically lock themselves into a particular career or profession. Those who have engineering degrees tend to work in operations. Those who have marketing degrees find themselves in Xerox or Procter & Gamble-style trainee programs. They become product managers and field sales managers on their climb up the corporate ladder. Bankers who have been victims of downsizing by large banks may continue to seek jobs at other big banks even though they might face a similar problem as the banking industry continues to consolidate. Careers don't have to be like this unless you want them to be this way. In fact, the average person changes careers five to seven times during his working life.

One of the major lessons in life is to make learning portable. You know you've mastered something once you can apply the skills elsewhere.

The elements you excel at can be arranged and adapted in new environments to present new opportunities, if you approach change from this perspective. Finding a position offering individual growth and advancement is only limited by your talent, persistence, and energy to find an environment that stimulates and rewards your professional development.

For example, Fred, a shop supervisor we worked with wanted a chance at greater challenge, variety, outside contact and recognition in his job. He was very interested in a position with the purchasing department given his knowledge of the components and process of making his company's products. Fred wanted to be more confident and qualified to take on a role in the purchasing department. Setting some professional goals for himself, he enrolled in night school to study the principles of accounting, and finance and accounting for non-financial managers. These courses are offered at community colleges, at high schools and evening classes, and through companies offering professional development and training services. He became actively involved with a professional association of manufacturing plant purchasers to educate himself about the purchasing function. He networked with and met other purchasing managers to learn more about their experiences and careers, and to gain additional resources.

Today, Fred is happy that his skills, planning and hard work have gotten him a job as a purchasing manager. He experiences greater career challenge, variety and contact with outsiders, and says that he has finally found his place in the corporate world.

In reviewing your career possibilities, what are your priorities? Look at the lists you created in Chapter 2 and your answers to the exercises in this chapter. These are tools for pinpointing specific areas of motivational needs, identifying the basis of those needs, and building action plans to meet those needs.

What are Your Basic Options for Employment?

For the *Type E^M*, the basic options for employment can be based on a number of dimensions. The following considers two of these: the degree of change, and the degree of risk.

Options	Degree of Change	Degree of Risk
1. Stay with Current Job/Stay with Current Employer	*No Change*	*Very Low*
2. Join a New Department/Stay with Current Employer	*Lateral Move*	*Low*
3. Perform the Same Job/Join a New Employer	*New Environment*	*Moderate*
4. Find a New Position/Join a New Employer	*New Career*	*High*

Stay with Your Current Job/Stay with Your Current Employer

If you are content with your current employer and you enjoy the people you work with, perhaps the most important action for you to take at this time is a skills inventory. That is, evaluate your current set of skills and capabilities against the set of responsibilities you have been hired to carry out. Then compare where you are now with where you want to be. For example, what skills does your manager have if you aspire to advance to his job? You can no longer rest on your laurels and expect seniority to propel you to higher pay scales and the executive suite. You must be vigilant about acquiring the necessary skills with people, information, tasks and responsibilities to keep up with the global marketplace. Who is your company hiring to do what kinds of jobs? Who is being terminated? What about your company's competitors? Look in the employment section of your local newspaper and industry trade journal for the specific skills and positions in demand. Ensuring that your skills are updated is one way of relieving job stress, maintaining interest in what you do, and challenging yourself to improve your career potential.

In addition to lifelong learning through reading, coursework, and seminars, you should strengthen your knowledge on the job. Whenever possible, take on challenging assignments to exercise new skills, and add variety to your regular responsibilities. Taking on additional responsibilities will give you a reputation of being a reliable problem solver which makes you a valued employee.

If your company is financially healthy, with no significant changes or turnover in employees or management, you are in an enviable, low-risk employment situation. Nonetheless, you need to stay plugged in to the informal as well as formal communication networks inside and outside of the company that will keep you abreast of any changes.

Join a New Department/Stay with Your Current Employer

If you enjoy the people you work for, but you don't want to continue doing what you're doing for the rest of your life, you may be able to make a career move right where you are with the people you've worked with over the years. Many companies promote from within and encourage lateral moves to retain loyal employees.

For example, it is not unusual to see an accountant or financial manager move into a general management role which may eventually lead to the president's office. In this case, a financial background coupled with a good knowledge of operations and marketing will help, along with the support of your peers and senior management.

Research your company as you would any prospective employer. What is its mission? How does this year's annual report compare with last year's? What is the company's standing in the industry? The community? Are the majority of employees happy or disgruntled? Is your product or service in an expansion mode, or has demand peaked? Where is the organization headed in the next year? Five years? How do these facts, figures, and projects impact your job and career aspirations?

How do your fellow workers regard you? What have your annual reviews told you about your strengths and weaknesses and the company's expectations of you? What is your visibility and standing in your industry or profession? Who knows what you do and how well you do it? If you are a strong resource for your company, the company might see how your experience and expertise can be valuable to them in another area of the business. If you can't demonstrate or promote your skills, it will be very difficult to convince the company of your value to them in any position.

Keep in mind that if you move to another department within the company, you may have some fence mending to do with the members of the department you worked with previously. It is useful to remember that part of your success has come from the people you've worked with, so be sure to acknowledge others and give credit where it is due.

Perform the Same Job/Join a New Employer

People tend to seek new jobs and companies for one of six basic reasons: For a change of pace or environment, to avoid being a victim of cutbacks, to seek new professional challenges, to be recognized for their contributions, to escape bad relationships with other staff or management, or to make more money.

If you are unhappy in your current job and are thinking of leaving to join another company, be sure to select your new employer carefully. Sometimes a person leaves one company to join another because he believes he will have greater autonomy and freedom of action. However, he soon realizes that regardless of position, someone will always be watching over him. The "grass is not always greener on the other side of the fence."

In thinking about moving on to a new employer, a good place to start is to evaluate whether the job and responsibilities in your current situation are consistent with the positive aspects you've included in your lists from

Chapter 2. Specifically, elements of your job and responsibilities should be reflected in List 3 — "Where My Interests Lie," and List 4 — "What Turns Me On." List 5 — "Getting Feedback from Others," should reflect positively on your abilities and accomplishments on the job. Assuming this is the case, a new employer offering a similar set of responsibilities to that in your current position is an appropriate path to follow. Just be sure that your move will get you closer to your career goals than your current employment does.

There may be elements of your company's environment that are motivating you to leave. These elements may include the company's culture briefly outlined earlier, relationships on the job, and the level of work-related stress you feel. By isolating those elements of your job that are causing you unhappiness, loss of productivity, and stress, you can constructively look at other employment situations and determine if the work environment will be more compatible with how you work or improve your work performance.

Looking for the same job with another employer comes with a moderate level of risk in two respects: it places you in a new work environment, and exposes you to a degree of uncertainty. This is true even if you are a knowledgeable outsider who has done your due diligence prior to moving to a new challenge. Exchanging a familiar environment and relationships for a new work situation comes with inherent stresses — the need to build new relationships with co-workers and staff, to become familiar with the dynamics and work style of a new management team, and to learn and understand the business, systems and peculiarities of the new company. In addition, a move to a new work situation is often accompanied by a loss of personal stature due to your lack of familiarity with the new situation, and a loss of seniority (particularly if you've worked with your previous employer for a long time).

Find a New Position/Join a New Employer

Looking for a new position and a new employer at the same time is the most risky of the four employment options. The unknown about a new job, new people, new expectations, and a new company is a major risk factor. Additionally, your risk is increased to the degree that you must change and adapt to new ways of doing things. For example, if you are thinking of moving into an account management position in technical sales from an internal technology development role, the novelty of servicing customers may wear thin. Reaching sales quotas by closing sales will be your focus and source of stress, especially if you are going from a salary to commission-based compensation.

In all cases, understanding the risks and rewards of your current and any potential new job will help you in evaluating your next steps. If a new job will enhance your career growth, productivity, and well-being, a change may be good for you.

In each of the four employment options we've reviewed in this chapter, there is a variety of opportunities for various levels of autonomy. Whether managing a business unit, or managing a large project, you are required to manage people and make many decisions that will impact the success or failure of the business unit or project. Most decisions are made in an environment with some degree of uncertainty. Therefore, you can test your general management skills, along with your ability to manage a business unit or project. This is an attractive opportunity to hone your entrepreneurial skills in a company-supported environment. It is an opportunity for "intrapreneuring." While you are self-directed and held accountable for outcomes, you can still fall back on the company to support the unit's or project's financial obligations and risks. This is the key difference between intrapreneuring and running a business on your own. In your own business, you will bear all of the risks — personal, financial, regulatory, and business. We will explore entrepreneurship in greater detail in Chapter 4.

While middle managers are vulnerable in today's business climate, they can still find their place in the corporate world. This is particularly true in environments where technologies are being increasingly applied, and outsourcing of contracts and workers is taking place. Somehow, these technologies, contracts and workers must be coordinated and integrated with existing personnel and processes. This requires managers to have the analytical and technical skills to understand the processes or products being contracted or purchased, as well as the ability to deal with outside contractors and consultants.

You'll note that money has not been a point of discussion in this section. While it is a significant factor, money tends to overshadow the importance of the various reasons for getting out or staying in your job. As you go through the process of decision-making, rank the factors that are important to you, including money, to shed the right light on your ability to make an informed decision.

Every new employment situation is two-sided. The company decides whether you're the right match of skills, capabilities and traits for it, and you decide whether the employment opportunity and environment are right for you. Every company has its own personality. For example, the president and chief executive officer of a small pharmaceutical company resigned after only six months on the job. The reason was that his background from a large pharmaceutical company didn't fit with the smaller company's entrepreneurial style.

Your compatibility with a new company is an important factor in your success and happiness. As in the example of the pharmaceutical executive, if you plan to leave a larger company, your experience with systems and procedures may make it difficult for you to cope with a lack of order and a loose and informal *seat-of-the-pants* style of management that is sometimes evident with many smaller companies.

Sometimes leaving one job for another only shifts the stress from one set of pressures to another. You may leave company A to escape the pressure to produce sales, only to feel burdened with unusually long hours at company B. Before making any move, imagine what your days and weeks are going to be like on your new job. What will the commute time be? What about the number of overnight business trips, non-reimbursable work-related expenses (e.g., parking, dress code, child care, etc.), and sick leave policies? Is the business subject to seasonal fluctuations meaning uneven paychecks for you?

Another consideration is the diversity (or lack of) in the organization. If you are thinking about joining a company whose management, executives or owners share the same religion, ethnicity, educational background, or culture, this will have a bearing on how people relate to one another, how decisions are made, and how promotions are made. If you aren't familiar with or don't understand the corporate culture and how to work within it, your employment may be short term.

We firmly believe that each individual needs to find that environment that allows him to thrive and perform at his best. Anything less will stunt your growth and rob you of long-term happiness, let alone employment security.

If you are considering joining another company, refer to your lists from Chapter 2. Your answers will give you a good idea of what job factors are important to you. Chosen carefully, a new career situation can make a considerable difference in your mental well-being, accomplishments, and satisfaction with life as an employee.

On the other hand, you could be setting yourself up for future problems by looking for the perfect job when you are better suited to create your own business. The never-ending search for the fabled "fountain of youth" or perfect job can leave you frustrated and unfulfilled. Finding employment with another company may only delay or suppress your feelings about what you really want to do.

The Next Steps

1) Review the lists and personal summary you prepared in Chapter 2 and make appropriate modifications, particularly as they relate to things you like to do or things that you dislike about job content, level of responsibility, or work environment.

2) Compare your answers with the benefits of being an employee and determine, at least in general terms, whether you lean in the direction of a *Type E^M*.

3) If you see yourself as a long-term employee, consider enhancing your skills to apply to your current job, or to prepare for a new employment situation.

4) If you see yourself leaning toward being an entrepreneur (*Type E^N*), the next chapter investigates what it takes to be a successful entrepreneur.

5) Determine if the fork in the road you are most attracted to is the right choice for you. That is, ask yourself what more you need to know to make a good decision. Additional information will help you determine:
- Whether or not to stay in your current job.
- How to transfer to another department within your company.
- What specific companies you might want to work for in a similar position or capacity.
- How you can improve your qualifications and sell your current capabilities to another company.

Now put your insight into an Action Plan:

1) Write down the attributes of an employee that describe you so that you can understand whether you are a *Type E^M* (employee) or *Type E^N* (entrepreneur).

2) If you are better suited to be an employee than an entrepreneur, what would be an ideal job for you? Discuss your attributes with someone you respect and trust who knows about your job and work.

Ask them how your capabilities can add value to the company's operations, then determine if your current job can include these elements of responsibilities.

3) Look in the classified ads to help you determine the types of jobs and titles that would include elements of these responsibilities. This will give you an idea of what positions in your company, or in other companies, can best use your talents. In particular, it might show who you would have to displace, work for, or report to in your company, if such a job were given to you.

4) Determine how your current capabilities could be enhanced to give you a greater chance to pursue this opportunity.

5) Talk with your manager about the possibility of such a job opening up so that the company can receive greater benefits from your set of skills and capabilities.

With action plan in hand, you are ready to make the transformation to being a re-energized employee.

Chapter 3 Checkpoint

The *Type E^M* individual prefers to work for a company or organization, and enjoys the familiarity of a structure, group of people, and definition of responsibilities, where the risk of failure is generally borne by the owners and top management.

✎ As a *Type E^M* individual, you have four basic options for employment, depending on the degree of change, risk and opportunity you seek.

✎ Your compatibility with the workplace environment and people in a company will play a large part in your performance and success as an employee.

If you are a *Type E^M* individual, ask yourself what additional information you'll need to understand your career options and to make a good decision.

SOME REASONS PEOPLE STAY IN A CORPORATE JOB

1. I feel a sense of camaraderie working with others. Over the years I've developed close social bonds and friendships with my co-workers. There is little pretension among the people I work with.

2. I've gained a sense of respect from, and am well liked by, my co-workers. The promotions and paychecks are a measure of my worth, and recognition for a job well done. I like that.

3. I enjoy managing others, and feel a sense of authority and control over results.

4. Others' skills complement mine. I feel a sense of relief that I am not responsible for knowing all the answers.

5. The company I work for provides on-the-job training and professional development. It invests in new technologies and work tools to help workers develop their skills.

6. The work environment brings a sense of structure and order to my life. It provides a sense of predictability (I know I have to be there every day) and familiarity, and lets me plan family, community and sports activities.

7. I feel an identification and association with the company, its products and services. I feel a sense of importance because our company's stock is traded in the financial markets.

8. The world and workplace are changing so quickly that I feel comfortable staying with what I'm used to. It may not be the best thing for me, but I know what to expect.

9. In today's work environment, leaving my job will bring a sense of uncertainty. I couldn't be sure about how long I might be unemployed. If I left my job, I would lose my seniority and level of pay.

10. I like what I do, and I'd rather work to live, than live to work.

Chapter 4

GETTING OUT:
Gaining Control Of Your Destiny

In Chapter 3, we looked at the *Type E^M* individual — the loyal employee — and the options of staying with your current job, joining a new department, or joining a new employer. In this chapter, we'll examine the entrepreneurial *Type E^N* individual and see if this profile matches you the best.

First, let's identify some of the signals that may be causing you some anxiety about your job security:

1) You feel apprehensive every time you see your boss.
2) You feel uneasy as Monday morning approaches.
3) You're bored with your work or responsibilities.
4) Your opinions don't matter to others any more.
5) Your overall responsibilities have been reduced.
6) You have no defined career path.
7) You believe that you cannot continue to grow professionally within your current position.
8) Your last pay increase happened so long ago that you can't even remember the date.
9) You feel that you are underpaid for the contribution you make.
10) You've been demoted as a result of a merger.
11) You have been told that your skills aren't needed in the new realities of the marketplace.

12) You're doing a lot of moaning and groaning about the cutbacks in your company.
13) Someone was just promoted, but he/she joined the company after you did.
14) Your mentor has been fired, and you're looked upon as "one of his boys."

More often than not, the signals of an impending dismissal are all too clear, but an employee doesn't want to recognize them for what they are. Many people wake up too late to do anything about them, while others spend more time planning their leisure time activities than their careers.

There are many reasons that people want to leave a corporate job voluntarily:

1. Company restructuring is on the rise
2. Lack of authority or autonomy
3. Too many bosses and too many levels of approval or authority
4. Long hours, stress and burnout
5. Sexual harassment
6. Racial or other prejudice
7. Age discrimination
8. Forced relocation
9. Conflict with the culture of the company
10. Conflict with the new owners of the company
11. Lack of team spirit
12. Requests to undertake unethical or illegal tasks

These factors can affect workers at all levels and in all professions. Even lawyers and doctors are no longer resistant to career-switching. In spite of their hefty paychecks, many lawyers are frustrated because the law doesn't excite them any longer. They become mired in messy divorce proceedings, tough litigation, and other non-satisfying endeavors, or have to deal with uncivil and uncaring opponents or judges.

Similarly, many physicians are terribly frustrated by their inability to provide a high quality of medical care because of the intervention of third party health care providers and the managed health care system. Insurance carriers today are perceived to have the power to induce physicians to join their provider networks, and to unilaterally change contract terms to impact the providers' profitability. Physicians translate this loss of control in their practices into an inability to best serve the needs of the patient, a core principle of the healing profession.

Whatever your particular situation, the factors causing you to think about leaving should be weighed against your entrepreneurial tendencies.

Are You Ready To Become Your Own Boss?

Becoming your own boss has a glamorous ring to it, doesn't it? But, don't be fooled or romanced by those inspiring stories and company profiles that turn up on the television business shows and in the entrepreneur magazines. According to the U.S. Small Business Administration, one in four new ventures fails within two years of start-up. The majority of the remaining three survive, but grow modestly. About five percent of these remaining companies will take off, and a smaller percentage will eventually become large corporations.

Despite these statistics, the idea of becoming one's own boss is an attractive one, a downright powerful one. But, you must think rationally and objectively about such a big move. Do you have what it takes to meet the challenge of being your own boss? According to a study by Scotland's Heriot-Watt University, entrepreneurs are described as:

1) Tenacious and willing to make sacrifices in their family life and standard of living to start a business.

2) Achievement-oriented. They possess a strong desire to succeed even in the face of several failures. They are able to thrive on crisis, while always putting on a happy face to customers and employees.

3) Visionaries. They have precise goals which they can clearly explain to others. They constantly re-energize themselves and others around them.

4) Responsible. They assume personal responsibility, seeking situations to assume responsibility for successes and failures; and believe that outcomes are within their control. They are able to give themselves the criticism that they deserve, accept the criticism of others, and remain humble.

5) Problem solvers. Entrepreneurs are able to find the best solutions to problems.

6) Observant. An entrepreneur appreciates variety and is able to see trends and catch details that others miss.

7) Flexible. Entrepreneurs tolerate ambiguity, remain productive and focused even under uncertainty. They can juggle a variety of chores.

8) Big picture people. They take calculated risks, lowering the level of risk by planning thoroughly.

9) Optimists. Entrepreneurs learn from their mistakes and see failure as temporary.

Considering the study, the *Type E^N* individual can be described as having:
- Endless persistence
- A little naiveté
- Some healthy self-confidence
- An open mind to creative solutions
- An inclination to be frugal
- Unending coping skills
- Determination

If you decide to go into business for yourself, entrepreneurs tell us their personal investment is rewarded by:
- More variety in responsibility and projects
- Less office politics and corporate bureaucracy
- An energetic and responsive environment
- Increased sense of individual involvement and control
- Short chain of command
- Setting their own pace and their own hours of work
- A great feeling of self-worth and accomplishment

There are early indicators of the *Type E^N*'s entrepreneurial flair. Think back to the games you played as a child, the decisions made as you grew up, and the roles you've played. Were *you* always the most adventurous when it came to the trek through the woods? How did *you* arrive at your educational or career choices? Did *you* choose your major and the college you attended? How did *you* determine which job to take after graduation? Did *you* make these decisions on your own, or did your parents or spouse make them for you? Can you identify the time when *you* began to think of yourself as being different from the conventional and conforming employee, either breaking away from the pack or seeing yourself as miscast? Have you always been a self-starter, or has someone else always made decisions *for you*?

As an entrepreneurial manager, your take-charge attitude has likely carried over to the way you do your job and supervise your people. The following checklist is adapted from the book *Bouncing Back* by Andrew DuBrin. It helps you evaluate if you are an entrepreneur type. Are you? Check the boxes that describe your style.

☐ A heavy motivation to get work accomplished, combined with a direct approach to giving instructions to employees.

☐ An intense sense of urgency that motivates many people and discourages some. Do you have such an intense sense of urgency that you expect others to feel the same way about work?

☐ Impatience and brusqueness toward employees because entrepreneurs are always in a hurry. Do you frequently eat on the run? Many *entre*preneurs operate more on hunches than careful planning. Are you discouraged with people who insist on studying problems for a prolonged period of time?

☐ A charismatic personality that inspires others to want to do business with the entrepreneur despite his or her impatience.

☐ A strong dislike for bureaucratic rules and regulations, which make the entrepreneur impatient during meetings. Have you done some job hopping because of your frustration with rules and regulations imposed from above?

☐ A much stronger interest in dealing with customers than employees.

☐ A strong achievement drive which translates into being a self-starter fueled by the need to succeed and accomplish something. Are you constantly keeping score?

☐ A willingness to assume personal responsibility for the success or failure of a given activity or event.

☐ An ability to spot problems and opportunities that other people overlook.

☐ A belief that one's accomplishments and failures are under one's personal control and influence, and that luck is not such an important factor in contributing to success or failure.

☐ An ability and a willingness to live with a certain amount of uncertainty in life. This uncertainty can relate to job security, business deals, and personal life.

☐ A willingness to take calculated and sensible risks. A calculated risk means that the chances of winning are neither small enough to represent a gamble nor so large to be almost certain.

☐ A willingness to accept setback, and then to recover and keep going. Do you have the required resiliency?

It may be no surprise that your experiences and past decisions indicate that you are a *Type E^N*. This may explain your outward attitude or internal feelings of dissatisfaction as an employee if the company you work for does not provide an entrepreneurial environment or an appropriate level of employee autonomy. Having the basic traits of an entrepreneur, however, does not ensure business success. Having the tools and knowing how to use them skillfully are two different things.

Whether or not you succeed as an entrepreneur will still depend on careful planning based on your particular circumstances. Do you have the right business idea at the right time? Do you have the drive and staying power to see the details of the business through? What about your family, finances, personal focus and emotional state? These are topics we'll cover later.

For many embittered victims of company cutbacks who have vowed not to cast their lot with another employer, the great allure of starting their own business is freedom. For others, it is the flexibility of self-employment while their children are growing up. Still others see an entrepreneurial venture as a bridge between the years of full-time career and retirement.

STATISTICS SHOW THAT BEING YOUR OWN BOSS IS GAINING POPULARITY

Based on a survey of professional women's associations, 19% of executive and professional women plan to go into business for themselves, and another 19% are considering taking the plunge. In fact, AT&T estimates that by the year 2000, 65% of women owned businesses will be home-based and 80% of new businesses will be owned by women.

Another study by the University of Minnesota showed that one in eight people harbor a secret desire to start a company. What's more, when contacted a year later, a quarter of them had actually gone out and opened a business.

In 1991, *The Wall Street Journal* reported that more stock brokers strike out on their own because they are tired of the pressure to push the product of the month, or they were forced out of the big firms. The main drawbacks of being on their own were the fatter medical and phone bills, and nobody to keep them company except research reports. At the time the number of solo stockbrokers nationwide was reportedly 2,000 and growing.

The Link Research 1995 Home Media Consumer Survey found that the work-at-home population has expanded by 3 million for the 12 month period ended June, 1995. Home workers increased by 7.6% to a total of 39 million. The survey found that this increase is largely attributed to company employees who bring work home and who use any combination of PCs, modems, fax devices and/or multiple phone lines.

The largest segment of the work-at-home population includes full-time or part-time self-employed people who work primarily out of the home. There are approximately 12.9 million households where at least one person reports self-employment as the primary income source, and 13.9 million households who report at least a part-time, self-employed home worker.

Getting Out 73

The following is adapted from a *Los Angeles Business Journal* article on women in business, "Leaving Corporate America...Is It The Right Move For You?" It cites the growing movement by women to leave large companies for careers in smaller entrepreneurial companies, consulting, and their own businesses. We believe that the article provides basic and thought-provoking questions for women and men alike. The article asks you to consider whether starting your own business will improve the quality of your life and satisfy your yearning for the following challenges. These are more good questions to determine whether you are a *Type E^N*.

1) Can you afford the financial risk? What financial resources are you able to devote to the new business and how far will they stretch before you run out?

2) Can you sell, market, and do the operating work also? Starting a business is a commitment to make the company successful with long hours and multiple responsibilities. You may not have some of the resources that were once available to you, like a secretary, a legal department, and a travel department to book your tickets and arrange your itinerary.

3) Is there a proven market for what you have to offer? Will customers see the need and pay for your product?

4) Do you know how to set fees for your services?

5) Do you have the credentials for what you propose to do?

6) Will this venture increase your chances of professional growth?

7) Do you want to do the nitty-gritty?

8) Are you persistent almost to a fault?

9) Can you handle rejection?

10) Are you a natural networker?

11) Can you adequately deal with conflicts of interest between your family and business?

12) Are you strong enough to cope with operational, personnel, and emotional challenges?

13) Do you want flexibility and freedom in your career?

If you answered "yes" confidently to seven or more of these thirteen questions, you should explore further whether leaving the corporate setting is the right move for you. By leaving the corporate world, you leave behind the guaranteed paycheck, the perks, status, good hotels and restaurants, first class air travel, and a support system. In return, you'll be your own boss, work fifteen hour days, bear all the risk, receive no regular salary, have no security, and maybe no future. But then again, there'll be no soporific meetings, reports and video presentations. You'll have to be more aware and prudent in managing your time and expenses. You'll be required to be more self-reliant in exchange for more business flexibility and a certain degree of personal freedom. Running your own business is selling yourself and your business all the time. Being out there all the time. You'll lick your own stamps and change your own light bulbs. The trade-off to the long hours is indeed the feeling that you can control your own destiny.

If it still sounds attractive, read on.

> **THIS SEAL OF QUALITY STARTED ON THE KITCHEN TABLE**
>
> Early in his career, David Power was a financial analyst at Ford Motor Company. After a short time as a consultant to General Motors, he started a market research firm, working out of his kitchen in Westlake Village, California. Today, you know his firm as J.D. Power and Associates, the premier market research firm that publishes quality and customer service rankings for the automobile, airline and computer industries.

Are You Prepared to Be Your Own Boss?

There are dozens of books, seminars, and magazine articles on the specifics of starting your own business. Our focus is to give you the big picture and a taste of what it takes so you can decide whether to pursue or abandon this career move.

In asking yourself this question, there are a number of things to consider. When it comes to starting a business, the phrase "Put your money where your mouth is" is the reality. Because the risk of starting a business is large, the financial risk and exposure are not points to belittle or ignore. A *Los Angeles Business Journal* article in which Benjamin Cole interviewed a partner from a large accounting firm focused on this very topic. The article highlighted the following:

1) You must be prepared to lose everything that you invest, and place a limit on how much you can lose. You need discipline to stay within your pre-set limit.

2) When you complete a realistic plan of operating costs, rents, packaging, promotion, etc., add 10% - 15% for unexpected events and expenses.

3) Do you have financing? If not, consider having your financing in place — a line of credit, a second mortgage, and increased spending limits on credit cards prior to leaving your company job.

4) Are you humble enough to operate lean and mean? You won't be able to spend in the same fashion as when you were employed; frugality will be your constant companion.

5) Spend your money on good quality letterhead and stationery, and a laser printer to make you look bigger and better than you are.

6) Pay for good legal and accounting advice, and be sure to build your business network. Do this before you jump out on your own!

7) Look for ways to get free publicity, and make sure you know who your customers are and how to reach them prior to spending money on advertising.

8) Know when to quit, and quit if it is taking too long to make money.

9) What psychological adjustments have to be made? Get comfortable with a less extravagant business and personal lifestyle than you were previously used to. Whatever the level was before, now it will be less.

10) Quickly build a vendor network so that you can keep your production and capital costs lower.

When you leave an employment situation and go into business for yourself, your financial resources and your plan will determine the level of risk you will face. By taking a realistic view of your willingness to take on the financial risk, you'll quickly decide whether you have sufficient entrepreneurial instincts to run your own business.

How Can You Prepare Yourself While You Work For Someone Else?

Whether you are thinking of joining another company or going into business for yourself, be sensitive to the need for retraining. You must have cutting-edge information, particularly in computer technology, business law, financing, and marketing. There are many managers who turn down opportunities to take professional development courses paid for by their companies because of the time involved. Don't be short-sighted. The more education you have, the more income-earning potential you have. The next time your boss asks you to go to an Internet marketing course or to attend a "diversity in the workplace" seminar, go. Lifelong learning is the mantra for the coming century. Broaden your horizons and skill base. You never know what you will learn, what new ideas you will develop, and the contacts you can make. Our advice: Do it!

For example, after years of working as an engineer, Joe decided to pursue his dream to develop a low cost desalination process that he invented. He gained some additional training in finance and marketing to accomplish his goal. People are making changes everywhere. Don't be surprised to learn that your doctor is completing an MBA program so he can transition from providing health care to managing it. Many teachers have left the school campus to become corporate trainers in the business world. You can make a change for the better, too.

Another way to exercise your entrepreneurial muscle is to begin a business while you are still employed. This reduces your risk of "starting from scratch" because you are earning a paycheck. This may be helpful until you gain a base of customers or have the equipment and a business organization in place. However, it would only be ethical if you are not going to compete with your employer, and if you are not doing anything for your own business while you are compensated on your employer's time.

Which of Your Assets Help You to Succeed?

No matter which fork in the road you take, remember that in the corporate world, the one-company, one-career era is over. You must discover the difference between what you *do well* and what you *like to do* if they are not the same things. And if what you like to do can be translated into a sound business concept, then you might enjoy a profitable future with your own business. There is a link between self-image and the job one holds.

Your hobby and leisure pursuits can indicate how successful you might be in working and relating with people. *The Wall Street Journal* reported the following:

> "If you're a bridge player, chances are you are not a team player. Card players, especially bridge aficionados, score poorest in corporate compatibility. Bridge players tend to be intellectually arrogant, cagey and eager to pounce on a rival's weakness. They are more apt to be highly critical of mistakes rather than sympathetic and helpful."

Organized sports activities such as basketball, hockey and football, work off anger and tensions and promote compatibility; fishing, boating, dancing, jogging, tennis, bowling and golf are avocations which foster camaraderie. It would appear that any outside activities, such as playing in a band or orchestra, line dancing, sailing — which involve team participation — are typically better for work groups, than activities which highlight strong individual competition.

It is clear to us all that we'll never escape the need to have business dealings with others, whether customers, vendors or employees. Your comfort level in dealing with small or large groups of people will influence the size of any business you're involved with and how much success you achieve.

So, What's Stopping You?

In 1990, an Accountemps survey concluded that one in three managers think most executives would flee the corporate suite to start their own businesses if they could get the necessary funding. In the same year, the United States Internal Revenue Service reported the number of people filing tax returns as independent contractors has been increasing each year. It has been reported that there is almost no job — from anesthesiology to zoology — that cannot be done on a contract basis.

Different people will have different levels of comfort with respect to their financial resources and the security they require. A good rule of thumb is to have cash reserves of at least six to nine months of your monthly paychecks before striking out on your own. This will help you to cover your monthly expenses during the startup period. The more specialized the job or career you are in, the larger the reserve should be. The size of the cash reserve will depend on how cash intensive or risky the business is, and how quickly you generate revenues. People tend to greatly underestimate how long it takes to build cash flow. Therefore, you might consider working as an independent contractor to test the waters of independence in your chosen field, and minimize your expenses. It's all a matter of planning.

An important point to ponder is that starting your own business will not automatically solve any problems of cultural, racial, or gender discrimination you might have faced as an employee of a company. Some problems may persist:

- Preconceived perceptions of your capabilities and expertise
- The openness and receptivity of potential clients toward a marketing call or business development meeting with you
- The willingness of banks and financial institutions to issue credit to your business

These are all realities that may affect you as a business owner even if you have not faced them as an employee.

Home-Based Business Facts

Compared with the overall mortality for new businesses, the figures here indicate a very high success rate for home-based businesses. We think that much of this has to do with entrepreneurs testing and refining their new business concept while keeping their expenses low. Then, when things take hold, the ingredients for success are readily apparent.

1. Nearly 8,000 people start a new business each day (one every 11 seconds, or about 300,000 per year)
2. Nearly 25,000,000 Americans operate a home based business
3. Most begin home businesses in their spare time.
4. They earn an average of $50,250 per year
5. 20% earn more than $75,000 per year
6. 95% will enjoy a profit in their first year
7. 85% will still be in operation after 3 years compared to 20% survival rate for conventional storefront businesses, based on a lower cost structure.
8. The average home-based income is 2 times greater than the national employee average
9. 50% of home businesses that start as a part-time endeavor turn into full-time careers

Other Benefits Enjoyed by Working from Home
1. Tax benefits
2. Flexible working hours and more freedom to structure your life to put first things first
3. A higher degree of career enjoyment and self worth than traditional employment situations. *Home Office Computing* reports a satisfaction rate of 95%.
4. The opportunity to set up in a rural area or anywhere you desire
5. Low overhead, risk and investment capital than having a separate business establishment
6. Security? Fortune 500 companies have been eliminating an average of 1,500 jobs per day in recent years. Small business (fewer than 20 employees) is the only area of employment growth in the business community.
7. Work in your jeans or sweats; no dress codes or uniforms to buy.

Report by the Link Resources Corp., a New York based consulting firm.

GETTING OUT OR STAYING IN:
A Look at Both Sides

List #1: What I Like Least

1. Writing up orders
2. Analyzing sales statistics
3. Dealing with returned goods
4. Disciplining staff
5. Meetings with my boss
6. Taking orders from my boss

List #2: Things I Find Difficult To Do Or Do Not Possess the Skills For

1. Following up with sales staff to make sure they're selling
2. Identifying new customers
3. Calling on new customers
4. Presenting to large audiences
5. Fixing broken machines

List #3: Where My Interests Lie

1. Like to work with computers
2. Enjoy learning new languages
3. Like to solve problems as a member of a team
4. Like to run with a project from begining to end

List #4: What Turns Me On

1. Meeting tight deadlines
2. Finding sources of capital
3. Reading about new technologies
4. Knowing where the competition fails
5. Understanding how to beat competition
6. Being hands-on in all aspects of a project or business

List #5: Getting Feedback From Others

What I'm good at ...
1. _____
2. _____

What I'm not good at ...
1. _____
2. _____

Where my interests lie ...
1. _____
2. _____

List #6: Why Do I Want To Stay in the Corporate World?

1. Steady paycheck
2. Enjoy working on teams
3. Develop work-related friendships
4. Build a corporate career
5. Like a more predictable work environment
6. I don't like making big decisions on my own

List #7: Why Am I Interested in Leaving the Corporate World?

1. Independence
2. I have know-how for a product
3. I love to sell
4. I know how to raise money
5. I understand how to beat the competition
6. I'm a very organized individual

List #8: Do I Willingly Take Risks?

1. Like to dabble in stock market
2. Don't get sensitive about losing money
3. I love bunjee jumping
4. Comfortable with dealing with money
5. I date often and love being a ham in the crowd

List #9: Why Do I Want A Business of My Own?

1. Have run a business
2. Like calling the shots
3. Know how to read P&L
4. Managing cash flow is a talent I have
5. Have a great product to sell
6. My brother has a business
7. People say I'd be good at running a business

Getting Out 81

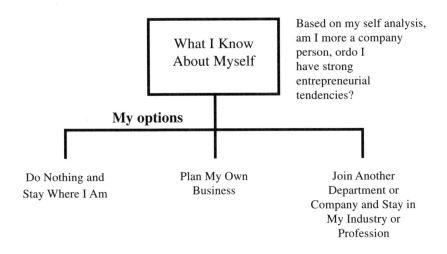

	What I Know About Myself	Based on my self analysis, am I more a company person, or do I have strong entrepreneurial tendencies?

My options

Do Nothing and Stay Where I Am	Plan My Own Business	Join Another Department or Company and Stay in My Industry or Profession
1. Steady paycheck	1. Less formal	1. Better fit for me
2. Paid hospitalization	2. More autonomy	2. Change of scenery
3. Paid vacations	3. Grow with a trend	3. New challenges
4. Company cafeteria	4. Quickly take advantage of a market opportunity	4. Opportunities for growth
5. Stock options	5. Less ambiguous	5. Surrounded by people
6. Surrounded by people	6. Greater achievement	6. Team atmosphere
7. Team atmosphere	7. Reward matches effort	7. Recognized for efforts
8. Shielded by others	8. Responsible for all decisions	8. Build on experience
9. Comfort with company culture	9. Greater risk	9. Expand reputation
10. Shared responsibility	10. More stress	10. Adjust to culture
11. Bureaucratic decision-making		11. Advance position
12. Corporate turmoil		12. Corporate turmoil

Our goal is to help you discover your strengths and weaknesses, your comfort zone, and your options. Avoid the temptation to procrastinate. Use your time productively while you're employed, and you'll gain confidence in your ability to make the right career moves.

The Next Steps

Complete the comparison of your personality, work style, interests, and habits with those of an entrepreneur. While our lists may differ semantically, you should have a good idea of whether or not you are a *Type E^N*, and if this is a path you would like to explore further.

1) Review the lists and personal summary you prepared in Chapter 2 and make any necessary modifications.

2) Compare the contents of each of your lists against the benefits of being an employee and the attributes of an entrepreneur. Does your profile match a *Type E^N*?

3) If you don't have many of the characteristics of an entrepreneur, you are probably a *Type E^M*. In this case, look for opportunities to develop or enhance your skills either in your current job or with another employer.

4) For you entrepreneurs, re-read Benjamin Cole's 10 points summarized earlier in this chapter. A big challenge will be your ability to understand the business you are developing, as well as the sources of help available to you from your personal and professional network.

5) Write a five step action plan that responds to the following questions. The answers will tell you what additional information you'll need to arrive at a good decision:

- What more do I need to find out about the level of risk I'm willing to take on?
- Do my home and relationship situations allow me to take on this level of risk?
- What types of businesses am I most qualified or suited to be involved with?

- If I were free to make a decision tomorrow, what would I do?
- How would I approach such an opportunity?

This exercise differs from that of Chapter 3 as it focuses more on determining whether you should follow an entrepreneurial direction. Now, take the next steps in writing your action plan:

1) Write down which attributes of an entrepreneur strongly describe you so you can understand if you are honestly and truly suited to be a *Type E^N*.

2) List the types of businesses that would best apply your skills.

3) Find examples of these types of businesses in your neighborhood or town if they exist, and talk to the owners about how successful or difficult it is to survive and be profitable.

4) Go to the library and find out how successful these businesses have been in the country, how large such a market might be, and what range of incomes these businesses earn. The county or state Economic Development Office has the wage and salary breakdown for a number of jobs, as do publications such as the annual *Information Please Business Almanac and Sourcebook,* and *The American Almanac of Jobs and Salaries.* Your accountant will be able to steer you to additional sources of information.

Talk with someone whose business judgment you respect about whether you would be suited to this type of business, and ask his opinions about your chances of success.

As you begin to formulate a plan for yourself, keep in mind these simple, yet key, points:

1) Do what you enjoy; all the better if you are truly passionate about it.
2) Find the right niche and get there early.
3) Move and move fast.
4) Make committed actions to get the job done.

5) Take care of your people.
6) Be resourceful.

Chapter 4 Checkpoint

The *Type E^N* individual is more likely to be tenacious and achievement-oriented, with a strong desire to succeed, and tolerance for ambiguity and uncertainty. Having the tools and traits, and knowing how to apply them effectively in your own business are two different things.

✎ As A *Type E^N* individual, you can prepare yourself by taking advantage of professional development opportunities to broaden your entrepreneurial and business skills while you are still employed.

✎ Your success as an entrepreneur will depend on careful planning based on your particular circumstances.

If you relate well to the attributes of a *Type E^N* individual, you'll want to build your base of information further, and to carefully evaluate the risks and the decision to go out on your own.

Reaching for the Right Answer

Chapter 5

GETTING FIRED:
The ABCs of Good Preparation

There is one overriding lesson to be learned from competitive sports: Prepare well and you will do well. Good tennis players know that it's not just hitting the ball that counts. Proper preparation means a practiced and well thought out response to an opponent's power on ground strokes and a quick study of your adversary's tendencies in shot-making over the course of the warm-up. All this takes practice and preparation.

The same is true for marathon runs. How many spectators truly appreciate the long hours of training – starting with two to three miles, progressing to 10 miles, and on to the epitome of physical fitness to run 26 miles? It's unthinkable for someone to attempt a marathon without proper preparation.

The reality is that all goals worthy of undertaking require detailed and intensive preparation. We want you to prepare yourself for the day when you may leave your corporate job.

Mentally, you're already traveling along the road that will take your life in a different direction. You are mustering up the courage to take that scary step out of the familiar corporate world into the unknown. How do you make such a move? What do you need to think about first? What kind of "homework" should you do? What kind of maneuvering is there to be done? Since you may not have been a "planner" before, this chapter will give you some direction.

Previous chapters have helped you gain a strong sense of whether you should remain employed or start your own business. If your leanings are entrepreneurial, you have a lot of preparation to do. You must agree that the decision does not have to be, nor should it be, made overnight! Regardless of how confident you might be, until you have a clear vision and plan for your business enterprise, you aren't ready to go out on your own. So think about your current job as a means of leveraging your way into a new job or business.

What Would Life Be Like In Your Own Business?

First, it's a good idea to create a description of what this other life might be like. Take the time to write answers in your notebook to the following questions, and jot down additional thoughts that pop into your mind:

1) What product or service will your business offer?

2) Because you are in business to earn a living, your product or service must be exchanged for money in a revenue generating event.

3) What events and effort will be required to get a buyer to the point of exchanging money for your product or service?

4) How will you cope with the competition, deal with the customers and suppliers, and handle the relationship with your banker and financial backers?

5) What will your typical day or week look like?

6) What will your business look like in five and ten years? Will you be a lone ranger or will you have a staff?

7) What will your lifestyle be like, particularly the relationships you'll have with your family and close friends?

The description of your business and your plan doesn't have to be perfect. For the moment, don't worry about whether it is exactly what you want. You have to start somewhere, and the best way to do it is to plunge right in. It doesn't have to be right the first time, or the second. People often change their minds about very important decisions in life. College students change their choice of study major an average of 2.7 times during their first two years in school. You may change your thinking several times, too.

Don't be afraid to keep challenging your decision by asking yourself, "Is this really what I want?" The most important thing is to be sure that you are serious and clear about what you intend to do. This is certainly not a moment in your life to act impulsively. Remember your parents asking you if Little League Baseball or piano lessons were what you wanted? You could have quit, but they encouraged you to finish what you started. Now, you can have a similar conversation with yourself about whether you are in the career you really want to dedicate your life's work to.

CHOOSE YOUR RUT CAREFULLY

A New England traveler came to a road well grooved by sand and mud, which had now dried out. A hand-lettered sign nailed to a tree by the side of the road read, "Choose your rut carefully. You'll be in it for the next 10 miles."

Take the time to think about where you're headed. We've all seen examples of well-intended resolutions and uncommitted goals based on vague and wishful thinking. The well-publicized five year plans of the former Soviet Union didn't materialize. Closer to home, we'll hazard to guess that many of your New Year's resolutions never come to pass either. With this in mind, why will your long range career plan work? A good reason is that you're taking the time to research and build a foundation based on solid facts about the person you should know best, you!

When Should You Strike Out On Your Own?

You started this chapter by answering some broad questions about being in your own business. We've challenged you to visualize what being in your own business would be like. Here are some additional questions to consider:

- If you do decide to leave your job, when will that be?
- Do you have some particular age in mind when you will make the transition from your corporate job to something else?
- If you want to wait until you have enough money to fund your plan, what figure are you targeting and when will you accomplish this goal?

You may want to wait until a certain milestone is reached, such as your children completing their schooling. You may not want to make a move while an elderly parent is living with you; or you might be waiting for that appropriate business opportunity to present itself. All of us have different needs and goals which determine the time frames of our personal calendar of events.

Like a space launch, the next phase of your life needs a timetable for a countdown. It could be a period of ten years, or five, or whatever suits your personal circumstances. But, be sure you give yourself enough time to consider all your requirements. Unless you've already been working on a plan to leave your company, a quick countdown of only a few months is probably not enough for such a major change in your life. Remember, you'll need time at every stage to:

- Research your options carefully
- Accumulate the necessary capital
- Collect critiques and second opinions of your plan from others
- Get objective and professional advice (your attorney and accountant will be very helpful)
- Revise your initial plan thoroughly (or even abandon it and start over again)

The launch of a space mission requires a countdown to a definite date and time because so much coordinating is necessary. Planning is no less important to *your* mission. The stakes are much too high for you to construct it haphazardly.

How Will The Changing Face of Business and the Economy Affect You?

Inevitably, there will come a time when the decision to leave your current corporate job will be made. How many of your friends and family have retired from the very same company that they started with? Probably not many. We noted earlier that even in Japan, the paternalistic relationship between employer and employee of guaranteed lifetime employment is on the wane. The days of the one-company career are over. With the rapid changes in the business environment, terminations and changes have become a way of life.

> **HAVE YOU DREAMED ABOUT BEING YOUR OWN BOSS?**
>
> In November, 1995, *Success* magazine reported that "96% of Americans aged 25 to 44 would like to be in business for themselves — not that 96% would succeed or that 96% would even try it, but just that they'd thought about it."
>
> A 1996 *Inc.* magazine/Gallup survey found that "32% of the adult working population, or almost 40 million people, have never owned their own business but dream of starting one."

How Can You Prepare Yourself While You Still Have a Job?

Any change in management or ownership of a company will almost surely result in changes in the atmosphere at work and how jobs are done. Given today's business climate and environment, how do you manage these changes so they are beneficial to your goals?

If heavy layoffs do occur in your company or industry, the best advice is to wait until things crystallize. Then listen to what the plans are and how they will affect you directly. While events affecting your company will certainly have an impact on you, you may actually benefit personally as you will see in Chapter 8.

Once you've decided to make some changes in your career life, then what? Use all the intervening time to your advantage. Remember our earlier reference about "doing your homework?" Here's what that means.

1) Get to know all there is to know about your present employer.

2) Learn everything you possibly can about competitors in your current line of work, and about any new endeavor or potential lines of work you are considering.

3) Find out where the numerous sources of outside information are, and use them to your advantage.

4) Get your personal finances in order.

Termination Time

It's a lot more comforting when *you* are in control of your own decisions and destiny. Decide *who* you want to make the decision about you. When decisions are made *for you*, instead of *by you*, your confidence and preparation are sure to be impacted by a new set of stresses at a time when you may already be reeling from adverse news.

Being laid off or forced into involuntary retirement because of a business downturn or consolidation can be devastating if you aren't physically, mentally or financially prepared. When white collar professionals and knowledge workers — people whose work responsibilities focus on finding, assembling and providing information — are caught in the crossfire of takeovers, global competition and efforts to improve shareholder returns, the results are swift and impersonal. The best defense is to be ready and prepared, so that it will not be devastating to your career, emotions, or finances.

What Can You Learn About Your Employer?

At the time of your termination — whether voluntary or involuntary — the flexibility in any severance package you might receive from your employer can be strengthened by the research you've accumulated about your company. Develop a base of information from two perspectives, that of an employee, and one of an inquiring journalist. Here is an easy way to start developing some objective data:

1) Start a collection of business and financial newspaper clippings on your company. This will tell you where your company is headed and what customers, suppliers and the business community think about your management team.

2) Get the most recent annual and interim reports. This is relatively easy if your company's stock is publicly traded. The corporate communications or investor relations department usually has copies, as do online services and reference librarians.

3) Be aware of new product introductions. Any event or activity that will give you an indication of the company's future will help you project how successful the company might be. This will add to your future planning should you decide to stay with the company, or to set up a business offering a related product or service.

4) Secure outside investment company reports about your employer to determine how the market perceives the growth and investment prospects of your company.

5) Scan the trade journals for articles about your company and the products in your company's industry. Will the market potential of the company make it a strong competitor in the future?

This type of information can help you form an opinion about what might happen given the decisions being made in your company. You may gain a good perspective on how well the company might perform in the future, and how some of the events might affect you and your continued employment with the company.

By developing a perspective on how strong the company is financially and competitively, you can plan your next career or business move. You will also get an indication of what you might receive or be able to ask for should a termination or lay-off occur.

Companies, particularly public ones, are extremely sensitive about the image they convey to their customers, the public, and to the investment community. An unusual number of employee terminations might be viewed as an upheaval and engender a lack of confidence by Wall Street. Many times, perceptions or opinions can be as powerful as whatever may actually be happening.

Reporters from business publications can make use of a minor event to spark interest in a company that otherwise receives little or no attention. Most companies, especially conservative ones, do not like any kind of publicity, particularly when it carries negative overtones. Companies will go to considerable lengths to avoid any adverse publicity. This can work to your advantage in the event of negotiating a termination and severance package.

There are numerous factors that may affect the timing as well as the nature of your termination from your company:

1) When is the fiscal year end? When are earnings reports released? *(The company may be sensitive to the impact that employee terminations and settlements may have on its reported earnings, and possibly delay* terminations until the following fiscal year.)

2) What is the date of the annual meeting of the shareholders? (*Any bad news around the time of an annual meeting can reflect negatively on its tone. A company tries to maintain a positive public image around this time.*)

3) Is there an upcoming stock offering? (*In addition to the cash that the offering is projected to generate, the company will be in a public relations mode, and will do whatever is necessary to maintain a positive image with the investment community. This will help to maintain a favorable impact on the share price when the offering enters the market. Terminations may not be consistent with the image that is being portrayed.*)

4) Is the company in negotiation for new financing? (*Debt financing will require that expenses be kept in check, and this may signal management's willingness to trim expenses, including accelerating the termination process for some of its employees.*)

5) How have new products fared lately? Have there been some blockbuster hits or dismal failures? (*Blockbuster hits may signify the building of financial strength, which may have a positive impact on any negotiated termination settlement that might occur.*)

6) Is the company currently negotiating a large business deal? (*Employee terminations may reflect the availability of financial resources in the long-term, or a tight cash situation in the short-term. Either will impact the success of the business deal, the timing of any termination and the size of potential severance packages.*)

7) Has the company changed its advertising agency recently? (*If this is a means to lower or cut expenses and improve profitability because sales per advertising dollar have not been strong, terminations during this time may not be accompanied by generous severance packages.*)

8) What is the depth of personnel in your department? (*Will this signal a degree of expendability in your staff?*)

9) Does your particular expertise demonstrate your great value to the company? (*If it does, is your supervisor spreading praise about you?*)

10) Did you sign an employment contract, non-disclosure agreement, or non-compete agreement? (*This would be a good time to review with your personal attorney what you might realistically or optimistically expect should you be terminated.*)

Having this kind of information may help you considerably when the time comes for you to seriously consider leaving. Understanding how well your company is doing, and whether its market and financial prospects are healthy or weak will at least give you a context for understanding your potential role in the future of the company, or any discussion on financial settlement should a termination become reality.

Here are some additional tasks to carry out if you are contemplating changing jobs:

1) Assemble and review all personnel manuals, policy bulletins, and new employee orientation materials to be clear about your rights as employee, while you are employed and should you be terminated.

2) Develop a list of names of recently terminated employees. Talking with them on an informal and confidential basis might give you an indication of the consistency and range of termination settlements provided by the company should they be willing to share their personal situations with you.

3) If there have been wholesale firings, get a copy of company handouts. Try to find out more from employees who attended termination meetings so you know what to expect. (Did the handouts accurately summarize the terminations that have occurred so that you will not be surprised the next time it occurs?)

4) If your firm has a legal department, determine which lawyer has been assigned to personnel matters. If you know who will handle employee termination matters, you may gain a better understanding of how your situation will be handled should your number come up.

5) In informal conversations with the personnel representatives in your company, try to get information about personnel trends in your company and other matters related to firings and layoffs (e.g., advance notices, termination settlements, references, outplacement counseling, and how long they will provide professional support). This will be helpful in finding out what support the company will provide should you leave the company, so that you can at least make assumptions about how to prepare for those support areas that won't be provided by the company.

Whether or not you finally make the decision to leave the company, completing these tasks will keep you in touch with what is happening, and help you anticipate, plan and make decisions. This gives you an opportunity to see how job positions and assignments might change, what promotions might be possible, which departments or products are the growth or weak areas for the company, and consequently how these events might impact you and where you might focus your future efforts – both within and outside of the company.

If terminations and reductions-in-force are a frequent occurrence in your company, you should document every meeting or discussion on the subject. Most people can't remember the details of what was said when they are under pressure and fear for their job. Later, when you make plans that don't include your current employer, you may need to recall specific things that were said and done months or years ago. If the circumstances surrounding your termination prompt you to seek legal counsel, this documentation will prove invaluable.

What we've suggested here is not devious, unethical or illegal. You are developing intelligence just in case you need it to make informed decisions about your career and future, whether your intentions are to stay or leave the company. As a forward looking person, assembling this information is a means of staying well-informed. You'll be able to make more intelligent decisions about your work or personal situation in the future, not only in preparation for going out on your own, but also in case you stay or find yourself in another corporate job. This information may even be worth thousands of dollars to you in increased severance benefits because you're more familiar with the company's history and trends in previous terminations.

We strongly urge you NOT to break any contractual agreements you have regarding confidentiality, and we certainly do not condone the removal of company documents or property.

What Can You Do to Prepare for Your Future?

If you are planning to become a business owner yourself, there are additional things that you can do during this period. Enroll in company training programs and seminars. While these programs may have been presented to you in previous years, you may not have seen their relevance. Now, employee relations, site selection, negotiation and motivation techniques and other topics may be of great interest and value to you in preparing for your "next life." If your company sponsors extension programs at a local college, you may want to take advantage of this resource, and see if any of the courses will be relevant and beneficial to your new business or career.

Use your remaining time with your present company to your advantage. While you have the security of a job, make the most of the time and resources available to you. This will help you stay in a positive and proactive frame of mind. *Act outwardly as an employee and think inwardly as an entrepreneur.*

How do You Gain an Information Advantage?

As you identify competitors, suppliers or customers, get into the habit of collecting pieces of information that may be of enormous value to you later. You may just find an opportunity to jump start a business by buying into an already-existing business. Or you may be the right fit with the current owner who wishes to scale down his/her involvement in daily operations. This may lead to the negotiation of a part owner/employee situation with an agreement to buy the business later.

If you are considering buying an existing business, here are some things you should know:

1) Name of the principals and key people. It is always advantageous to know who's in charge.

2) Age of the owner of the company. This person might be close to the age of wanting to sell all or part of his company.

3) Additional family members active in the business. Lots of family involvement in the business may not open the possibility for outside ownership.

4) Is there an heir apparent? How qualified is he/she? If it is a family-owned business, what is the relationship between the parents/owners and children/participants?

5) Are there any divorces or feuds in the family which may cause tension and result in split loyalties? This may lead to a willingness by the owners to sell the business to an outside party.

6) Has the owner ever discussed selling the business? What's the scuttlebutt in the trade?

7) Have there been articles about this company in the trade press? This may provide some expert opinion and insight about the company's future.

8) Is this a one-man company where everything revolves around a single person? While it's always difficult to deal with a strong individual business owner, you may find that he or she may just be willing to talk about the succession of the company.

Who Will Your Competition Be?

If you eventually leave your present job and become self-employed, it makes a lot of sense for you to stay in the field that you have the experience and where you have the contacts. Your comfort level will be higher. Likewise, lenders and investors will have a much higher degree of confidence in you. Just about the last thing a banker or potential investor wants to see is a business plan to open a restaurant from someone who has never been in that business.

However, whatever industry or business you eventually choose for yourself, you should assemble a complete dossier on all your potential competitors. Visit competitors' exhibits at trade shows to learn what they are doing and become familiar with the key people in their organization. This does not have to be in the form of a spy mission. Look at the situation as another opportunity to network in a friendly business setting. It is always wise to develop good relationships within your industry. It's much easier to do this well before you leave your present job. Once you start your own business, attending trade shows may be a lower priority in your budgeting and spending.

If your potential competition includes public companies, get their annual reports and any other information that may be available. This may tell you where their business and marketing efforts are placed and the types of products or services they're planning to launch. This may also help to confirm that you're on the right track for your future business. What's the reason for all this? Your previous knowledge of competitors' products may not be as detailed as you need now that you're considering a decision about whether you're going to compete against them. As far-fetched as it may seem to you now, there may come a time when you may be involved in acquiring a former supplier of goods or services, or all or part of a competitor's company. You may even think about launching a product or service that will appeal to those companies in your field of interest. It's amazing that much of this information is available for the asking if you want to seek it out.

As an example, one of our interviewees (we'll call her Sheila) was a graphic designer who was responsible for designing and producing her company's internal publications. When the workload in her employer's corporate communications and investor relations areas became unmanageably large, she was sent to the department to assist them. Her expertise was used in completing annual reports and other high quality publications circulated to the investment community and the company's shareholders.

Sheila accumulated a database of specialty outside vendors. They specialized in scanning film output and photography, software solutions and support for high quality desktop publishing, and the production of bound reports for the financial and investment communities. After Sheila took a leave of absence from the company to have a baby, she wanted to remain at home to spend more time with her new daughter. Because her family could not afford the loss of a second income, Sheila started a graphic design business, specializing in producing newsletters and investor communications publications. Her company targeted small companies who were planning to undertake initial public offerings to the investment community, and who could not afford the expensive fees for such assistance and publications. She developed a niche in the marketplace by mining a database of contact names, competitors and vendor sources to build her own business.

The theme here is to **be prepared**. Just by looking at your ideas and thoughts about what the future will hold may convince you that your ideas or goals may not so far-fetched after all.

What Can You Find Out At Your Public Library?

Not surprisingly, one of the best sources of information is your local public library. In our experience, there seems to be great reluctance for people to visit libraries if they no longer are full-time students. Your first visit to the library might be to chat with the librarian about the extent of their business section, the periodicals they carry and the reference journals and book titles that are available. Librarians are there to help you. In fact, they enjoy the prospect of a challenging request. If you know your way around a library, you'll know where to find reference publications on businesses in just about any industry. Look for *Moody's, The Thomas Register, Standard Rate and Data Service* (SRDS) and *Standard & Poor.* Most libraries carry copies of local and regional newspapers, along with issues of business magazines and other publications.

Are Online and Technology-Based Services Really Helpful?

Today, you can access Dun and Bradstreet's databases of businesses across the country on micro-fiche or CD-ROM (the CD-ROM versions are updated quarterly). Company profiles from both *The Wall Street Journal* and your metropolitan newspaper on a fax-back service, or even computer-based online delivery of information about particular businesses, products or services are also available.

With the age of technology, you may already be an online subscriber to *The Wall Street Journal's Personal Journal*, which customizes *The Journal* to your specific requirements. This gives you business and worldwide summaries, and the news columns, companies and stocks you want to track, all via a telephone line and modem with the convenience of your own personal computer.

As another resource, if you're not already an Internet service subscriber, many public libraries provide computer access to the Internet which will also be of great value to start your information searches. The Internet is a system which ties a network of computers and informational databases together from thousands of points around the world. If you have a computer and a modem, you have the opportunity to access this extensive network of computers and databases.

The Internet gives you access to the Library of Congress and the Small Business Administration, for example, where you can get a wealth of basic information on how to start a business, write a business plan, find reference data on various industries, including demographic, employment and economic indicators. Many companies are increasing their marketing exposure with home pages or web pages on the Internet, which are similar to advertisements in a magazine or on television, but made available through computers. If you choose to find these home pages, they'll tell you about the company, their products and services and where to contact them (by letter, telephone or e-mail), and give you ideas about online marketing and merchandising. It's a good place to start a search, because the Internet can point you in the right direction with addresses, people to contact or reference materials to look for in the library.

Sources of Information: Periodicals

Now that you see the value of the information searches, let's look at some additional sources of information available to you. Along with the data you are compiling about your own company, its competitors, and suppliers, you should be assembling other information and data in your field of interest. Fortunately, there are many sources which are readily available to you. This fact-finding phase can be most interesting, very intriguing, and as you gather steam, downright stimulating.

To scratch your entrepreneurial itch, several magazines come quickly to mind:

- *Success*
- *Entrepreneur*
- *Salesman's Opportunity*
- *Business Start-Ups*
- *Sales & Marketing*
- *Inc.*

The articles may provide you with just the spark you need to consider a new venture. For example, *Inc.* Magazine provides good case histories of new business ventures. And, to its credit, the magazine also does follow-up stories and reports objectively on failures as well as successes.

Forbes, Fortune, Business Week, Inc., and *The Wall Street Journal* offer a wealth of information, and should be read regularly. Staying abreast of movements in the economy, industries and companies of interest to you, changes in executives and management positions, and interesting articles about business and industry in general is a must, particularly if you need to know how best to offer a product or service, or approach potential customers or suppliers. You never know when the news you read today will be valuable in the discussion you have tomorrow. It isn't necessary to purchase these publications; most are available at your public library.

Fortune deals with the larger, more established companies. In many instances, this may not be relevant to the entrepreneur or small businesses. However, reading *Fortune* is a good way of keeping in touch with the goings-on in the corporate world. *Forbes* is one of the few real "whistle-blowers" in business journalism today. *Forbes* does not hesitate to report on management failures, weak strategies and corporate wrongdoing. In their pages, you'll also find case histories of well-performing companies. In all of these publications, opportunities can be found from examining high performing companies, as well as companies that haven't done so well.

Day in and day out, *The Wall Street Journal* is the most comprehensive source of timely business news, trends, and new products. If you're not a regular reader of *The Journal*, consider at least scanning the first page for the capsule summaries, and the Marketplace and Mart sections which report on marketing trends and list new opportunities. Many readers will gravitate to specific columns or features and read them on a regular basis. This is a way of staying abreast of industries or trends that are most meaningful to you.

If you are keen to have your own personal copy, then take the perspective that if you can get just one good marketing idea, be motivated to develop just one new product, or secure just one important phone contact, then the cost of a subscription pays for itself.

Most large metropolitan cities have outlets that sell out-of-town newspapers. Their classified sections give you an indicator of where the economy is going. As an example, if companies are hiring production engineers, you know that they are preparing to develop and manufacture new or more products. The following Sunday editions have voluminous classified sections and should be scanned for business opportunities:

- *Los Angeles Times*
- *The New York Times*
- *San Jose Mercury News*
- *Chicago Tribune*
- *Miami Herald*

Sources of Information: Trade Publications

If you are going into a new industry, you can accomplish a lot with a small investment of your time. The first step is to make a list of the trade publications that serve the industry that you are interested in. How do you make such a list? *Standard Rate & Data Service* (SRDS) publishes a complete listing of all newspapers, business publications, consumer magazines and the like. SRDS is available in separate editions; get the volume on business publications. The book is arranged by business classifications, such as Advertising and Marketing, Automotive, Banking, and so on. Within each of these classifications, you will find the various journals that serve that particular industry.

Next, find a library that subscribes to the publications that you want to read. If there are colleges in your city, their libraries are usually very complete, particularly if they have a business school. While you are there, get to know what other resources are available in their library either in hard copy, on microfilm, microfiche, or online. There may be books, pamphlets, and government data on the industry in which you have particular interest. If you don't find the information you are looking for, the librarian is usually quite resourceful, and can help by pointing you in the right direction. The library uncovers the approaches to find information. Learning to use the library may be one of the most advantageous lessons you master.

In addition, seek out regional trade publications, newsletters, and company-sponsored journals. Within a particular trade journal, there is a wealth of information, including a great list of contacts on the masthead page. Editors, other than the most senior people, are usually very willing to talk about their particular industry. Call them! They may often send you a sample copy. In addition, some publications have analysts on their staff whose job it is to track specific industries very carefully. Another great source of information, if the publication has one, is the in-house librarian. This person maintains an unpublished index of the contents of previous issues of the magazine. We have found that trade publications are an invaluable source of grass roots information and ideas.

There are many free publications which are industry sponsored or in "controlled circulation," meaning they're paid for by the advertising and sent free to qualified subscribers. If you're interested in information technology, there are bi-weekly publications on networking systems, trends in the industry, hot new products, and the Internet, to name a few. There are also banking publications which track movements and trends in the financial markets. The list goes on and on.

Information From Sellers of Companies

For those of you who intend to go into business for yourself, peruse the "Business Opportunities" and "Businesses For Sale" sections in the classified section of newspapers and magazines. Contact the business brokers or principals who have listings. Much useful information can be gleaned from calling sellers of businesses. It is amazing the level and types of detail that will be furnished over the telephone to a stranger.

If the seller withholds confidential data about his business, it is quite understandable. But other data, such as competitors, industry trends, overall profit margins, effective advertising media, names of key people in the industry are yours for the asking. Before you make the call, prepare by making a list of the information you would like to have. Present yourself as a serious and qualified potential buyer, but don't overpower the person. You may know more about the industry than they do. Don't allow yourself to get to the point of intimidating the person at the other end of the telephone. In many instances, the seller has prepared a packet of information about his business and will send it to you upon request.

Other Sources of Information

Other sources of information include venture capital companies that specialize in particular industries, trade associations, civic groups, chambers of commerce, patent office filings, trademark registries, retired executives, banks, entrepreneur groups, as well as business departments at colleges and universities.

The Internet is another valuable resource. If you go to your local library, the reference librarian can help you onto the Internet, and show you how to find business sites.

A new source of information, the business incubator, has become popular over the past few years. The people involved provide a forum in which you can test your new ideas, present a business plan for critique and develop relationships with entrepreneurs. Your local economic development agency or chamber of commerce will probably have access to the consulting services that incubators offer. Chambers of commerce generally have an arrangement with retired executives (e.g., SCORE, the Service Corps of Retired Executives) who volunteer their time to help start-ups and other small businesses with advice and critique on a no-cost basis. Colleges and universities are often linked to business incubators through their graduate business schools, extension offices or career/alumni centers. Many colleges and universities offer business, advertising, computer, marketing, accounting, or legal services to the small business community as a class project. These can range from no-cost to modest cost programs.

How Do You Get Your Financial House in Order?

As you gather information to start a business venture, don't overlook the importance of your personal and family financial situation. When you leave your current job is largely influenced by your personal finances. If you haven't given serious thought to your unique situation, here are some pointers to get you started on gathering information about your finances.

We'll point out some of the considerations that you should look at. Please consult your accountant, certified financial planner, or tax advisor before you make your final decisions. These are merely suggested areas for exploration. We are not qualified financial counselors, and our suggestions should not be followed as professional opinion or advice.

Personal Finances

Whether your long range plan includes your own business or corporate retirement, the status of your personal finances will become a major factor in the implementation of your action plan and timeline.

If you intend to buy an existing business or launch a new one, you'll need financing. This requires your ability to show that you are credit worthy. Therefore, you have to get your affairs in order while you are still employed, and before you take on any more responsibilities. It is easier to borrow money or attract investors if you have money, a steady income, tangible equity, or some combination of these.

Essentially, this calls for an accounting of your assets and liabilities, a clear picture of what funds or credit you need to make the business profitable, how you are going to use the capital, when and how you're going to repay it. By doing this in advance, you'll be prepared with a clear understanding of your cash needs, and the "war chest" you have set aside to sustain yourself and your plan. If you leave this until the end, your banker may lend a sympathetic ear, but may not be helpful at all. Here are some things we learned on the subject that you need to know.

Secured Loans

Your home mortgage is a good example of a secured loan. The loan is secured by the home you live in. You always want to keep your account and payments current. Most loans of this type have a ten day grace period for payments to be made without penalty. You may want to set up a pattern of making payments that will not vary much from the present time to later. While you have a steady income, you are probably making payments exactly on the due date. Later, when cash may be tight, an extra three to eight days will be very important to you. If you anticipate that this will be the case, start sending in your payments one day after due date, then two days after due date, and then gradually make payments six or seven days after due date...but within the grace period allowed. You will not be penalized and your account will not draw notice, as it will be consistent with your prior payment practices.

Home Equity

Equity in your home or other real estate, in most cases, will be your single most important asset when seeking additional funds from venture capitalists, financial institutions, or private investors. If you already have considerable equity, you may want to prepare for your "next life" by taking an additional loan now while you are still employed. You will incur additional interest charges, which may be tax deductible. Putting the proceeds into money market accounts, certificates of deposit or other non-speculative interest-bearing instruments will be productive in the short term. The important concept here is that you must secure the loan or capital while you are gainfully employed with a steady income rather than when you're not working or just starting out a business. In essence, you're borrowing money when you don't need it in order to get the best rates and service from investors or creditors. Timing is a key factor.

Two cautionary notes:

1) There may be tax implications for you, so you should discuss this with your accountant.

2) With the volatility of the real estate market over the last few years, it would be wise to establish a new and current fair market value for the real estate you own and compare it with your mortgage balance. In this way, you will determine an accurate amount of equity that you have.

Credit Lines

Bank lines of credit have become very popular for individuals. They provide you with a pre-approved amount of credit that is restored by making payments. These are usually check-credit accounts, with no interest charged until you actually use the funds.

It is always easier to secure access to funds in this manner when there is not a critical need. Therefore, think about applying for this type of loan well in advance of when you might actually need the funds, and before the time when you may not meet the lender's criteria.

Automobiles

If you already own one or two automobiles, reduce the remaining balance owed as much as possible, and make sure that the automobiles are in good working order. If it is a valuable collector car or expensive late model automobile, keep it in first-class condition. You may have to get an appraisal because you want to be able to list the vehicle at its maximum asset value. During your transition period, do not make any new commitments for automobiles, either for purchase or lease. Definitely make do with what you have.

Unsecured Loans

When you prepare a personal financial statement, the list of liabilities should be as short as possible. If you have unsecured loans for furniture, appliances and the like, pay them off as quickly as you can without upsetting your cash flow requirements. In fact, if you have any unsecured debt in the form of outstanding credit card balances or unpaid bills, try to pay them off without impacting your cash flow. The reason for doing this is that the real cost of borrowing has risen significantly over the last fifteen years. In the early 1980s, credit card interest rates rose to over 18 percent as inflation topped 10 ½ percent, making the real cost of credit card borrowing about 7 ½ percent. Today, with credit card rates hovering around 15 ½ percent to 16 percent, and inflation at 2 ½ percent, your real cost of borrowing has risen to about 13 percent to 13 ½ percent. It is just not good value to carry debt at these real rates where it is not necessary to do so. The less debt load you carry, the fewer things you have to worry about later.

Credit Cards

You certainly do not want to abuse the open ended opportunity that consumers have today to increase their credit card indebtedness, as interest rates charged are quite high relative to other consumer and equity loans. But, many entrepreneurs have financed themselves with this type of credit.

You can open credit card accounts and be assigned credit limits based on your current financial condition. But you do not want to be tempted to overuse the funds available to you. You run the risk of getting into a major problem if you do not use this credit judiciously. Just when you need the funds that are available to you in the credit card accounts, you may find yourself deep in debt with monthly payments that you cannot handle. What you should do here is similar to the treatment of lines of credit. Build a "war chest" and have comfort in knowing that the funds are there if and when you need them.

If you do not have any of these revolving bank credit cards, we recommend that you establish your credit worthiness and secure the cards while you are employed. Once you leave your position of employment, your application stands a good chance of being denied.

Lifestyle

If you anticipate the need for funds in the future for a business enterprise, you want to make sure that you present yourself to lenders and investors as having a lifestyle consistent with what a lender will be comfortable. Lenders and investors are not interested in supporting a grand manner of living for you and your family. Therefore, don't purchase an expensive automobile or jewelry, or show outward signs of affluence shortly before or after you will be seeking funds. It's terrible for your credibility. Show that you live within your means and know the value of a dollar.

Assembling Your Information

In this chapter, we have brought numerous sources of information to your attention. There are valuable things to learn about your current employer, your potential suppliers, competitors and customers. Gather all the information you can on any and all businesses that you may be interested in. Doing it in advance of your last day of employment will stand you in good stead for your big move.

Putting all your financial information together is also important. In fact, you won't get very far without some facts and figures. All too often, people who are leaving full-time employment don't give this enough advance thought, and end up suffering. Many times, this results in a devastating situation for the family, and has a significant negative impact on the ability of the individual to move a new business forward.

If you are not willing to invest your time and don't possess a high degree of curiosity in all that we've covered, maybe you're not the *Type E^N* that you thought you were.

Preparation Means Success

Let's go through a checklist to make sure that you've covered all the bases before you hand in your resignation.

1) In your notebook, summarize what life might be like for you as an entrepreneur. This will include details about your proposed business and what you'll be selling, how you'll generate revenue, what your typical day or week will look like, and what your business will look like in ten years.

2) Make a list: When the right time to leave your job will be; at what age you will be; what family and financial circumstance or milestone will have occurred; whether it will be you or the company who will initiate the separation and how you would like to see the event occur.

3) List the names of people whose advice you respect, and whom you might ask to critique the plan you will formulate for your new venture.

4) List the things you will research and information you will gather about your present employer, along with where and how you will find this information.

5) Make a list of the various activities, including seminars and training, that you plan to attend while you are still employed.

6) Make a list of the potential competition to your venture, the type of information you will collect about them, and where and how you will collect this information.

7) Take a trip to your local library to find out what business resources it has. Prepare a list of questions you need answers to. Find out about the periodicals and other resources they carry, learn about their Internet service capabilities, and familiarize yourself with the publications we've mentioned.

8) Create a checklist of the things you'll need to follow up on to get your personal finances in order. In Chapter 9, we'll tell you more about dealing with your banking officer or account manager, and in Chapter 10, we'll help you to prepare your personal financial statement. Make sure that you give your accountant a call and jot down the items he/she feels are necessary for you to include in your plans. Know your net worth, spending habits, and tax bracket while you have time to make adjustments.

When you have gone through this chapter and collected the information we've described, you'll find out just how useful this exercise is. In fact, the steps that you take in doing these exercises will be beneficial to you time and time again. Keep in mind a little success in carrying out the above steps will give you the confidence to move forward. This process will help you to think about things you would have never thought to ask.

Chapter 5 Checkpoint

Whether it is two weeks, eight months or five years, good preparation can bring you greater control - whether you anticipate termination, or are thinking of leaving voluntarily.

✎ You have a number of sources of information available to you about your current employer, suppliers, competitors and customers. You'll find tips on getting your financial house in order.

✎ You understand the changes that will affect your future, how to prepare and what to look for while you are still employed, and where to find the resources that will help you move forward with confidence.

Whether or not you leave your current job, you'll be better prepared, knowing you have to use your time wisely, and gain an information advantage.

GETTING READY:
WHAT TO DO BEFORE YOUR LAST DAY

> *Start by creating a vision of the other side*

Gathering Intelligence

> *The Economy*

Competitors	*My Employer*	*Personal Finances*
Am I confident that my idea/business will succeed?	Do I know what to expect and whether I can realisticaly negotiate a good settlement when I leave?	Have I adequately planned to review and get my personal and family finances in order?

Sources of Information

| *Publications* | *Organizations and People* | *Online* |

Do I at least know what information is available and where to find it?

Where Am I Now?

- Am I prepared?
- What additional information do I need?
- Have I set a realistic time frame in which I expect things to happen?
- Am I clear about my next steps and time frame?

Chapter 6

GETTING FIRED:
What If It Happens Before You're Ready?

It's a moment everyone dreads. Your boss walks in, says your job has been eliminated, and tells you what the arrangements for termination and severance pay package are. Your worst nightmare has just come true. You're hurt; you're stunned; you're helpless. You feel that there is nothing that you can do.

Wait a minute! There may be a lot that you can do. Leaving as you've been asked to may cost you rights that you didn't know you had. If you are prepared, you have an opportunity to at least understand what you can do if it happens before you're ready to move on to your next opportunity.

In an environment of downsizing and consolidation, not only are reductions of staff and the elimination of people a regular occurrence, there is also pressure to improve productivity among the surviving employees. This creates a much greater need for team players, taking initiative and responsibility. You may have made the first rounds of cuts, but you're not out of the target area automatically because "no one's left" and they need you to do the work. If you are perceived not to be a team player, if you are outspoken about all the change, or if your typical response to new tasks is "It's not my job," don't be surprised if you are soon joining the ranks of the walking wounded.

118 Entrepreneur Or Employee?

Usually the public announcement of a company's merger, relocation or restructuring is accompanied by soothing statements from the public relations office that "nothing will change." Employees and managers alike often take an optimistic view that things will be okay, and that they will be unaffected by the turn of events. The truth is that these occurrences *always* bring the dynamics of change. The chances of not being affected by them are rather slim. Regardless of whether it's a mega-deal like the Walt Disney Company acquiring Capital Cities/ABC, or something of a smaller scale like Acme Tool & Die Co. merging with City Machinery Co., none of the companies will ever be the same again.

Once people, places, and things are set in motion, nothing can stand still. Every event of this magnitude will affect each and every employee in some way. There is a tremendous impact on wives, children, housing and schooling as well. In the end, when terminations occur, the corporation doesn't fire individuals; it fires families.

LAYOFFS IN THE HEADLINES – IS YOUR EMPLOYMENT REALLY SECURE?

Today's business headlines are not helping us to gain a sense of security:

- *Startling increase in layoffs, with merger mania and the deadly combination of rising costs and a worsening economic climate are frequently cited as the key reasons.*
- *The changes and cycles affecting key industries are causing considerable insecurity and stress.*
- *Layoffs are impacting prominent corporations.*
- *Staff cuts are affecting all levels of staff within the corporation.*
   Are you prepared if you should be next?

The Wall Street Journal, September 11, 1990. "A White Collar Guide to Job Security"[1]

In some cases, administrative, bookkeeping, and accounting systems are merged; sales staffs are combined to eliminate duplication; and perhaps advertising or back-room operations are consolidated. Entire computer systems may be replaced. The goals are to reduce costs, eliminate redundant systems, and/or close low-producing units. Behind the systems, units and costs are living, breathing people and their families. While badly run companies will have problems whether they are recession-resistant or not, the best-run companies will survive and enjoy the spoils from the fallen.

This chapter focuses on the topic of danger signals, how to know your job is coming to an end, and how to prepare for it. Before reading further, get yourself in the mindset that you are not very knowledgeable about firings and terminations. After all, they have not been everyday occurrences in your life. Think of yourself as an advocate for yourself — that you're going to find out as much as you can, and prepare as well as you can, for any termination that might be in your future.

What Signs Should You Look For?

There are industry signs, company signs, as well as signs in your relationships at work which indicate that your future with your employer may not be a bright one. Open your eyes and look for these warning flags:
- Your company has experienced financial losses, low profits, or you hear complaints about costs being too high.
- Your company has high debt and low cash flow – products aren't selling or accounts are difficult to collect.
- Your firm merges with another that duplicates your work.
- The company as a whole is going through a downsizing.
- There is divestiture activity in your particular division.
- A new person from another division with close responsibility lines to yours has just been moved in. Your boss or your boss's boss has gotten the ax.

- Consolidations of job functions and departments begin to occur. Management has already tried an early retirement buyout.
- People begin to take care of their own when staff reductions are in the offing.
- A hiring freeze is put into effect.
- Salary increases become less frequent.
- Projects which seem important to the future of the company are put on hold.
- You're not invited to meetings that you used to be expected to attend.
- Expense checks and commissions are not being paid as promptly as before.
- You receive memos and announcements from the top about cutting expenses and allowances.
- There are cutbacks in advertising expenditures.
- Office plants aren't being watered as often as before, and other maintenance functions are being neglected.

Be alert to these dangers, and you will be able to sense when "something" is coming.

Are You and Your Job Safe? Assess Your Situation Objectively

Rather than getting caught up in the rumor mill, stay in touch with your immediate supervisor. Get a feel for how he or she thinks you're doing. Try to get a formal assessment from your supervisor or human resources manager if the company does not already have a procedure for this in place. This will give you an indication of the mindset of your supervisor and other management personnel.

Then ask yourself about your responsibilities and the functions that you perform. The safest workers and job titles are those that contribute directly to the bottom line. Salespeople are the lifeblood of the organization. They bring in the revenues, and they are closest to the customer. The farther you get away from the customer, the more difficult it is to justify your salary, particularly in a crunch. This is an important concept to understand, particularly if you are in accounting and other administrative support functions. Long-term employees may be replaced by newcomers who earn half their salary. Companies look at who is the most expendable and who is the most expensive. If someone falls into both lists, look out.

With today's *delayering* of corporate America, middle-managers are on the way out if their main function is to shuffle paper and oversee people. Many of these tasks are being automated. The managers who are in demand are facilitators. They have the skills to get the most from their people by making sure they have the information and resources to achieve the company's goals. Job security will be determined by your ability to recruit, train, and retain highly productive, loyal workers. You will be accountable for the results you get from your collaborative teams and diverse workforce.

Companies always need people for personnel, collections, billings, or operating key company databases (e.g., customer and employee records and files). However, the more you're in a peripheral position, the more expendable and insecure you are. Advertising, public relations, and research and development are important to the company's future, but are common targets for staff reduction. One reason continues to be the difficulty in measuring their contribution and benefit to a company's present and future performance. If you can quantify the results of your efforts, your position is better protected.

WHO IS BEING LET GO?

A 1991 *Wall Street Journal* brief stated:

Among fired executives surveyed by outplacement consulting firms, 47% are sole support for their families and 48% have children at home. A third of the furloughed executives had over 11 years of service with the company and 41% lost their jobs due to mangement changes.

No one is immune to termination. Frank Biondi, Jr., former CEO of Viacom International, was the right hand man for the famed and shrewd businessman, Sumner Redstone for over eight years. In 1994, the duo had successfully purchased both Paramount Pictures and Blockbuster Entertainment. Mr. Biondi was fired unexpectedly in early 1996 because Redstone wanted the company to "move faster." Biondi's laid-back, decentralized management style no longer matched the needs of the company. Even though Biondi's quick mind and solid grasp of numbers were valuable business skills to Redstone in the past, they were no longer the right skills. It happens to the best and the brightest.

What are Some of the Reasons for Termination?

There are many reasons for termination, some very just and some very unfair. The following brief list of indicators may offer warning signals that termination may be close at hand. They are presented to provide you with a greater awareness and to help you anticipate and be adequately prepared should you find yourself in these or similar circumstances.

1) Performance reviews that worsen dramatically suggest that an employer is formulating grounds for dismissal. During your term of employment, document all promises, criticisms, commendations, and conversations related to your performance.

2) Medical and social issues such as employees suspected of having HIV, AIDS, back problems, or cancer.

3) Personal grooming habits such as men having long hair or excessive facial hair, wearing of garish clothing, and persons who are overweight.

4) Alternative lifestyles.

5) Religious practices such as wearing a skull cap or worshipping during the workday.

6) Cultural incompatibility. Your religious beliefs may differ from the majority of employees in the company. The same holds true for native language, and ethnic backgrounds.

7) Strong regional differences (e.g., the familial aura in many Southern-based companies, or the hiring by some companies of candidates with degrees from the "right" universities).

8) Non-inclusion in the cliques that dominate the internal "political" structure of the corporation.

9) A whispering campaign that identifies you as being involved in a clandestine office romance.

10) Being caught sending what is considered offensive e-mail messages at work about any employee, manager or the employer. Because the computer and anything on it is considered company property, e-mail messages can be reviewed and judged as cause for dismissal.

11) Rules that prohibit employees from engaging in outside businesses. This is a particularly sensitive issue when a company employee (for the purposes of his own business) contacts the company's suppliers. Moonlighting, seemingly non-controversial, can cause friction and resentment. For example, an employee who is a part-time real estate agent, spends too much time on the phone during business hours, might be fired because of his outside business activity.

During times of consolidation or breakup, decisions to terminate employees might seem to be without any rational basis and occur "out of nowhere."

What About Some of the *Hush-Hush* Reasons for Terminations?

As progressive as companies have become — and in spite of the protection offered employees by labor laws — we often witness instances of terminations which are related to the following factors:

Age: As an employee's age increases, the cost of health insurance premiums paid by the employer rise. Profit sharing plan payouts can also be more if they are structured to reward employees based on seniority. Hence, older employees may simply be too expensive to maintain. Because employee costs are perceived to be lower with a younger employee base, some companies are willing to terminate older employees as a means to keep overall employee costs down.

Gender: Sexual harassment continues to be an issue in the workplace. In the majority of situations the violator is appropriately dealt with. In other cases, the unfortunate victim is further victimized for making it known that he or she has been sexually harassed.

Lifestyle, Race or Religion: "Our customers just don't like interfacing with minorities," along with alternative lifestyles, "far out" as well as mainstream religions, and other religious biases, can often give rise to prejudices which lead to unfair and unlawful terminations.

Personal Habits: Smoking, hair styles, attire, drinking and social habits can be a source of displeasure in the workplace.

Health: The health of the employee or of the employee's family affects the productivity or time spent by the employee at work.

Compensation Level: Where your compensation may be higher than others in a similar capacity, it can cause dissension in the ranks.

Vesting rights: Vesting rights in profit sharing, retirement or seniority profit or benefit plans can sometimes be a determining reason for letting an employee go.

So-called Personality Clashes: These can be real, perceived or fabricated.

Not a Team-Player: A subjective call often related to personality clashes.

While we'd all like to believe that the business world is a fair and ethical place, these and other similar reasons for termination, while not overt, still play out daily across America. Because they are related to how your employer conducts its business, each situation can bring about its own sensitivities and biases. Be aware!

EMPLOYEE BEWARE—THIS MEAL COULD BE YOUR LAST

These days, if the boss surprises you with an invitation to lunch, you may be wise to say you're not hungry. Odds are, before the waiter hands over the check, your boss may hand you a pink slip.

OR ... THIS RIDE COULD BE YOUR LAST

If you have use of a company car, beware the boss who asks to "drive along" with you on a Friday afternoon (or any afternoon for that matter). The boss may spring the news of your termination on you, then drive you straight home for your last ride in the company car.

Who Are Losing Their Jobs?

Pink slips, termination notices and the like are crossing all lines in the corporate hierarchy. Some groups previously thought to be immune are finding themselves vulnerable. In the past blue collar workers at big manufacturers bore the brunt of layoffs. Then it was office employees and mid-level management people who fell victim. Now employees in service industries such as banking, real estate and retail, and the professionals who support them — accountants, consultants and even partners at big law firms — find that they too are expendable. Many unemployment offices, previously frequented by only blue collar workers, now see quite a mix comprising all income levels in the ranks of the terminated or unemployed.

The Effects of Job Loss

Terminations often come suddenly and without warning, with employees being asked to clean out their desks and leave the building within the hour. Most companies handle terminations poorly. Firing an employee brings out our worst fears and few people know how to talk about it. The result is that there is very little effort to help the employee save face, restore self-esteem, or to take a positive look at the employee's future. This adds to the trauma and the residual anger, and can lead to depression. Reactions that follow a termination parallel those that follow any loss:

1) Brutal rejection: "After all the years I gave them, how could they treat me so callously?"

2) Denial: "They'll get that contract next week and hire me back."

3) Self-blame: "If I was really good, they would have fired someone other than me," or "I should have been more politically astute," or "They know what's best."

4) Anger & Depression: Often people in this situation begin to think that they are crazy, but they are not. It's their way of responding to a loss.

For men, masculinity is oftentimes falsely equated with earning power. Impotence is a common, but temporary, reaction to job loss. Additionally, people avoid friends and colleagues because they feel that they've lost status. But this isolation only makes depression worse. Joblessness usually is accompanied by helplessness, particularly if the termination came as a surprise and the employee had no control whatsoever. The effects of someone's discharge ripple throughout the company and the corporate community.

A good approach is to deal with it head-on and face up to the reality of it. This is easier said than done, of course. While it may be a shock, there should be no shame unless you have been engaged in illegal, unethical activities, or there was just cause for dismissal. Taking into consideration the many reasons for terminations, you must take responsibility for your actions. Absenteeism, accidents on the job, sub-par performance, and no personal improvement top the list for employer dissatisfaction.

What About Your Agreement?

Every employee has an employment contract, implied or written. If one person is an employee and the other is an employer, there is a contract. It doesn't have to be written. When you were hired, someone may have said words to the effect that "as long as you do what you are told, you'll have a job here." As a result, there is a set of rights that employees have that they are genuinely unaware of. However, it does not mean there is a guarantee of lifetime employment.

The "Covenant Of Good Faith And Fair Dealing" recognizes that a special relationship exists between an employee and an employer. Some courts may interpret a breach of this covenant between employer and employee in the following situations:

- An employer may not wrongly characterize a person's performance.
- An employer may not arbitrarily terminate a 30 year veteran employee because they contracted an illness that requires a longer than normal recuperation period.
- An employer may not inflict undue emotional distress on an employee.
- An employer may not terminate an employee who refuses to do something unethical or illegal.

Note that these rights do not automatically accrue to, or benefit an employee. The traditional concept of employment-at-will, which implies "I hired you, therefore I can fire you," has come under repeated attack. This has led to the following clarifications to protect the rights of all employees, and place some limits on employers' "at-will" contracts:

1) The law protects whistleblowers who expose company wrongdoing, people serving jury duty, and people who file worker's compensation claims.

2) Employees who have been promised numerous things in employee manuals and personnel sessions.

3) A legal doctrine, known as "promissory estoppel," holds that if an employer makes a promise, and the employee relies on that promise and suffers because of that reliance, then the employer can be held liable for breaking that promise.

4) Both sides, employer and employee, are expected to conduct themselves in good faith when dealing with each other.

5) An employer may not show extreme and outrageous behavior when discharging an employee.

Caution! We certainly are not implying that every termination has a legal twist or loophole which benefits of the employee. Not every firing or termination will provide the employee with recourse.

What Should I Do if I'm Being Terminated?

Often, when employees are terminated, fear causes them to sign the release forms and leave with a severance check in hand. This is why advance preparation is so important. Before you accept the first severance package that is offered to you, here are some practical questions that you should get answered:

1) Which of the benefits offered to you are mandated by law? Exactly how were these benefits calculated in your case?

2) Can all of your unused vacation be converted to a cash payment? Or, can you remain on the company's payroll during your unused vacation time and continue to receive medical insurance coverage during this period?

3) Has every option been explored to find you another position within the company?

4) Are there any conditions put on the acceptance of the severance package being offered to you, such as not being able to work for a competitor?

5) What are the details of the "extended benefit" package being offered, or mandated by law? When do these job benefits end? What happens if you accept another job?

6) Can you get reference letters in writing from your boss or other company executives if you are leaving on good terms?

> **The best piece of advice we can give you is that every termination is unique. You, the employee, are what makes it unique. Because there is no other individual like you, it follows that there is no "typical" benefits package. Once you accept this concept, you will have a greater chance of securing a better severance "deal" for yourself.**

What Not To Do

After the initial shock of being fired wears off, you will likely experience a desire for revenge and retribution. Get these thoughts out of your system quickly. Don't be vindictive and don't burn bridges. It is debilitating and taints your overall objective. What is best for you in all likelihood is to get on with your life.

Should You See a Lawyer?

Whether you want to take legal action or actually have grounds to do so are two different things. Laws vary by state, but there are usually three areas where a suit may be appropriate:

1) Violation of anti-discrimination laws.

2) Violation of the Plant Closing Act (The Federal Plant Closing Act requires that companies with 100 or more workers notify employees 60 days in advance of a plant closing or the layoff of two-thirds of a plant's work force. Companies have to pay workers two months' wages and benefits or put them back to work for the same period if they fail to give timely notice.).

3) Wrongful discharge.

Remember that a lawsuit may not always be appropriate, even though your lawyer or someone else has encouraged you to initiate one. Be careful that a lawyer doesn't draw you into a lawsuit which may drain you emotionally and financially, and which may potentially not be resolved for years. Recent trends indicate that courts are taking a very hard line on frivolous lawsuits and legal actions without real merit. Because the court dockets are backlogged, legal remedies take a long time. Do not automatically look to the courts to solve problems that can be resolved without litigation.

Sometimes, an event in your life like this is better handled by putting it behind you. In short, moving to a new job or starting a new business, and otherwise getting on with the rest of your life, may be the best revenge.

On the other hand, consulting a lawyer doesn't automatically mean a lawsuit. Sometimes, a letter or phone call from your attorney to your former employer may clear up some of the details and may even get you a better severance package. This can vary greatly with the circumstances. All is not etched in stone, as your soon-to-be ex-employer might have you believe. Whether out of conscience, compassion, fairness, guilt or even fear, employers will, on occasion, modify their "published" offers to people being terminated.

What Severance Benefits are Available to You?

Regardless of the position you've held in your company, a termination becomes a great equalizer when it comes to benefits that may be available to you. The usual "company line" may state that the same severance package is offered to all employees. Don't believe it! Some benefits are not readily volunteered by employers; you have to ask for them. Here is a checklist of the benefits and other "goodies" that may be available to you:

1) Salary continuation or lump sum payment.

2) Separation payment or cash settlement (apart from #1 above). When should you accept the payment? Is there a deadline? Depending on your tax situation and family income, deferring your payout to the following year may positively affect your income tax bill for the current and following year. Alternatively, accepting a monthly payout rather than a lump sum can affect your eligibility for unemployment benefits. Note also that mandatory payroll tax deductions may be greater in a large, lump sum payment. These would be good topics to review with your accountant.

3) Is the severance package offered appropriate considering your age, tenure and position with the company? In addition to the company's pre-set payout formula based on tenure, there may be additional money available to you based on your age depending on the types of profit sharing or employee stock and option programs in place with the employer.

4) Allocation or proration of anticipated bonus over the part of the year worked. While the "company line" is that the bonus is only payable to employees of record as of certain dates in the fiscal year, terminated employees have a good chance of receiving prorated amounts.

5) Pension payment or annuities.

6) Earned or vested interests in profit sharing, thrift or ESOP plans.

7) Accelerated vesting in pension plan or profit sharing plan.

8) Credit for unused sick leave, vacation, or personal days, particularly when you've accrued many unused days.

9) Bridge payments related to Social Security eligibility.

132 Entrepreneur Or Employee?

10) Life insurance coverage. You might want to ask to have ownership of a company-paid life insurance policy put in your name if you want to continue paying the premiums. This might be beneficial if the premiums are at such a low rate that the benefit it ultimately provides cannot be bought less expensively elsewhere, given factors such as your age and the company's ability to buy the policy for less.

11) Long and short term disability insurance.

12) Health insurance extensions. Depending on your age, you may have your company buy medical insurance coverage for you until Medicare takes effect. The federal COBRA law requires companies to permit workers to buy group coverage under the company plan for as long as eighteen months after termination, with the possibility of extending this period further in some cases. This regulation may not apply to small companies.

13) Discounts for car rentals, airline travel, hotel accommodations. This is especially valuable to terminated employees who may be searching for new employment or business opportunities away from their current city or town.

14) Purchase of computer or company car (often at their depreciated values).

15) Career-transition counseling and outplacement services (ask for them or the cash equivalent if you don't need them).

16) Relocation services.

17) Use of company office space, telephone, computer, copier during a job search.

18) Recommendations, letters of referral, and personal references.

19) Personal financial counseling.

20) Family counseling.

21) Psychological counseling.

22) Extension of notice of dismissal to coincide with next anniversary date of your employment.

Let's take a look at some of the severance packages major companies have given their discharged employees. In a downsizing maneuver, ABC, the television network, gave two weeks pay for each year of service and two weeks pay for each $10,000 in current annual salary and other benefits. In the downsizing of Times Mirror Company, higher level editors were offered referrals to job placement counselors. Employees were offered $3,000 to help in their job search, and severance packages ranged up to one year's pay for employees with ten years seniority.

As an added note, when lower level editors and reporters learned of a major reorganization at the Times Mirror flagship newspaper, *The Los Angeles Times,* they returned to their desks to literally wait until their phone rang to tell them that they were next to lose their job. Bizarre as it may sound, this is true.

In another example, General Motors Corporation introduced a "career transition" program in 1993. Paid leave was offered for as long as fifteen months (depending on length of service with the company) while the employee looked for another job. Once a GM employee entered this program, they were obliged to leave the company.

The point here is that large companies, in particular, have developed many novel programs to assist terminated employees. Because these programs don't appear to be fixed, presenting a strong case for your personal circumstances may provide an opportunity to receive a better severance or termination package if it happens to you.

> **POINTERS FOR THE TERMINATED**
>
> Here are some quick pointers you may wish to consider if you become terminated:
>
> - *Roll over your retirement fund into an IRA.*
> - *Even if you get a large, lump sum settlement, don't pay off your mortgage.*
> - *Know your rights concerning insurance continuation.*
> - *Ask for outplacement help.*
> - *Cut back personal expenses within reason.*
> - *Don't be ashamed to file for unemployment benefits. You supported this fund through your paycheck, and you've earned the right to collect unemployment benefits now that you need them.*

Wrongful Terminations

Today, companies are becoming much more sensitive in handling terminations. Large companies offer management training sessions specifically designed to teach the right and wrong ways to handle such matters. In addition, many companies have initiated grievance procedures to ward off lawsuits by ex-employees. This resulted from companies discovering that some terminations backfire into costly defamation suits.

The Bureau of National Affairs, a non-government firm based in Washington, D.C. reported in 1990 that 25,000 wrongful termination suits were filed; the number continues to grow. The number of cases doubled from 1987 to 1988. Some of the more commonly listed reasons for the suits were:

- Promise of promotion
- Promise of continued employment
- Discrimination due to sex, race or age
- False accusations of stealing or lying

In the late '80s, the average age discrimination award was $722,294 while sex discrimination cases resulted in an average award of $475,181. Clearly, it is in the best interest of large companies to avoid such costly settlements. In addition, the bad publicity generated by these suits can bring a negative impact on company morale, and possibly the value of its stock.

Hush Money

Many companies ask employees to sign waivers of their right to sue in exchange for sweetened retirement or severance benefits. As an example, ARCO, the petroleum company, offered employees three weeks pay per year of service in addition to the normal severance payment in return for signing a waiver that they would not sue their former employer.

Hefty severance pay packages are sometimes linked to employees' promises to keep their mouths shut. This is rather common in divisions of large public companies, where the separate reporting of a division's performance is not required. This leads to public statements such as "left to pursue other interests," "resigned because of differences about the future direction of the company," and "took early retirement." These may highlight attempts by some companies to gloss over their internal problems or avoid negative publicity, which could result in a negative impact on their business.

Sealing the lips of former employees is the corporate equivalent of a gag order. Distinctly different from confidentiality clauses that prohibit workers from divulging trade secrets, these orders prohibit someone from saying anything about the company, whether good, bad or indifferent. While they are in the minority among severance packages, the use of these waivers and clauses is growing. An outrageous example of this was Ross Perot's departure from General Motors in 1986. He was paid $700 million to go quietly.

Negotiating Pointers with Your Soon-To-Be Ex-Employer

Should you find yourself on the way out of a job, the following items will help you to focus on elements we believe will help you in your negotiations with your *soon-to-be* ex-employer:

1) Always check out what other companies have offered in circumstances similar to yours. Look for magazine and news articles on the topic. Also, talk to others who are leaving your employer at the same time you are, and try to reach former employees who were terminated over the last few years. The more you know, the better your negotiating stance.

2) Never sign anything without getting something in return. For example, in exchange for signing a non-compete clause, you might ask for additional lump sum cash. Be careful about signing anything without the advice of *your* attorney, not the company's.

3) Do not permit your company to deduct unemployment payments from severance pay due you. Each carries with it different tax implications. Make sure that whatever payments you receive will have the smallest impact on your income tax obligations. Check with your tax advisor.

4) Take advantage of any "feelings" you're leaving behind. Remaining employees, including your boss may show signs of guilt, sympathy or compassion toward you. Capitalize on this and work it to your advantage as it relates to your termination settlement. Ask for letters of recommendation to aid you in your relocation.

5) Get copies of your personnel file. Some states have laws that oblige the employer to share these with a departing employee.

6) Ask for everything that you are entitled to... and more, using the various checklists and pointers in this chapter.

Without being confrontational, you should let your boss (or whomever is handling your termination) know that you are fully aware of your rights. You will gain much respect for this. Going quietly does not mean going meekly. You are neither a patsy or a scapegoat, but a person of dignity and substance. Don't forget it.

Our message to you is to start thinking differently about the company. If it will soon be your former company, start looking out for *Number One*, YOU! This will be the last chance you'll have with your current employer. If you are being terminated, and you've negotiated fairly, you'll be treated in a like manner. Should there ever be a future possibility of a business relationship, whether as an employee, supplier, or customer, view it as a new beginning with no ties or conditions bearing on your settlement agreement. Don't think that by being a *nice guy* and giving in that your chances of working with the company again will be improved in the future.

Whistleblowers

Workers who blow the whistle on bosses often pay a high price. Nobody likes tattlers. Even if wrongdoing is eventually uncovered, the company usually takes the position that the termination of the whistleblower is unrelated to the employee's disclosures. Many such cases wind up as wrongful discharge lawsuits. However, there are many adverse side effects such as stress on the family, loss of friends, and the inability to work in the same industry. The company may suffer as a result of inflammatory remarks by its employees and ex-employees, and shareholder lawsuits may result against these employees and ex-employees. Most corporations, particularly those that are publicly traded have an overriding desire to control unflattering publicity that may harm the company's image. They may take whatever actions within their means to avoid such publicity.

By the same token, some forced resignations are a result of a company wanting to get rid of a "bad apple" in their ranks. Employees are cautioned to get legal advice before "going public" with statements of company wrongdoing. These are dangerous waters, and you may indeed suffer great losses as a result of pursuing such a course of action.

Other Considerations When You Face Termination

Think about these issues:

Timing: Some companies will delay the announcement of layoffs, large scale downsizing and the granting of severance packages to avoid disclosure and discussion at their upcoming annual meeting of shareholders. Unusually generous packages must be disclosed in proxy statements. If layoffs are pending but haven't been announced, soon-to-be announced quarterly results or an upcoming company annual shareholders meeting may be the reasons.

Takeovers: If you anticipate that your company will be acquired by another corporation, the best advice in this situation is to *wait and see*. Don't leave hastily. Wait until things sort themselves out. Your current employer may be in poor financial condition and your potential new boss may rejuvenate the company, and offer an improved wage and benefit package and better advancement opportunities for you. In the event that the new company will eliminate many jobs, you are better off waiting to examine what their severance package will be. It may be very advantageous to you. We know of several instances where employees left too soon and lost many benefits such as early vesting of a pension/profit sharing plan.

Non-Compete Clauses: When this topic is discussed, most of us think that it only applies to senior executives. Not so. There are many instances where relatively low level employees are asked to sign these types of agreements (e.g., plant workers who mix ingredients at a food company may be prohibited from working for a competitor). Even without a non-compete agreement, be aware that a company has many tools at its disposal to protect itself from harm caused by ex-employees. As an example, eleven sales and marketing executives left a company at the same time to start their own competing company. Their former employer obtained a restraining order which enjoined the former employees from soliciting other employees, contacting their customers, or using confidential information obtained while previously employed.

There are no hard and fast rules; each case is judged on its own merit. Intent, planning, targeting of former company customers and employees and collusion are factors which may come into play. Be forewarned. A company generally has legal and financial resources that individuals just cannot compete with when it comes to launching a suit.

Your Peers: Many of your friends and associates may be leaving at the same time you are. Some may decide to "do something together." Don't be pressured into a joint activity just because you know them and the comfort level may be high. It is important to realize that you may be distressed and highly emotional. This can lead to decisions about your future that may not be in your best interests or good for you in the long run.

On the other hand, you may have developed an idea and business concept with a coworker with whom you have worked with over a long period of time. Many successful high-tech start-up companies came about as a result of people who previously worked together. If you are so inclined, examine your ideas and concepts while you are still employed.

Contract Employment: A new trend is developing among employees being terminated. The function that they previously performed is contracted to an outside contractor. The contract service provider hires you and leases you back to your former employer. Sometimes, this works out better for the employee as it leads to better pay and improved benefits. While the work may not be permanent, it may provide you with breathing space while you plan your future.

Exceptions To Company Policy: In some cases, the Human Resources and/or Personnel Departments manage the exceptions to the company's rules and regulations regarding terminations. In other cases, department heads are able to influence variances to company policies. Still, in other situations, the best resolution may come from direct contact with an executive with whom you may have developed a good rapport. Remember that there can always be exceptions to company policy if you can present the right arguments.

In this chapter, we've presented some ways of anticipating your last day if termination is a strong possibility. By understanding the impact of the business environment on your industry and company, how to read some of the danger signals for termination, and what to look for and how to prepare in case of termination, you'll at least have a plan of action to keep your career or track.

The more you know about how recessions work and the inevitability of business cycles, the more you will grasp the concept that there are always winners and losers. Hopefully, by demonstrating your willingness to think seriously about your future, you will be a winner. A winner's label is a tough one to wear, particularly if you've been told that today is your last day.

Don't Get Caught Off-Guard

1) Note whether you are in an industry or company that is facing market challenges and operational struggles. Are there some obvious danger signals that your career is about to be derailed?

2) Schedule a time to have a frank discussion with your immediate supervisor about your performance and the future of the department and company.

3) List any reasons you can think of that may cause you to get fired, and assess objectively whether this is indeed an imminent probability.

4) Research what you are entitled to at a minimum, should a termination occur. This can be done by talking to others in your company who are being terminated, finding out what other companies have offered in similar circumstances, listening carefully to the grapevine, talking to previously terminated employees during this and the recently past year. Some of the sources of information can be found in Chapter 7.

5) Have at least a preliminary meeting with your accountant and lawyer to review what your response should be to the initial package offered, and what to find out, what to ask for, and what they'll need to help you make an informed decision and possible personal changes should you be terminated this year. Make this subject part of your annual review of your affairs.

6) Review the checklist in the section "What Severance Benefits Are Available To You?" and determine which of these (among other items you may think of), are relevant to your situation. Make a checklist for yourself so you can be prepared for any termination negotiation that may occur.

7) Put your financial house in order early enough while you are still receiving a paycheck. This will be helpful so that you don't run out of time, or break under the pressure of stress and poorly negotiate your severance package.

Once you have gone through the above steps in this chapter and collected the information we've described, you won't be defenseless or set adrift if you lose your job. You'll be better prepared for termination discussion and negotiation should you find yourself facing the circumstance. Our objective is to help you put things in perspective and in order just in case you will be forced to face your last day of employment with your company before you are ready.

Early preparation will give you the confidence to face facts. It will also give you the ability to negotiate a settlement that is more in your favor than you might have thought at the outset of the termination process. Information is power. It will help you focus more on moving on with your life plan, rather than stewing over what just happened.

Chapter 6 Checkpoint

There are a number of danger signals that can help you to anticipate when your job is coming to an end.

✏ You'll see danger signals that relate to your work or personality, the company's actions or performance, or the economy as a whole.

✏ You can be better prepared with the tools to understand your rights, and what is available to you in negotiating your termination and severance.

By putting things in perspective, you won't be forced to face your last day of employment before you are ready.

In Transition: Alone in the Wilderness

Chapter 7

THE DAY AFTER:
Finding Yourself in Transition

You said your good-byes to fellow workers and associates. You promised to keep in touch. You put on a brave, tough exterior. That all happened on your last day on the job. Now, what happens? Regardless of how important you think you are as the department head, purchasing agent, director of management information services, night shift production supervisor, or payroll manager, the day after you leave your job, be prepared for one helluva letdown.

Sometimes job loss seems to occur for no apparent reason. Employees with large salaries are usually the first target of cost-cutters because they can be isolated as a single cause for an ongoing expense item on the company's income statement. A high salary history can be quite a burden in seeking new employment. Whether you are in a new business or a new job, you require a particular level of compensation in order to meet personal financial obligations that were based on your previous "safe" and "stable" job.

Now that the ties with your income stream have been severed, the fear of not being able to pay your bills threatens your peace of mind. For the thousands of workers who find themselves in this situation, flexibility is a strong factor to survival. You can adjust, rehabilitate yourself and go on. As with the old adage: "Necessity is the mother of invention."

Did You Ever Think They Would Forget You So Quickly?

Once you have been earmarked for dismissal, it is as if the world learned you have some type of communicable disease. How quickly word of your plight travels through a company and industry is one of the mysteries of the modern business world. People who previously curried your favor, invited you to lunch, offered football tickets to you, or called to ask how your son is doing in Little League Baseball, disappear.

Your old boss, whom you felt really close to, may not even take your calls. You may be given any number of different reasons for calls not received or returned. But in the end, you're an outsider now. The sooner you recognize it, the sooner you'll be able to get on with the rest of your life.

Are the Feelings You are Experiencing Normal?

Once you are no longer employed, you become quite aware of a number of things happening that distress you:

1) You start to comprehend that you are not indispensable.

2) You feel a loss of power. If you were in a purchasing position, you've lost the power of the pencil to generate orders. If you were in general management, you've lost the power of directing subordinates. They will now respond to someone else, and switch their allegiance accordingly.

3) You seriously question your self worth. You may begin to rationalize the reasons that you were let go, or vehemently justify why you should not have been let go.

4) You have considerable self doubt about your abilities. This will be particularly so as you begin to realize the great amount of effort needed to find a new position in a competitive job marketplace, and what you "could have done" when you "saw this coming."

5) You are bitter. The initial shock of being let go is transitory; it goes away. But bitterness is long lasting and almost a universal feeling among discharged employees.

6) You feel empty. We all attach a great social significance and status to our work. Most people equate being unemployed with being a loser, regardless of why you lost your job.

7) Increased stress hovers just beneath your consciousness. Be assured that everyone in this situation goes through this. Take some comfort in the fact that you're not alone.

Your challenge is to accept the fact that it happens to millions of people every year. People rarely die from it. Life goes on. Successful people are those who have the resiliency to bounce back and shake off the "loser" label, work through the "survivor" period, and move on to the "winners" circle.

Will I Ever Get Over These Feelings of Stress?

Stress, as opposed to fatigue, creeps up on you, is silent, and can have devastating effects. It is an internal mechanism that your body and mind mobilize to gain the needed energy to cope with challenge and change. Stress is the physiological and psychological response to any demand made on you. There is helpful stress — the kind that brings you victory in sports and keeps you alert in business — and there is distress, the tension that keeps you awake at night and fogs your thinking.

You may feel down, sad, rejected, and frustrated, and wonder what you're going to do and how you're going to cope with unemployment.

Each person has a slightly different bodily response to such a stressful situation, ranging from neck tension, to teeth clenching, to queasiness, to loss of appetite, to frowning. The ability to cope with stress is yours alone; you are responsible for how you feel and act. When tension builds up, you lose some degree of control over your behavior. The result: You snap at your spouse, labor over easy decisions, smoke one cigarette after another, overeat or withdraw from social contact. You can learn to defuse your anxiety before it leads to despair and physical illness.

The most common signs of distress are:
- Headache, stomach pain, back pain.
- Inability to sleep restfully, or not at all.
- Clouding of the thinking process.
- Loss of appetite, or over-indulgence.
- Your emotions and temper are tougher to control, or you become very sentimental about everything.

The key principle of maintaining a low-stress lifestyle is balance, arranging your days in such a way that your needs are fulfilled in healthy proportion and you don't become overloaded by your worries to the point of intolerable stress. A delicate balance includes the following elements in a variety of settings:

Work and play	Challenge and ease
Stress and relaxation	Striving and taking it easy
Companionship and solitude	Exercise and rest
Discipline and self-indulgence	

There are some rather simple and inexpensive ways to handle the extra stress: walking, involvement in hobbies, social work or activities that give you temporary relief from your problems. Properly managed, the stress you experience can become a positive factor, a motivator, and a stimulant rather than a threat. Harness the energy that is bubbling up within you to decide what you're going to do next.

Some Other Disorders

So that you won't declare yourself to be suffering from something that you are not, here are some of the disorders that you may experience:

Depression: A condition of general emotional dejection and withdrawal; sadness is greater and more prolonged than warranted by objective reasoning. It's long lasting and not traceable to a specific cause.

Anxiety: Distress or uneasiness of the mind caused by apprehension or fear of danger or misfortune.

Tension: Mental or emotional strain. It is an intense and suppressed suspense, anxiety, or excitement.

Hostility: Antagonism or opposition in feeling, action or character.

Anger: A strong feeling of displeasure and belligerence brought about by a real or supposed wrong.

Revenge: To want to punish someone for a wrong in a resentful or vindictive spirit.

You may experience a little of all of the above. This is to be expected and quite normal for a short period of time. A word of advice: Don't indulge yourself for very long with these feelings. Get professional counseling if you are immobilized or destructive. Work through your grieving period, then stop feeling sorry for yourself. If you don't, it will only make things worse.

Typical Reactions of Those Who Have Been Terminated

If the following list of thoughts are very familiar to you, you are running through the normal thoughts of people recently terminated. Take some comfort in the fact that you're not alone, and know that your turmoil will pass.

- I'll never get over the rejection…never!
- It hit me like a ton of bricks.
- I was caught totally off guard.
- I was in a state of shock.
- Here one minute; gone the next!
- I couldn't believe it. It took 21 years to build up a career here, and 10 minutes to tear it down.
- All those years went down the drain.
- Those ungrateful S.O.B.s.
- After all I've done for them … this is my reward?
- What's the definition of loyalty, anyhow?
- Why me?

The experience of a lost job is often similar to the psychic journey that follows the death of a loved one. There is usually denial, then anger, then bargaining. Your mental and emotional state may vary widely until you finally come to a healthy state of acceptance. This process, along with a shift in your priorities, usually takes from six months to a year, depending on the individual. Regardless of how well you believe you are dealing with your situation, seek out someone close to you with whom you can talk about your feelings, and who can help you keep the total picture in perspective.

Do's and Don'ts

What do you do when you wake up "the morning after" and have no place to go? Your daily routine is totally disrupted. Your daily planner is empty. What do you have to talk about? Think about? Do? This can be very trying.

Allow yourself to experience the range of emotions we've been talking about. By anticipating the events and feelings described, you'll be able to keep the big picture in view and let go of what was. Begin building what will be.

In order to enter this new phase of your life unencumbered, you need to address the issues. Why were you terminated? Why did it happen to you and not to someone else? How do you feel, and how are you reacting? If you do bring hostility, vengeance, or any other emotional chip on your shoulder with you, you'll only hurt yourself. It will stand in the way of clear, intelligent and objective decision-making. Try to focus on steps that will be beneficial for you to move forward.

Here is a short set of dos and don'ts to help you meet with your next challenge:

1) Get over the feeling of low self-esteem. Lack of confidence will have an adverse effect on your ability to raise capital for a new venture or hurt you when interviewing for a new job.

2) Avoid giving the appearance of being defeated (sometimes referred to as the "hat in hand" syndrome). Your body language, dress, voice, and choice of words will telegraph any feelings of insecurity or desperation. Make up your mind to stand tall and go after what you want.

Everyone wants to be associated with a winner, and if you project yourself as one, that is how you will be seen. Don't be brash and cocky either. A little humility never hurts. You must be the kind of person others want to do business with. If you're having trouble getting yourself together, perhaps this is the time for a vacation or hiatus to get your batteries charged.

3) If there is someone in your industry that you admire greatly or have established a rapport with, seek this person out, and ask for a meeting. Over the phone, tell him briefly about your situation and request some time to get his counsel. Very few people will turn down a genuine call for help. Most people, regardless of how big and important they are, will be flattered by your request. Network, network, network!

4) Take all calls. You never know who is on the other end of the line and where it may lead you. Learn how to listen, then listen. Be available to anyone who can possibly help you.

5) Call former competitors. Tell them about your situation. You may not be comfortable to ask them for a job. However, you should tell them about your new status, and inquire as to whether they know of any good opportunities for you in the industry. Be certain they have your home phone number. Ask them when you may call them back, then follow-up.

6) Explore the Internet. It offers a new and exciting vehicle for you to gather information about companies, business and job opportunities, and ideas. The Internet can also quickly disseminate information about you to a worldwide audience. E-mail is a non-obtrusive way to put your message before the right individuals.

This is where the preparation you've started while you were employed will really pay off. Chapters 5 and 8 will help you create a list of names, addresses, phone numbers and e-mail addresses, which will be quite handy. Changes are happening so quickly on the Internet that new services are introduced every day. There is a wealth of resume services, job banks, career search services, and industry and business information to help you with your research. You may even be able to have an interview without leaving your home.

7) Shake off who is to blame for your situation. Now is the time to plan and think ahead and act positively. Don't be distracted by negative preoccupations. Think of the baseball player who just made a costly fielding error. He shrugs it off, goes to bat in the next inning and drives in the game-winning run. That's positive action and a wonderful demonstration of resiliency.

8) Stop complaining, mumbling or being ornery. Stop thinking about running away and starting over somewhere else, or about doing harm to yourself. Don't get into a long-winded dissertation on "what's fair;" don't threaten to sue, and don't make rash outbursts about blowing the whistle on what's "really" going on in the company. Stop whining, don't tell people about how you were shafted, and don't hurt the ones you love. Take a walk (or however many walks you'll need) in a quiet and serene place to get all this "stuff" out of your system.

9) You may question the "ladder of success." Losing a job in middle age or in mid-career can trigger a re-appraisal of your beliefs and goals. Some say they would not return to a corporate job if it were offered. As a result of their recent experience with being terminated, they might now conclude that the rat race for prestige and possessions is a sham.

The key point is to get yourself beyond the feelings of self-pity, hostility or vengeance, and back to a positive, clear and forward thinking frame of mind. Deal with the nasty feelings so you can get on with life.

How Do I Pick Myself Up to Get Started Again?

Many newly terminated employees find that they are at peace with themselves after leaving the pressure cooker or *rat race* they were in. They are happy to no longer be caught up with "keeping up with the Joneses." This comes with a change in personal and family priorities, or a clearer perspective of what their priorities are.

People say that women adjust quicker to job loss than men. This is particularly true for those who have cared for children or aging parents. Their maternal instincts, natural resilience, upbringing, and ability to juggle a number of priorities, gives females strong coping skills. This helps women to deal with the transition easier than men, who generally derive their identity and self-worth solely from their work outside of the home and family.

A pressing issue for detached workers is how they're going to pay for their children's college education. The best approach is to deal with it directly by talking candidly and honestly with your teenager. When they say "level with me, dad," do just that.

The transition period between jobs may be a good time to do some volunteer work. This can be very helpful in regaining your confidence and self-worth, and building a network of friends, colleagues and potential business or employment contacts.

You may need to reassign household tasks with your spouse being the breadwinner and handling the family finances while you do more cooking, childcare and other duties. While you have a flexible schedule, make time for your friends, family, and significant other.

For many ex-employees, one good that may result from a forced career move is the lowering of your expectations of work itself. You may reach the decision that you will no longer totally invest yourself emotionally in your job. You may begin looking elsewhere for sources of satisfaction, and may do things that you never thought you would do. For instance, one ex-IBM executive never saw a customer in the last eight years of his term with the company. Now, he sells crafts made by his wife at weekend fairs, and has rediscovered his love for interacting with people.

How Do I Get Rid of Those Nasty Feelings?

After losing your job, can you really afford the time to do some of those things around the house or in your life that don't seem to be very productive in finding you a job? Guilt or family pressure can often force you to rush into finding a new job before you're mentally or emotionally prepared. While this book can help you decide whether a career or business option is right for you, it cannot define the period of time that you will need to be in a frame of mind to begin your journey.

Should you paint the house during a point of transition? If you really like painting, have all of the proper tools, and have confidence that you can do it well, go ahead and do it. Set aside the time and assign a realistic completion date. However, if you contemplate painting the house just because you now have the extra time on your hands, stop a minute and do some serious thinking. If you're really not very good at this sort of thing, you may be injecting additional stress into your life when your mind and body can least afford it.

If you are not disciplined to do it every day and complete it on time, this painting project may become a source of irritation between you and your spouse just when you both need each other's support. You may be taking valuable time away from initiating a plan for yourself. In other words, if you're using some projects as excuses to avoid taking care of business, don't kid yourself. Stop procrastinating.

What About Forced Retirement and the Over 55 Group?

You may feel that you have been forced out of your job because of your age, and as importantly, before you are ready to leave or retire. Terminations are a fact of corporate life whether you are aged fifty-five or thirty-five. But there are additional considerations that an older person has to deal with.

First and foremost, don't lose your confidence in the skills and experience you have accumulated over the many years of your working life. Give yourself time to reflect over the circumstances of your termination. Don't let your misplaced anger and guilt prevent you from solving your predicament in a rational and measured manner.

If you have the luxury of time, a steady source of other income or financial reserves, then the self-evaluation exercises, and determination of whether you are a *Type E^N* or *Type E^M* might be worthwhile to go through. If you are not in this fortunate situation, it may be best to stick to your proven skills, and not make dramatic changes in your professional life.

What is working in your favor? What business situation or companies might your skills be best transferred to? What contribution can you realistically make to the management of these companies? As you answer these questions, you may want to update your skills and capabilities, add to your strengths, and make yourself more marketable.

There is an increasing number of placement and executive search firms for professionals over forty years of age. Given your experience and years of employment, you will have accumulated a range of professional and personal contacts over the years, such as friends, attorneys, accountants or bankers who work with small businesses. Your skills and experience in sales and marketing, operations, finance or business management may be exactly what a small business needs to help it succeed. Timing and the right network of contacts may put you in touch with small businesses involved in a product launch, merger, or plant expansion, who may need your expertise.

You should also explore opportunities to sit on the board of advisors for a small business, or participate in a political, community or local public service group. This could be very helpful in exposing your skills to a wider audience. Search every opportunity to make valuable use of your contacts, and to build strong new ones. This will increase your chances of finding new employment or a business opportunity.

As an example, the company that advertising executive David had been working for was purchased by an international conglomerate. Although the acquiring company initially promised that everyone's job was secure, eventually the pruning started. David was suddenly terminated at age 57. He had hoped to work until age 65. David was devastated. After all, who would want to hire a 57 year old "has been?"

David had accumulated a healthy amount of savings over his career, but had no hobbies, and did not play golf. With nowhere to go after his termination, he had a void in his life. He struggled to find a job suitable for someone with his qualifications in the twilight of his career.

Creativity and persistence paid off. David approached several small community newspapers and asked if they knew of companies who needed some advertising help, but could not afford high-powered talent. The papers were all too happy to refer him to small retailers and professionals. It turned out to be a win-win" situation for everyone. David's clients got the services of a very talented and experienced advertising man at prices they could afford, and the newspapers received a greater volume of advertising from these satisfied businesses. And David? Well, he's doing just fine. His business is growing by word of mouth, and his circle of business contacts is expanding to keep him busy.

Sudden job loss produces different reactions in different people at different stages in their lives. For David, money wasn't the motivation. He needed something to do. He now derives great personal satisfaction from owning a successful medium-sized business.

You Can Do It

Once you've had an opportunity to look at some of the career options in Chapter 8 that you may not have considered, you can organize your thoughts and look at how to approach a new career or pursue your own business. You've learned how to strengthen your employability, to detect the winds of change, and to face life without a job.

You don't have to go it alone. There is a wealth of information and a group of close family, friends and advisors who will be more than willing to help you. At the same time, understand that it all starts and ends with you. We know you can do it. We did.

Chapter 7 Checkpoint

Job loss is distressing and all-consuming, particularly if you don't know what to expect emotionally.

✎ There are normal and abnormal feelings that can result from being fired, and you will certainly experience them should you find yourself in transition.

✎ Whether you are 35, or over 55, you can identify your strengths and the positive steps you can take to build your esteem and gain your confidence again.

Flexibility and a healthy mindset can help you to organize your thoughts, pick yourself up and get yourself and your career started again.

Chapter 8

CAREER OPTIONS YOU DIDN'T KNOW YOU HAD

Before those darn computers became so popular, I was happy being a typewriter repairman. There wasn't a week that went by without someone jamming the carriage, or bending a key, or fouling up the platen to keep me busy. Sometimes I got lucky because a clumsy writer got correction fluid into the typewriter's innards, or too many eraser shreds into the moving parts. I thought typewriter repair was my meal ticket, until the computer came along. All office jockeys want today is speed and efficiency. Where's the craftsmanship? I'll tell you, "The computer will never replace the typewriter! I'll always have a job. Mark my words!" And then one day, my son walked in from school and asked, "Hey dad, what's a typewriter?"

Is your job going to lead you down the same path as the type writer repairman? Have you kept up with the technological changes so there's a place for you in business or industry tomorrow? Change in the way we all carry out our responsibilities and job functions is inevitable. Are you going to stay with your current employer? Are you considering leaving? Whatever direction you choose, it is healthy to keep in mind that you have many career options open to you in these changing times.

Are You a Victim of the Changing Times?

In 1979, *Business Week* published a University of Michigan survey which concluded that 36% of Americans felt their skills were underutilized; 32% believed they were over-educated for their jobs; and 50% complained about a lack of control over the days they work and their job assignment. These figures indicated a high degree of frustration on the job that even in today's times, has gone unabated. Worker discontent is nothing new in the corporate world; moreover, it continues to rise.

In today's business environment, uncertainty rules the day. Competition has taken on global proportions and profit margins continue to dwindle. With the exponential growth of computer automation and information technology, efficiency dictates that the productivity and revenue generated per company employee must increase to combat competition.

It is no longer only the old rust belt industries that cut the work force. From consumer products, to the automotive industry, to the traditionally unaffected public sector, to real estate, and retailing as well as our financial institutions — no industry is safe. Even relative high-growth sectors or newcomers like telecommunications and financial services are vulnerable to cuts.

Technology and the desire to build shareholder value have given rise to the reengineering of operating and business processes for improved efficiency and profitability. The physical and psychological impact on people has been significant. Moreover, as millions of baby boomers move into positions of authority, the opportunity for advancement for others declines.

Middle managers saw over 1.5 million jobs disappear in U.S. companies in the 1980s, particularly in large companies such as IBM, General Motors, Chevron and Kodak. In the '90s, there appears to be no end of downsizing in sight. The scope of the management function continues to blur as middle managers take on much more hands-on roles, as doers, managers, motivators and trainers of people. The focus on higher individual productivity continues to eliminate the layers of middle management, duplicate staffs, and administrative functions.

With the continued shifts in the market, changes in corporate structure, and the use of computers and new technologies, it is not surprising that people in their 40s and 50s find themselves in situations where they are writing resumés they thought they would never need.

Change Means Opportunity - What Will It Mean for You?

As a middle manager, career vitality depends on your ability to increase your skills and knowledge as a hands-on operator, information provider, and motivator of people. Today, age, initiative and common sense can be helpful qualities for those who can shift their paradigms to learn the new ways of doing business.

Transferable skills are essential to survival. If you don't have a skill that's salable to firms other than your old employer, then you have no job security. Lifelong careers with one benevolent, paternalistic employer have gone the way of the typewriter repairman; they are few and far between. Why? For one thing, today's companies have to react more quickly and effectively than ever before to the challenges they face in the marketplace. As chaotic as the employment world looks to you right now, the world of business looks even more unpredictable to the people who are trying to build profitable companies. As we approach the next millennium, global enterprises will emerge, grow, and fail overnight, thanks to a home page on the World Wide Web and other communication vehicles we aren't even aware of yet. We live in a world in which demand for once-essential products and services can be superseded in an instant as a result of technological and political developments.

What does this mean to you? Adaptability is everything. In today's economy, a person who can perform only a single set of tasks is seriously handicapped. Portable skills give you the flexibility to move from one company to another. Today's employers want people who can spot problems, independently resolve them, and pass the necessary information along to colleagues as circumstances require. Companies want employees who demonstrate the ability to adapt well to brand new ideas and procedures. They want people who show initiative and creativity.

The watch words in today's economy are efficiency and creativity. Employees who live simply by the clock will not enjoy much career success or stability. Companies seek employees who have a marketing orientation and the ability to present the company's products and/or services in a compelling way to prospective customers or investors.

Find out what other companies in your field are doing by getting to know a few people who work for your major competitors, reading your industry's trade magazines, and going to trade shows and seminars. You will learn how companies in your industry are affected by change, and how this will impact the evolving range of skills and career options that will present themselves.

Do the New Job Descriptions Create Opportunities for You?

Job descriptions are undergoing radical changes as a result of changing demographics and other developments. These are most obvious in communications and computer technology, process automation, and information management. While old job categories are disappearing, new job categories are being created on a daily basis.

There are four essential ingredients for success in the 21st century:
1) Computer technology – At least develop a working knowledge of personal computers and software applications to keep pace with the growth and innovation in technology.
2) Collaboration – Manage relationships in diverse, self-directed, work teams, while servicing and selling to customers within and outside an organization.

3) Continuous learning – Sharpen and update your core skills and capabilities at every opportunity. Be curious, ask good questions, and listen to the answers.

4) Knowledge about knowledge – The amount and speed of information increases through technologies and techniques. Develop outstanding abilities to locate, customize, organize, package, and apply information to solve problems and create new business opportunities.

Therefore, to take advantage of tomorrow's business opportunities you need to take action.

1) Update and reinvent your competencies continually to apply the latest accounting, marketing, negotiating, quality control, selling, or production skills. For example, if you are a production manager, how knowledgeable are you of the purchasing function? Have you continued to develop relationships with your suppliers or vendors? Are you familiar with the most recent quality standards relevant to your current business or the businesses you are interested in? How familiar are you with the financial aspects of the production function (production costing), demand forecasting, just-in-time (JIT) planning and production methods, and your department's impact on the bottom line?

2) Become conversant with computer and communications technologies. As one example, the Internet and workgroup technologies allow you to collaborate on one or more projects with a remote team connected by computers over telephone lines. Expertise can increase your productivity.

3) Apply and enhance your skills in marketing and communications to develop and sustain working relationships with co-workers, customers and alliances. Interpersonal skills are very influential. If you're generally a quiet person, and it is not in your character to promote yourself overtly, at least demonstrate your awareness of self-promotion from a political point of view.

4) Discuss your progress, responsibilities and results regularly with your manager. Be sure to communicate and get feedback regularly.

5) Demonstrate your skills even in challenging situations to show your ability to think, act and achieve results under pressure. Remember to take credit when it is due.

6) Join outside trade associations. Always remember to report back to your company on at least one aspect of value from any professional meeting you've attended on your company's behalf. Talk favorably about your department's, manager's, and company's activities (where they are not proprietary) so that outsiders view you as a good company representative. If you don't have anything worthwhile to say about your company, don't say it. It's a small world, and you just never know who is listening, and how it might affect you.

As our working years become longer, even the over fifty-five year olds cannot avoid computer know-how, multi-tasking, and cross-disciplinary projects. The old rules of the workplace no longer apply in the leaner, flatter organizations. Read. Read. Read. Attend lectures, workshops and seminars through your professional association, at a community college, or community service organization. There are hundreds of accelerated learning classes for adults. There are even video- and audio-taped courses for home study, and college credit courses which can be taken over the Internet (better known as "distance learning"). There is no excuse for not riding this new wave of information and technology.

Jobs on the Extinct List

A *Los Angeles Times* article dated August 20, 1995 listed jobs that were "on the way out." Most are jobs that can be replaced by some application of technology and computers.

- Secretary
- Bank teller
- Telephone operator
- Receptionist
- Middle Manager
- Public librarian
- Wholesale merchant
- Medical specialist
- Farm operators, managers and workers
- Newspaper carriers

Secretaries are becoming less popular in a time when the middle manager ranks are dwindling. Additionally, today's business world is calling for managers to self-manage and organize, including doing their own correspondence and typing with the computer. E-mail, computer networks, workgroup technologies, and the Internet have drastically changed the way people work, and reduced the need for large and slow-moving organizational structures. Support staffs have been cut in number, leaving smaller teams to collate, finalize, post, and ship letters and packages, and to handle broader office functions. Gone are the days of the secretary who is dedicated to one or two managers. Receptionists are also less in demand given the efficiency of automated call management and routing systems. Aside from the employee cost savings of telephony, companies have discovered that not only are these systems efficient, they aren't as temperamental as employees might be.

As automated teller machines (ATMs) and online banking services become more popular, banks are encouraging customers to use these services to reduce the number of tellers required to service customers. The number of banking jobs is declining.

Even in health care, many positions are not as promising as they once were. The sophistication of medical equipment, managed care, emphasis on prevention and wellness, home health care, and the widespread availability of information is changing all aspects of the industry. For specialists, the field has become less lucrative than it used to be.

Jobs for the Future

As technology and demographics change the face of the economy, new jobs and careers are being invented every day. Many of the new job descriptions are being strongly influenced by the increasing need for workers to be technically qualified and literate. In addition, there is an increasing emphasis for both managers and staff to establish service relationships among themselves and with customers. It is interesting to note that while the positions offer something new, they have often evolved from positions which existed in the past. Clearly, they demonstrate the need to adapt your core skills and capabilities to a more technologically- and service-oriented workplace and culture. Much of this relates to employees fundamentally providing or offering value-added talents and capabilities to their companies.

The same *Los Angeles Times* article cited earlier predicts a growth in the numbers of the following positions, many of which emphasize the requirement to adapt knowledge to the emerging electronic information age we now live in:

1) Interactive Advertising Executive - offering traditional advertising capabilities for print and television media, and expanding to online, multimedia and computer-based networks, while interjecting a two-way communication of the message with the audience.

2) Web Master - working hand in hand with the interactive executive, managing the company's presence on the Internet by combining both technology and marketing elements, and developing a means to communicate to customers and other interested parties, about the company's products and services. This will be a prominent position, particularly in light of the growth of the Internet and the increasingly wired world companies compete in for customers.

3) Cyber Librarian - adapting library science to the need to research and retrieve information stored online around the globe in cyberspace. It is consistent with the notion that knowing where to find information and how to organize it is valuable to tomorrow's successful companies.

4) Answer Network Technician - making answers and resources for technical support more accessible to the growing number of small to large companies who need to keep their computer and information systems up-and-running to remain competitive. In this light, knowledgeable technicians who can respond instantly to a technical support need, and who can provide instant answers to help their companies prevent information systems downtime, are a valuable resource.

5) Community Concierge - facilitating the process of bringing people together in virtual communities. With the increasing popularity of telecommuting and the rise in mobile offices and workers, keeping track of where employees, staff, managers and alliances are, and ensuring that customers are provided high levels of service and response will be the prime responsibility of this position. Strength in coordination and the management of relationships will be a much sought after capability in the coming years.

6) Net Technologist - ensuring that a company can communicate with, and has access to, both the market and the many sources of information and resources available through the Internet. There will be a differentiation of skills among today's network managers and administrators, information management and support staff, and systems design engineers, with the net technologist taking a more strategic view of the management of and access to information sources.

7) Intellectual Mercenary - working beside the net technologist, finding and collecting information which will be used to manage the affairs of tomorrow's company. It will collect competitor and market information to best position the competitive profile of the company and its products and services.

8) Electronic Security Guard - taking two forms: (1) surveillance over a myriad of valuable assets – from information to physical assets; and (2) security of systems and information which might otherwise be accessible via the Internet by "computer hackers."

9) Para-professional - providing traditional specialized knowledge on demand in accounting, legal, real estate, investment or other specialty area. This will be important to large companies on a continuous basis, or to a number of smaller companies on a demand basis. Their services cost less than licensed professionals, and they are able to provide a set of full services, including the administrative logistics (preparation and follow-up of forms, delivery of filings, and correspondence) of their specialty area.

10) Volunteer in the non-profit sector - contributing their time, energy and expertise. This will be a means to "give back to the community" and to develop new skills and contacts for future career opportunities. With the growth of non-profit organizations and the continual need for strong support and community participation, interest in these organizations may help you to develop skills which can later provide a source of employment and income.

These new jobs are not outlandish stretches of the imagination, but logical extensions of job descriptions or positions which exist today. They demonstrate the opportunities that you can create for yourself by staying aware of the trends and changes in the workplace, and capitalizing on them. The truth is that while many "good" jobs are falling by the wayside, the economy is creating a great number of new jobs to support business in the information age. Most, if not all, new jobs must enhance the business

Career Options 169

and add to the bottom line. If the jobs don't add to the business, chances are that they will be marked for extinction.

What Should You Do?

An important aspect of career survival is to reinvent yourself, just as companies have, to keep pace with the times. It is interesting to note that companies experience a life-cycle in the marketplace after which they either adapt to survive, or die. People tend to offer the same product or service year after year, albeit at a more sophisticated level. While acceptable in the past, the fast changing economy and workplace call for a reinvention of self – not only to offer continued or renewed value to our employers, but to maintain the marketability and competitiveness of our capabilities.

The first step in this process is to identify the core skills you already have. This may be as easy as listing the responsibilities you have in your current job as Accounting Supervisor, Marketing Manager, Director of Quality Control, Production Manager, or another position.

Next, evaluate the position in light of the information covered in this chapter. Ask yourself, "How current are my skills, and what needs to be upgraded? How conversant am I with basic computer technologies? How strong are my computer skills? What do I need to do to improve my competitive advantage in today's marketplace in view of the trends for tomorrow? How effective are my skills to market myself and my capabilities, and can I do so both verbally and literally?" These questions help you develop some sense of what you will need to do to be competitive.

As an example, an accountant/auditor left her position with an accounting firm to join one of her clients as a division controller. In addition to her monthly financial reporting responsibilities, she saw the need to analyze production and selling costs which had a large impact on the division's profitability. Soon she was negotiating better contracts with vendors and contractors, and even helping the production department schedule production shifts to optimize the costs.

She realized that the financial records didn't give her or the management in charge of the division sufficiently good information about the division's customers, customers' buying patterns and cycles, or which products customers might buy or have to replace over time. She learned about management information systems. She took courses to keep abreast of the latest developments in finance and accounting, and sharpened her management and negotiation skills. She also worked with the division marketing manager to help him develop a marketing information and intelligence system that provided better information with which to manage the marketing function.

When a new corporate position for a Regional General Manager was created to oversee market development and the management of the divisions, she was the best candidate. Her co-managers respected her ability to understand the business from a base of solid education and experience. She had developed strong business relationships over the years with both division management and the corporate office. All of this preparation allowed her to move from a financial management position to the new Regional General Manager role.

Opportunities Abound

Whether you are a financial manager who aspires to the role of general management, a marketing manager who could one day have an opportunity to be the company CEO, or an entrepreneur-minded manager who hopes one day to make his fortune in his own business, it is your responsibility to create opportunities for yourself. Don't sit back and wish something good will happen.

"Help Wanted" on the Web

The Internet provides a wealth of opportunities for posting electronic resumes, answering online ads and finding information through company databases. Job seekers can network by e-mail and news groups, and cultivate business contacts with managers and recruiters who seek new employees or candidates with various specialized skills.

Some sites provide classified job ads that appear in the top newspapers in the United States. From the comfort of your own home, you have the ability to substantially widen the scope of your job search, and network with great numbers of people, companies and recruiters – an opportunity that was unavailable to you five years ago. With access to a variety of career search sites, the idea of researching another city or town, and finding a new job and relocation opportunity is now a reality. The Internet provides great tools and versatility to help you search the entire job market and find a new job or career opportunity.

Search and Personnel Placement Firms

What if your current job has not provided many opportunities to update your professional skills, particularly those necessary to your core capabilities (e.g., accounting, sales training, marketing research techniques)? You will be glad to learn that personnel and search firms and brokers do provide skills training and upgrading to prepare candidates for temporary or full-time positions. These newly acquired or updated skills are then appropriately marketed to various industries and companies.

A relatively new service is that of employee leasing. Such companies maintain and offer an elastic workforce, usually by placing the company's employees (other than critical or core employees on their payroll) and performing the personnel function. They can hire and fire less expensively than the company could manage. When companies' employee needs change, employee leasing companies provide additional qualified staff where clients need them.

The number of contingent workers has more than doubled in the last few years as corporate "rightsizing" and the need for worker flexibility continue. Contingent workers are temporary hires, part-timers, freelancers, and independent contractors, who allow companies to meet seasonal or cyclical demand or short-term expertise in specific specialty areas.

While numerous companies have put restraints on new hiring, many still allow their managers to utilize temporary and contract help to supplement their permanent staff. Over one-third of companies surveyed report that they use contractors for a specific kind of expertise. This area of employment is experiencing major growth.

If you are considering using the services of search or personnel placement firms, look into their reputation and the success rate of their placement and leasing services. Ask what kind of training and skills updating services they provide to prepare you for the emerging careers, and be leery about requests for contingency fees. Note that personnel leasing and temporary employment agencies normally pay wages only and no benefits. You will have to pay for your own health insurance if you take a temporary job.

High-Tech Corporate Training

Corporate training, retraining and development in the United States is an estimated $50 billion a year business. The effectiveness of corporate training is enhanced by interactive, computer-based multimedia that allows employees and instructors to be at different locations during the training sessions. If you are in the training field, become familiar with distance learning and multimedia technologies to ensure your continued value to current and potential employers. Mastery of these areas can also help you sell your services and products to the broader corporate and adult education marketplace.

Online Marketing and Customer Support

Practically every facet of business is now impacted by computers. Whether you're in marketing, accounting, sales, quality control, manufacturing, purchasing, or customer service, you must have the ability to collect and distribute information by computer. More and more people are now connected to the Internet, and perhaps 200 million people will be connected by the year 2000. The Internet is the communications and data movement medium that is rapidly defining how business will be done from now on. This international network of computers offers dramatic opportunities to improve business productivity, establish personal relationships with customers, communicate with employees, and open untapped markets on a global scale. Savvy business people who become accustomed to conducting business in cyberspace will see their companies growth parallel the exponential growth of electronic networks.

There are many books and courses on how to profit from the Internet. A challenge for many marketing managers will be to experience the "surfing" process, and what other organizations are doing. Understanding what to research, staying abreast of the rapid changes in Internet technologies, and learning how to collect, analyze, and use the market data will bolster your marketing management skills.

A major shift in business over the last decade has been that from mass manufacturing to customer service. Technology that is manufactured into products and services will require after-sales customer support and training to ensure repeat sales and word of mouth promotion. The skills required to manage and develop relationships with customers, both external and internal to a company, will rival the technological skills upgrading required to effectively manage the marketing function. Being prepared for these key shifts in technology and customer support is imperative in broadening your career options.

International Career Options

The phrase, "It's a small world" takes on much greater meaning as global competition dismantles international trade barriers. Therefore, fluency in at least one additional language will open more positions for you as an employee or an employer.

1) Translators - to negotiate agreements; discuss product research and development; deliver presentations for marketing, corporate finance, mergers and acquisitions; enter into consultation arrangements, train employees, and communicate with customers or strategic partners.

2) Writers and ghost writers - to support advertising and promotion copy, publications, screenplays, training materials or contracts.

3) Seminar leaders/speakers

4) Research projects - to ensure communication and effective project management for collaborative efforts which are international in scope.

Contract Assignments

If you have specialty skills and technical know-how that can be adapted or applied to other companies, you could be an outside resource to your employer. For example, you could manufacture a product line or single product, manage the quality control process or function, or provide the component sourcing function. The company might receive a cost savings from outsourcing a function in return for an appropriate level of expertise and support. A potential contracting solution might enable you to provide your services to several companies at a time.

The Opportunity of a Downsizing

A corporate restructuring may be a boon to you. To eliminate long-term, committed, or fixed expenses, more and more companies are farming out jobs, procedures, and services that were formally handled by an in-house staff. These include some accounting functions, market research, production activities, health benefits administration, and human resources/personnel. If you are considering a business of your own, one of your first customers may very well be your ex-employer. After all, you understand their needs, and already have an accepted working style and the personal contacts to make this a real possibility.

What About the Consultant "Thing"?

In recent years, the word "consultant," has come to mean "out-of-work and looking for something." Before you hang up your shingle and print up business cards and letterhead, go through the business planning fundamentals that you would expect other businesses to go through. If you think your former current employer may be a major client who will get your consulting practice off the ground, ask yourself the following questions:

1) How real is the expectation that your former employer will provide you with a strong base of business and revenues? Will you be able to have a signed contract to ensure that this occurs?

2) Have you created a consulting fee structure? If you are in a position to negotiate a consulting agreement with your old boss, is there a reason that you would charge him a rate that varies from your standard rate? Is this reason a realistic one given your skills and expertise relative to your competitors?

3) What are you anticipating as the amount of time required on your former employer's project? How will this impact your ability to secure new business? So often, we are enamored with the notion that we are successful consultants because we are generating billable hours. If you are committed to starting a consulting practice, an equally critical measure of success is the ability to secure a client base of new business that is more than just one client!

4) Have you reconciled any need to perform beyond what would be reasonably expected of a consultant? That is, do you realize that you don't have to prove anything beyond the services and skills that you are selling?

5) Are you clear about the scope of your work and who you will be responsible to? You are not bound by the same chains of command and reporting structure that governed your previous employment relationship.

Be forewarned that marketing your expertise, and convincing others that you can do the job, may be a big challenge for you the first time out since you don't have a title or an established company behind you.

WILL I MAKE IT AS A CONSULTANT?

1. A 1991 report stated that of the nation's 1,300 management consulting firms, about 100 of the biggest, most-established concerns account for 75% of the industry's total revenue. That means 1,200 other firms are scrambling for less than 25% of the market!

2. Most start-up consulting firms haven't thought things through or gone through the business planning process that they advocate for their clients.

Pursuing a Hobby as a Primary Business

No matter how much passion you may have for fly fishing, stamp collecting, and such, beware! While turning a hobby into a business sounds good, it may be quite risky. A hobby-based business must be treated like any other business. Very few successfully make the transition of turning a personal passion into a business. Much has to do with losing sight that you must sell and collect revenues to stay in business. Along with the selling, once you turn a hobby into a business, you may lose interest in your hobby.

A second factor is that objectivity is a rare commodity among enthusiasts. You may conclude, much of the time incorrectly, that everyone else loves ice fishing as much as you do. Making some extra money from a hobby is one thing when there is no risk of having to earn a living from it. To "quit your day job" to turn your hobby into a business is another thing entirely.

On a positive note, if you are already experiencing success in another field of business, chances are that you are less likely to commit errors of enthusiasm and unrealistic expectations of how well your hobby might do for you financially. As an example, Martin Davis (former chairman of Paramount Communications and now an investment banker) and rock 'n roll artist Neil Young, teamed up to buy Lionel Trains, the famous toy-train manufacturer. While the partners share a love for toy trains, their primary motivation for becoming involved in Lionel Trains is business related. They see profitable opportunities modernizing product features, and incorporating new systems for marketing and distribution.

If you are considering turning your hobby into a business, it might be best to start by working for a business that serves the market in which your hobby or interest lies, to see what it is really like. Alternatively, you may wish to start a business in your hobby on a part-time basis to test the waters. Some of the challenges might include the risk of losing interest in your hobby because it is no longer fun, not having the skills to make the business run beyond the initial excitement, or not being able to raise capital for the business because bankers and venture capitalists perceive the venture as borne out of an emotional, rather than a business decision.

CAPITALIZING ON YOUR STRENGTHS

People who have left companies have used their creativity to fill a market opportunity.

- An ex-fireman developed a successful fireman's supply catalog, including memorabilia, models of fire engines and collectibles. Similar opportunities were found by an ex-pilot and an ex-soldier.

- An ex-controller of a savings & loan bank started a consulting firm which analyzed the accounts of forty S&Ls seized by the government.

- An ex-attorney formed a firm that specializes in pro bono work based on his intolerance for corporate greed and sympathy for the plight of the average citizen.

- Ex-advertising executives and agency people with creative abilities find work in other fields that can tap into their talents.

- Ex-IBMers found a market in publishing a newsletter for ex-IBM employees.

By maintaining a positive awareness of your working environment, you can profit from finding similar ideas.

SOME INNOVATIVE CAREER OPTIONS: IF THEY CAN DO IT, YOU CAN DO IT

- A woman combined her para-legal expertise with a team of graphic artists to prepare demonstrative evidence for trials and utility rate cases.
- A registered nurse who opened new branch offices and developed new business for a temporary help nurses agency founded her own company to provide home health-care services to minority communities.
- Two former volunteers at Los Angeles County Museum of Art's rental gallery now happily operate a gallery that leases art works, and generate a steady income stream.
- An electrician at Universal Studios teamed up with a sewing machine operator at Paramount to form Matthews Studio Equipment Group, which manufactures, rents and sells lighting equipment, dollies, camera cranes and other moviemaking gear to film studios, TV production houses, and advertising agencies.
- Two art and wine collectors who ran out of space in their own homes to house their collections opened up a fireproof, temperature controlled building to offer a storage service to other collectors.
- A woman with a passion for numerology started a dating service based on numbers.
- A writer of romance fiction now publishes three magazines, sponsors an annual romantic writers conference, and evaluates manuscripts for would-be Danielle Steeles.
- A salesman who manned his company's exhibit booth at many trade shows now uses closed-circuit TV (CCTV) to bring exhibits from the trade show floor right into their hotel rooms.
- Well-known film critic Leonard Maltin, a film buff at a very early age, published a film enthusiast's magazine at age fifteen and created an encyclopedic guide to the movies at 17. His business now includes several movie guides, a radio show, furnishing reviews and data to the television show "Entertainment Tonight" and on-demand reviews via telephone lines and CD-ROMs. His childhood hobby became a multi-million dollar business employing 12 researchers and writers.
- Two attorneys in Los Angeles searched for someone who made creative and tasty pizzas, and founded California Pizza Kitchen, which they later sold to Pepsico.
- Henry Lambert, a successful real estate developer, parlayed an interest in cooking into Pasta & Cheese, a retail and wholesale distributor of fresh pasta and other gourmet items. He later sold the venture to Carnation/Nestle.

There are many examples of people who turned their interests in food and cooking into very successful businesses; computer whizzes who applied their talents to graphic design and desktop publishing opportunities; or wanna-be major league baseball players who focused their interests on sports memorabilia businesses (baseball cards, shirts, etc.), many of which have become profitable operations.

In fact, there is an infinite number of potential business ideas and specialized niches that are possible in our enormous economy. As an example, the variety of software programs and the relatively low cost of computers make the entry into magazine and newsletter publishing relatively easy. All you need is the interest, the right concept, and the willingness to research the opportunity thoroughly, plan, and implement the plan. Your boundaries are truly only limited by your enthusiasm, motivation, creativity and persistence. If you have particular insight into a field, you may create an opportunity for yourself, provided you can support it with clear thinking, and the requisite business skills to get it up and running. The axiom "Do it with your head, not your heart" is very appropriate here.

What's In It for Me?

Let's return to the lists in Chapter 2, and in particular, Lists 2 to 4 – "Things I Find Difficult To Do Or Do Not Possess The Skills For," "Where My Interests Lie," and "What Turns Me On," and the paragraph you've written about yourself. As you review the lists and paragraph:

1) Update them based on additional thoughts you may have gathered through this and previous chapters.

2) Look for elements which highlight your interests and strengths, and which might help to form a career option that would play on these interests and strengths, given today's work environment. You may arrive at more than one attractive possibility.

Now, list these options, and add others you hadn't previously considered. More importantly, you will be getting closer to capitalizing on your career strengths and interests.

Creating Options

If you have particular insight into a field, you may create an opportunity for yourself, provided you can support it with clear thinking, and the necessary business skills and fundamentals.

1) From the list of options you created in the previous section, rank them from the one you are most passionate about to the one you're least passionate about.

2) Talk with your spouse and closest friends about the options you've created. See if you can create convincing points about how you can be successful in one or more of these businesses. Ask what you would do to find a job or create a business that would allow you to carry out this option. In these discussions, the objectives are to test your passion, interest and thought process, and to listen to others' opinions and thoughts to help you focus your thinking and choices. There are many inventors who display beautifully framed certificates on their walls to identify them as patent-holders. They are probably the same inventors who have closets and garages full of prototypes of their inventions waiting for successful marketing.

Inventors

If you like to tinker and invent gadgets, understanding the risks that accompany your choices will be helpful in keeping a sense of reality. The *New York Times*, September 10, 1995, suggests that you don't quit your job just because you've invented what you believe to be a kitchen gadget that no cook can live without. Statistics show that for every 100 patents issued, at least 98 of the products failed in the marketplace. At $10,000 per patent approval, patents are quite expensive. Additionally, the patent approval process takes years, and if granted provides twenty years of protection. However, the protection will not give you free reign to produce and sell your product without competition.

A patent does not protect you from an onslaught of imitators who may not be successful in challenging your patent but can cause you grief and enormous costs to defend your rights.

We take for granted products like the zipper, *VCR Plus®*, *WD-40®*, *Post-It Notes®* and the telephone, which were marketed successfully in the mainstream of commerce. While your new invention may indeed provide a superior technology or application concept, remember that most inventors suffer from an inability to commercialize their bright idea.

Big Company Executives

It is not unusual for corporate executives at large companies to fail when they try to become entrepreneurs, and much of the problem has to do with power. Big corporations have it; small ones don't. Here are some general thoughts which differentiate how entrepreneurs and big company executives work and think:

Entrepreneurs
- Do just about everything "guerrilla-fashion."
- Try to outsmart their competitors.

Big Company Executives
- Just have to make up their minds and exercise the power to assign staff to implement their decisions.
- Have the ability to outspend and outlast opponents.
- Usually get equity, provide an infusion of capital, obtain very generous employment contracts and severance agreements.
- Tend to act more from emotion and monetary reward when moving to a small company.

The Challenges of Moving from Large to Small Companies

In 1990, an Arizona-based business consulting firm reported that corporate middle- and senior-managers who start their own businesses are more likely to fail than blue-collar workers who become entrepreneurs. Although many blue-collar workers lack education and business experience, they have a higher success rate than their management counterparts because of their willingness to listen and take advice. Humility offers them a much better chance of success.

Thorndike Deland Associates, a leading New York executive search firm, also reported in 1990 that less than a quarter of senior marketing executives making the transition from a large company to a small one did so successfully. As well, three out of four senior marketers lasted less than three years in their new jobs with small companies. The reasons cited were:

1) Even experienced managers fail to realize that marketing at a large corporation is entirely different than marketing at a small company. For example, few trained marketers are prepared for the quick decision-making and emphasis on trade promotion required at small specialty firms.

2) Marketers from big corporations work with long-term programs. Because small companies need someone to come in and produce quick results, conflicts often arise.

3) Marketing positions at small companies often require overall business skills because their staffs are small and less sophisticated.

4) Small companies rarely understand how much money is required in order to sustain a serious marketing effort.

The consolation is that having failed at one small company, big-time marketers are much more likely to succeed the next time around. History has shown that for many first-time entrepreneurs, what seems to be a new adventure quickly turns into a humbling and costly experience. Many ex-executives say that more frightening than the financial concerns is the question of whether they have what it takes to fly solo in a business of their own. Even so, the American Association of Retired Persons estimates that one-fifth of its members have serious plans to start businesses or at least work for themselves.

Competing Against Your Former Employer

Starting a business that competes with your former employer generates a host of potential issues and potential accusations including:

1) Misappropriation of trade secrets – you discovered and developed the technology for your business while you were with your former employer

2) Unfair competition or contacting their customers – you know your former employer's customers and cost structures, and have targeted their customers with lower bids to steal the business away

3) Conspiring with others to damage the business of the former employer – delivering information, whether rumors or fact, about your former employers business, e.g., treatment of employees, cutting corners on products, etc. that may be harmful to them

4) Hiring employees away from your former employer

Given how delicate the legal environment is today, consult your attorney to review the exposure you may face if you are thinking about going into business for yourself and competing against your former employer.

We've offered these common precautionary situations to help you choose the best options for you. It's easy to get caught up in a moment of emotion and lose your wits and objectivity. No matter what opportunities come your way, if you're not ready to act, and your intuition tells you to look at it a little more carefully, listen! A little precaution will go a long way.

Regardless of whether you wish to find new career opportunities with your current employer or a new employer, or go into business for yourself, there are a great number of options open to you if you are open to them. By staying in tune with the times and upgrading your skills and capabilities accordingly, your chances of finding career happiness and success are much greater.

Chapter 8 Checkpoint

Change and uncertainty in the business environment mean opportunities to update and adapt your work skills. Staying abreast of computer technologies and continuing to build professional networks are essential ingredients for your success.

✎ The marketplace can tell you which jobs will become extinct, and which ones will gain increasing importance in the electronic age.

✎ While specialized skills and knowledge can lead you to business opportunities, remember that emotions can often lure you to a business opportunity for the wrong reasons.

By staying in tune with the times and focusing on career options that are realistic and appropriate for you, you have a better chance of being successful.

186 Entrepreneur Or Employee?

Navigating the Minefields of Entrepreneurship

Chapter 9

ON YOUR OWN:
Navigating The Minefields

There is nothing more exhilarating than opening the doors to your business for the first time, knowing this is now your main source of income and survival. Excitement builds as you receive the first order for your product or service. Then when the check arrives, you frame it to celebrate your first dollar earned truly at your own hand. Your business is officially up and running!

"How did I get here?" I ask myself. I more than vaguely remember the experience: Doing my own office and equipment maintenance; deciding whether to pay for janitorial service or doing it myself; debating between meeting payroll or paying valuable vendors; finding an affordable health care plan or "planning to stay healthy;" making sure the computer, fax machine and telephone were in sync, and getting used to having the telephone glued to my ear and being calm and polite on every call. If I could just have another pair of hands and more hours in every day!

If you are a *Type E^N* individual, starting a business on your own is met by both reward and challenge. No matter how much experience you've had, there will always be a detail that you will not have thought through completely when you embark on your own business. This chapter looks at some of the more basic considerations to help you get started and to point you in the right direction. We will take a broad look at the various options for going into business on your own, some of the challenges you will face as a business owner, where to go for assistance, and how to cultivate relationships that may be valuable to you in the future. By being aware of the potential obstacles to your success, this chapter will help you navigate the minefields against those unexpected setbacks that can drain you of your time and money.

With the growing interest in starting small businesses, high quality resources such as books, computer programs, government publications, and the Internet are becoming increasingly accessible and available to help you get your venture on its way. They cover everything from writing a business plan, to understanding site selection criteria for office, warehouse or retail space, and negotiating financing with banks and venture capital groups.

What Business are You In?

The fundamental question is, "What business are you in?" If you have experience, first-hand knowledge and a tremendous number of contacts in the field you are pursuing, then you have three strong components for success. Unfortunately, many would-be entrepreneurs gravitate to the things they would like to do, regardless of whether it is a sound business opportunity.

Without proper investigation of the marketplace to accurately define your product or service, the size of the potential market, and whether the product or service is salable, the odds of survival are not in your favor. You're making a decision from the heart, not the head. And if your business concept is emotionally based, at least confirm rationally that this will

be a viable business venture. You may begin by researching the following questions:
1. What business am I in?
2. What unique product or service am I offering?
3. How big and where is the market for such a product or service?
4. Whom will I be selling to?
5. Why would they buy from me?
6. What is my unique selling proposition (or USP)?
7. How much can such a product or service sell for?
8. Is this a profitable business?

You may have had an idea in your mind for some time now and have done some research on it, or you may just be starting to think about your business. To address questions 1 and 2 above, let's return to the lists you created in Chapter 2, "Why Am I Interested in Leaving the Corporate World?," "Do I Willingly Take Risks?," "Why Do I Want a Business of My Own?" Do your answers give you more resolve to leave your corporate job? Do you have a good level of comfort and willingness to take risks, and strong business reasons for wanting your own business? In other words, are you a *Type E^N*? Have your thoughts of starting your own business been reinforced by the feedback you've received from someone whose business judgment you respect (see List 5 – "Getting Feedback From Others," in Chapter 2)? If you need more clarity in what business to pursue and what products or services to offer, then the following steps may help you:

1) Bring out a copy of your most recent resume.
2) Highlight your accomplishments, then paraphrase them.
3) List your hobbies, education and personal strengths.
- Do you teach or train others well?
- Do you interview others well?
- What specialized functions do you excel in?
- What specialized knowledge do you possess?

- Are you a strong project leader and manager?
- What types of assignments and projects have brought you the most success and enjoyment?

4) What did you contribute to make these ventures successful?

5) Which of your attributes or skills have proven to be most important?

Look back at your Lists 1 through 4 in Chapter 2. Are your findings consistent with where your interests lie and what turns you on? Do they further confirm what you like least and the things you don't do so well?

Getting Ready to Begin

Review your lists, notes and answers to these questions in light of current trends in business and what is forecast to be hot in the next five to ten years. Can you arrive at a business that would apply your best attributes or skills? What product or service would this business sell to prospective customers?

If this exercise has been easy for you, then you have some basic elements and direction to develop a business plan for your new venture. If the exercise is difficult, review your lists again. See if they need to be modified, and talk to your friends and associates to see if they might spark another idea for you.

Whatever the outcome, don't be discouraged. Arriving at a viable business idea can be a major challenge. It is better to take the time now to point your business in the right direction while you still have time on your side, than to experiment with your life savings on an idea that is not fully developed. Give yourself a reasonable period of time to refine your lists, talk to your confidants and try the exercise again. Sometimes it takes a few tries to arrive at a sound business concept. Don't be surprised if it is different from the idea you started with initially.

> **CAN YOU OFFER A UNIQUE SERVICE?**
>
> What services can you offer to a company that you could do better and less expensively than the company could do for itself?
>
> One individual built a strong business servicing companies who operate their computer systems with COBOL, an archaic computer language. The number of companies using COBOL based computers is relatively small and declining. However, they do exist. This factor, coupled with a shrinking pool of COBOL experts, led this entrepreneur to offer a unique service in a strong niche market.

There are some good creative sources of business ideas, concepts and ventures around you. Numerous magazines and publications can add to your thinking process. For example, the Lifestyle section of *USA Today* runs stories that sometimes furnish names and phone numbers of the businesses they feature, or of local trade associations and industry resources. *People* magazine writes about new business ideas, some of them off-beat, that you might be interested in.

Additionally, if you're good at referral prospecting and sales team development, network marketing programs continue to proliferate across the country and around the world.

The key to finding the right path for you is to match your skills, capabilities and interests with sound business ideas that will most favorably apply your talents. This will allow you to enjoy not only the fruits of your labor, but the day to day operations as well.

I Have a Clear Business Idea. Now What Do I Do?

You have three basic choices about going into business for yourself: start a new venture from scratch, buy an existing business, product, process or technology, or invest in a franchise.

Two major reasons for business failures are poor management and insufficient capital. This can happen if you haven't planned well. It also occurs when a business owner faces an unplanned event that becomes a drain on limited cash resources. For example, a pizza restaurant operator may unexpectedly have to upgrade the plumbing in his twenty year old premises to comply with current building codes. He may not have anticipated this $12,000 expenditure when he developed a budget for his business. Other unplanned events might include:
- Shifts in interest rates which increase borrowing expenses
- Unexpected and costly machinery breakdowns
- Rises in the cost of scarce components such as computer memory and chips
- Security deposits for utilities, leases, etc. from first time business owners because they lack a track record
- Required modifications to office and warehouse premises to conform to new regulations, such as providing access to the disabled
- Required postings of bonds for sales tax and other state, local or other regulatory deposits
- Changes in local, state or federal laws

How Much Capital is Enough?

What amount of capital is sufficient? The rule of thumb is: You never have enough cash. Seasoned private investors know that if they are going to invest in a venture, they have to be patient and prepared to invest double or triple the amount they think it will take to ride the company through tough times. Early investors often overvalue a company, buying a stake in a company for much more than its true worth. When additional capital is required to build the business or help it to survive, the original investors become disgruntled that new investors buy ownership stakes with proportionately less capital than the original investors and dilute the ownership stakes of the original investors. Moreover, the amounts of additional capital invested are often less than expected to support the cash needs of the business.

The amount of capital required can also rise if sales in a new venture do not grow as quickly as owners might expect. This, coupled with the continuing outflow of expenses, places a strain on the cash flow necessary to support operations and expansion.

A National Federation of Independent Business (NFIB) survey of one year old companies in *Inc.* Magazine, December, 1990, reported the following gross sales:

Less than $50,000	35%
$50,000 - $99,000	25%
$100,000 - $199,000	17%
$200,000 - $499,000	14%
$500,000 - $999,000	4%
More than $1 million	4%

This may call for more realistic expectations of revenue growth, so that expenses are more aligned with the cash you have available, and you can better project the level of required capital to start and run your business.

Cash Flow

Managing cash flow (i.e., the amount of cash that remains after you subtract the cash expenditures from the cash received from the sale of product or services) is based on understanding when cash comes into the business, how it is used, and when cash is needed to pay expenses. The major component of cash flow is the cash received by a business from sales.

There is a distinction between making the sale (gaining a contract or recording that a sale has been made) and collecting the cash for the contract or a sale. The collection of cash, and the timing of the collection is what is important in determining cash flow. A second major component of cash flow is the cash paid for components, either for sale or for use in the manufacture of products. Other sources and uses of cash include receiving loan amounts, paying for operating expenses, buying machinery and equipment, repaying debt, etc. The objective of cash flow management is to maintain a steady, positive and growing cash flow, and to manage the timing of receipts and payments to maintain a healthy cash flow.

In analyzing cash flow, an important contributor is having adequate gross margins. Gross margin can be defined as the difference between the selling price and cost per unit of product sold. The higher the gross margin, the fewer is the number of units that needs to be sold to cover other expenses, and the longer your capital will last. As an example, if the selling price of a washing machine is $549, and the landed cost to the retailer of that washing machine is $328, the gross margin per unit would be $221 ($549-$328). Each unit sold would then provide $221 to cover other of the retailer's expenses of operation. Having adequate gross margins to cover the numerous expenses of a business is frequently overlooked by inexperienced entrepreneurs.

The entrepreneur is in constant need of cash to operate the business and to meet his own living expenses. Generating and managing a healthy cash flow from the business becomes a way of life. It emphasizes the need to do your market research in order to arrive at a realistic view of your sources of business revenue. This is a major factor in the success of the business and the well-being of the entrepreneur, and could affect the choice of which option might be most appropriate for you to start a business. Whichever way you go — startup, buyout or franchise — these are important points to consider as you further research these options.

Should I Start My Own New Business?

An August 5, 1994 *Wall Street Journal* article reported that new business start-ups are driving our economy at the rate of more than 700,000 new businesses a year. This is double the rate of a decade ago and eight times that of the 1950s. However, after five years, only one in twenty will still be in business.

Entrepreneurs who concentrate on industries with which they are familiar have a better chance of succeeding than those who get into unfamiliar enterprises. If you don't have the experience, align yourself with people who do have the experience or stay away from the so-called "fabulous business opportunity." Stick to an industry, product or service that you know well. This very fundamental piece of advice will serve you well.

Some successful start-ups are started on the misfortune of others, e.g., purchasing assets of failing companies, or turning around a bankrupt company. These companies have a good chance of turning a profit because they get a fresh start without the enormous debt that may have led to their downfall under previous ownership.

A self-owned business represents freedom, opportunity, independence, being your own boss, and working at your own pace. Principally though, it is an occupation for winners. In addition to doing your homework, a positive and winning attitude is imperative. If you go into business with the attitude that you will fail, then you probably will.

Business success is more a function of what you do to make the venture work, than of who you are. A recurring problem among new ventures is that the idea, product or service is sound, but the distribution method has to be changed to make it work. With this in mind, do your research, talk to industry experts and get advice before you go too far and too deep with your new gee-whiz venture. If you are inflexible about how your product might be distributed, you stand a good chance of failure. Many ventures are started on the assumption that everyone needs or likes the product they have created. Often the owners have not given much thought to whether they can make a living by selling their product.

An example might be an automotive after-market cup holder that a company develops and tries to sell to the large retail chains like Sears and

Wal-Mart. While the product is very popular, and is a great after-market product, buyers for the chains generally do not buy from a one product company. It is too risky. The cup holder company has no track record, might have an uncertain supply should demand soar, may not have the ability to finance and follow-through on a warranty program, and could drag the retailer into a product liability suit, etc. These circumstances might preclude many large buyers from buying products from the business regardless of how good the product is. Sadly, without available distribution channels, a company is doomed to fail.

SOME PEARLS OF WISDOM ON STARTING YOUR OWN BUSINESS

1. Be able to clearly articulate, verbally and in writing, what makes your business concept unique and viable. If you are unable to tell people why you will succeed where others have failed, you probably won't.

2. A successful business idea may mean a hectic life.

3. Size isn't everything. A one million dollar business is small to one person, but very interesting to someone else.

4. Hiring advisors before rather than after is expensive, but it's usually more expensive not to.

5. Consider deferred or reduced payment, or equity in lieu of payment for services from your accountant, lawyer or consultant.

6. Don't become too complacent and comfortable with your customer base.

7. Becoming too dependent on large customers puts you at their mercy. They may dictate packaging, pricing and terms of sale.

8. If you are dependent on a small group of customers, what happens when you lose them?

9. Ideas and concepts are rather easy to come by. Execution, implementation, distribution, marketing and financing are much more difficult.

10. Small entrepreneurs must make up with energy what they lack in size.

Should I Buy an Existing Business?

Business opportunities are available everywhere. A friend, accountant, lawyer, banker or someone in your professional and business network may give you a lead. Conferences and seminars travel around the country telling people about the "hottest" business opportunities. Business brokers earn their living by bringing a potential buyer and seller together for a fee. Unless you clearly specify the type of business you want to buy, they may not be able to help you. Understand precisely what the role of a business broker will be as you begin to seek candidates for your investment. And, don't forget newspaper and magazine ads in trade journals and mainstream publications list businesses for sale and business opportunities.

Forbes Magazine reported in its November 8, 1993 issue that 250,000 businesses changed hands in 1992 at prices of $5 million or less. According to business brokers, four out of five small businesses that were sold are still in business five years later. By contrast, the Small Business Administration (SBA) claims that two in five startup businesses survive for six years. This is because a business that is in operation already has a base of customers, a proven product, and a history, particularly when you look at its cash flow.

With some research and analysis, you might be able to make assumptions about the risk of buying such a business, calculate a predictable stream of cash flows from the business, and arrive at a value for the business from which you can determine an appropriate purchase price. Here are some thoughts to consider before buying a business:

1) Why is the owner selling and what are his plans? Is he retiring or does he plan to continue his involvement in the business?

2) Do I have good professional advice? Make sure that in addition to your lawyers, accountants and financial advisors, you have the expertise required to understand the operations and the technical aspects of the product and business.

3) Does my business experience fit? What value does your experience bring to the new business?

4) Do I have the right attitude about going into this? Am I willing to walk away from the deal if I can't get the right terms?
How strong is the company's market position? Is it a growing or shrinking market? Are sales for the product, in both unit volumes and prices, stable or on the decline?

5) Can the business pay me an adequate salary? Is the return on my investment one that I can live with? A ten percent return on investment may be good for other investors, but not for you.

6) Is my family behind this new business deal?

7) Do I have enough cash to support myself and my family until money starts coming in?

8) Do I need an appraisal? How will I value the business, and what is a fair price for it?

Do your due diligence by critically reviewing the customer base of the business you wish to buy, including the relationships the company has with its customers. Then ask more questions:

1) Is the business you wish to buy selling a product that is a strong seller in the market?

2) Is there a strong source of product supply? Will this continue into the future?

3) Does the product provide a reasonable gross margin (market selling price less cost of the product)? There are rules of thumb for different industries which you should research and make comparisons with.

4) What are the other costs of running such a business?

It would be advisable to develop projections for income and expenses, and arrive at projected cash flows as far into the future as you can (usually three to five years). Be reasonably sure that the assumptions you've made for product prices and costs, and units sold will realistically hold for the years projected.

Take an inventory of the equipment and machinery used in producing the company's products for sale, and get an independent and reliable source to appraise their values.

1) What are the replacement costs? Is newer or more advanced technology available? How many years of useful life does the equipment have?

2) What condition is the equipment in? How much maintenance and downtime are involved?

3) Are spare parts readily available?

4) What are the costs of insurance and service contracts for the equipment?

You'll need a valuation of the business and its components. You'll need to review the appropriate business structure and tax implications of any purchase you are considering. You'll also want to review the contracts and obligations of the business to its employees, suppliers, customers and others, and the obligations you have to the seller. Are there any liens, pending lawsuits or back taxes due on the business?

Establish a relationship with the seller to build rapport and establish mutual trust. This will go a long way in helping you to arrive at a well-informed buying decision. Find out who prepared the prospective seller's financial statements. Was it the owner/operator, a one-man accounting firm, or an established, reputable mid-sized firm? This will help you determine the credibility and confidence you can place in the items reported on.

From a banker or investor's point of view, anything you can do to increase the credibility of your information and presentation will go a long way in supporting your financing discussions and negotiations. Unless you have a strong business reputation with bankers and financiers, the use of a reputable accounting firm will be to your advantage. Moreover, the higher quality the firm, and the more recognized it is in the business community, the better you'll fare with bankers and investors.

Seasoned entrepreneurs agree on the following:

1) Don't place too much reliance on outside financing, no matter what people say, prior to the actual writing of the check. In most cases, your own savings and that of family will be your prime source of funds.

2) The start-up costs and early "maintenance costs" almost always exceed your forecasts.

3) During a recession or when buyers are scarce, the opportunity to leverage a small amount of cash on hand may be great. Where investors and lenders see a tremendous upside because of the strength in a new management team or in the market potential of the company, the likelihood of financing a larger part of the purchase price increases.

4) Some franchisors might accept a smaller cash investment if they develop a high degree of confidence in the franchisee. However, this is offset by a long loan payback period and high interest rates, the requirement of financial statements, caveats and conditions placed on the borrower.

"If it sounds too good to be true, it probably is." Don't get caught in the emotion of a hot deal! If you are required to make an immediate decision, don't! As you go through all these items, your financial advisor and your lawyer can provide you with invaluable assistance to guide you in the right direction which could save you money in the long run.

Franchises are Always Successful, aren't They?

Many entrepreneurs buy franchises because they think the franchisor's formula and guidance will save them from failure and provide an easy means of generating income. There are many outstanding franchises which have brought great success to individual franchisees. However, less than ten percent of franchise companies account for over half of all sales and franchise establishments.

Start-up capital to acquire the rights to these franchises is high given their success rate, relative risk and potential for long-term capital appreciation. Franchise costs range from $25,000 to $2,000,000, with an average investment of $150,000. If you don't have these sums of money available, less expensive franchises seem more attractive at first because they may potentially become the next superstar. But for every set of golden arches, there are thousands of tarnished dreams. Many people have lost their life savings in ill-conceived, low quality, and exploitative franchise concepts.

The Insider's Guide to Franchising, by Bryce Webster, outlines the many advantages a strong franchise organization offers:
- A recognizable trademark
- Consistent quality and uniformity in products and services
- Proven systems for business, marketing and operations
- Well researched sources of supply and service
- Excellent training programs and support to operate and manage the franchise
- Available sources of financial assistance for investment capital

But Webster also offers some cautions and pitfalls in franchising:
- Franchises are not always money generators; don't expect to be "rolling in dough" immediately.

- Franchises can and do fail.
- Franchises do not guarantee success, and require hands-on management of the daily operations and all its details to be successful.
- Franchise contracts are not written in the best interests of the franchisee, unless the interests of the franchisee coincide with those of the franchisor.
- Franchises may not be the best alternative for entrepreneurs because they have a well-defined and clear set of operating systems and guidelines which franchisees must adhere to. Entrepreneurs will generally have a preference for more personal discretion in how the operations are run. After all, that's what makes them entrepreneurs.

As with any important investment decision, do your homework. If you are interested in pursuing an investment in a franchise, check and verify every fact and figure put forth by a franchisor, just as you would if you were purchasing another business. Ask questions like:
- What is the real failure rate for this franchise?
- Is the franchise company in good financial health? What is the risk of franchisor bankruptcy, and how would this affect a franchisee?
- Do the franchise rights provide an exclusive geographic territory for the franchisee? Does this exclusivity also protect you against the franchisor's company-owned units?
- Am I experienced in the industry or business of the franchise? (If it is a retail franchise, and you do not have a background in retail business, you are in for a big shock.)

Federal Trade Commission rules require franchisors to provide prospective buyers of franchises with the information they need to make informed decisions. However, there are many instances of exaggerated claims and statements, inflated sales figures based on unrealistic levels of projected growth, and cases of outright fraud. The Small Business Committee of the U.S. House of Representatives and the Federal Trade Commission investigate allegations of deception, wrongdoing and abuse in the franchise industry. Complaints from franchisees regularly arise, and almost every year, there is a call for new legislation.

Year after year, franchising continues to grow, even though franchise failures are more common than most people think. It has been reported that during recessions, the rush into franchising increases. It seems that numbers of newly terminated middle-managers eagerly invest their savings, or the proceeds from their severance packages, into what they hope will be potentially lucrative franchise opportunities. They are looking for a route to fame and fortune, and a means to satisfy the desire to own their own business.

There is wide disagreement about the rate of failure between franchise and non-franchise businesses. Some sources indicate that sixty-five percent of non-franchise businesses fail, while only five percent of franchisees fail within five years of start-up. Many feel that the truer rate of failure among franchises is between thirty and forty percent over a ten year period. Large corporate franchises tend to be more profitable and successful than smaller franchises. Franchises which remain in business for four years have a much greater chance of making it to ten years.

Be clear on what the franchisor's and franchisee's obligations are before investing. Once you have purchased a franchise, some franchisors do not follow through on what you thought they were going to do. Advertising and support are usually the areas where they fall short. We interviewed a California business owner, who reported that he was very impressed with the people who "romanced" him to buy the franchise in the beginning. After signing up, he never saw these individuals again, and found it very difficult to reach them by telephone. He now only sees the local franchise director, a position that seems to experience a high turnover rate. The franchisee claims that the franchisor over-promised the rewards of the franchise and the assistance he would receive, and overstated everything from sales to income potential to special pricing. After several years as a franchisee, he resents having to pay royalties on sales, and additional assessments to support the company's advertising, whether it is beneficial to his location or not.

Once you are a franchise owner, be aware that the sale of a franchise, or leaving the franchisor's system, can be extremely difficult and expensive. The franchisor gets a good deal of money from you up front for the right to operate its franchise. In terminating your franchise agreement, you might find that the penalty and cancellation fees would allow the franchisor to buy back and takeover the operation at a fraction of the cost of a new franchise. Be aware that the original franchise contract is weighted heavily in the franchisor's favor. It may not be negotiable because you are not the only buyer of the right to operate their franchise.

If you are considering a franchise, choose one wisely. Make sure you understand obligations that the franchisor is imposing on you, both from an operational and financial point of view. Good sources of information on investing in franchises include Francorp, a large franchise development and consulting company located in Olympia Fields, Illinois; the American Franchisee Association, in Chicago, Illinois; and the Federal Trade Commission, Washington, D.C.

Special Situations

There are special considerations for those of you thinking about home-based businesses, family businesses, retail operations and partnerships.

SOHO (Small Office, Home Office Businesses)

Home-based businesses have become very popular. The availability and sophistication of personal computers provides professional and effective office technology. There are substantial cost savings from not having to pay rent for office space in the home; and, there's no travel time or parking costs. There are several professional organizations that support home-based businesses in areas such as health and business insurance, financing and marketing.

If you are considering starting out at home, you should be mindful that home-based businesses can run into many unexpected problems. In particular, when you are doing business in a residential area, how will your operation affect or disrupt the community? Do the local zoning ordinances allow such an activity in a residential neighborhood? Will the neighbors eventually resent your employees' and visitors' cars taking up parking spaces? What about the increased activity, traffic and trash? These are certainly considerations that will affect how supportive your neighbors are of your business.

Retail

If you're planning to start a new retail venture, you may note that the mid-90s has seen many retail vacancies due mainly to the difficulty retail establishments have had in surviving in a competitive marketplace. It is extremely difficult for start-ups to rent space in large, established and successful enclosed malls, which are like exclusive clubs in many respects. If you're not a member of the club, you rarely get invited to lease space. For the inexperienced, lease negotiations can be prolonged and rather testy. The posting of security bonds can be difficult, and the costs can be enormous due to stringent build-out criteria, hours of operation, common area maintenance and other costs.

It is extremely difficult for a new retailing venture to secure prime space. The mortality rate of new retail business ventures is very high.

You may be enamored by the Saturday or pre-Christmas foot traffic in the malls and the visions of ringing cash registers. Just remember that the rent you'll pay for the prime space will be the same on those deserted Tuesdays from 10 a.m. to 4 p.m. when there is little or no business activity.

A new retail trend has developed with the creation of kiosks. In some cases, these can be temporary (e.g., having limited exposure for the period from Halloween to Christmas) and allow a newcomer to test a concept without an expensive and long-term lease. While many mall operators now encourage off-beat, niche-type businesses, they can evict you on very short notice. In the last few years, several of these kiosk operations have developed into full blown, serious retail operations. Some have expanded into "real" stores. The huge Mall of America in Bloomington, Minnesota, reports thousands of requests from people interested in becoming kiosk and cart merchants. With low start-up costs, typically comprising a security deposit of $3,000 on the cart, one month's rent of $1,500, and inventory costing $10,000, these outlets have become very popular across the country.

There are many instances of a kiosk offering a variety of products only to find a great deal of interest in one or two specialty items. Within a short time, the whole offering and name are changed, and the kiosk becomes successful by highlighting the new specialty line that maintains good market and product appeal.

Family Businesses

Family businesses are growing in numbers and popularity, too. As a result, there are more business school extension classes and seminars being offered on the subject. These programs cover such topics as managing culture, race and ethnicity; managing multiple roles as owner, manager, employee and family member, and succession and estate planning. If you are considering starting a business that will involve investment or management by other family members, there are a number of aspects to consider:

1) Legal and Estate Planning Considerations
These include the type of company and proportions of ownership. The proportions of ownership may impact your working or personal relationships with other members of the family. There are also estate issues which can be dealt with to minimize the tax impact of ownership transfer on the growth in value, capitalization or solvency of the business. This would be a good time to seek the advice of your accountant or financial advisor, lawyer and an estate planning specialist.

2) Relationships Between Family Members
Whenever one works with other family members within the same organization, the dynamics of the work relationship are further complicated by the familial relationship that exists in a multiple role environment.

Additionally, the expectations of the family, both parents and children, are often assumed and not clearly communicated at the outset, creating opportunities for various problems to arise:

a) Sometimes the children that parents are counting on to run the business decide to pursue their own dreams, even if those dreams differ from the parents' plan.
b) In other cases, children who want to manage the family business prove themselves unqualified to do so.
c) Charges of nepotism arise when non-family employees perceive that family members are given preferential treatment with regard to promotions and raises.
d) Sibling rivalry occurs, regardless of the reason.
e) Parent/child conflicts can arise.

A major issue for family businesses is management succession — passing the business on to the next generation of managers. While parent owners may wish to pass on the business to their children, often the children aren't interested in or capable of taking over the business. Part of your planning for a family owned business will be to understand the objectives of all the family members, particularly as they relate to the ownership and management of the business.

Where it would be possible to pass the baton to a family member, be sure of both the capability and commitment of the family member in assuming charge of the business. It might be a good idea to have a mentor or an experienced interim manager continue running the business. This will help the successor round out his capabilities and confidence prior to assuming the reins completely. Alternatively, it may be advantageous to have an impartial board of advisors or directors assist in making a more objective decision concerning succession.

Partnerships

Partnerships, like family businesses in some respects, should be based on a clearly defined, clearly communicated, and clearly understood definition of the roles and responsibilities of the partners. Partners should state their goals clearly to one another and commit them to writing. Yet even with this in place, partners should have skills and capabilities which complement one another, and should have work habits and ethics that are compatible. Partners should feel comfortable being very "open" with each other. A helpful thought is that partnerships don't always focus strictly on investment funds. Partnerships can involve some partners providing the financial investment, while others contribute the ideas, or required technical and operating expertise.

Many entrepreneurs shy away from partnerships because of the horror stories. For example, where partnerships involve family members, such as brothers, it is not surprising that the sibling rivalry continues. A pair of siblings who have been very competitive throughout their lives, whether in sports, school, or outside activities, may find the perfect environment in a family business or business partnership, to resume their rivalry. If this is not controlled, the rivalry, rather than the business, could become the focus of their efforts. This could be detrimental to the orderly operation and growth of the business. As a second example, what if one sibling is required to fire another? This might lead to actions or avoidances of actions which might not be in the best interests of the company.

Where Will the Money Come From?

When it comes to funding and financing, the key questions are: "Where can I get funding?" and "How do I get financing?" According to *The Wall Street Journal* (June 4, 1990), much of the money invested in start up companies comes from private investment funds, usually from wealthy, individual investors (known as *angels*). Private investors back more than 30,000 start-up companies a year, while venture funds back only 2,000. There are many occasions when companies reach the later stages of their development and outgrow common sources of financing, like loans from family and friends, traditional bank loans, and those guaranteed by the United States Small Business Association (SBA). In such cases, they may seek financing from angels or venture capital funds (pools of investment funds created by groups of investors used to invest in particular businesses or ventures).

To improve access to capital sources, the SBA provides a service to match small businesses in need of capital to compatible sources of angel financing, using the Internet to bring them together. This helps entrepreneurs to save time in searching out potential investors, and gives angel investors potential investment opportunities which better meet their criteria for investment and return.

Bankers

Much has been written about bankers and their conservative ways. Most of what you read about them is true. As a result of the unbridled real estate activity in the late '80s and the problems of the savings and loan institutions, regulators have come down hard on the lending practices of banks. However, make no mistake about it — banks are in the business of lending money. Cash is the commodity they trade. Who they "sell" their commodity to becomes increasingly critical as you move from being securely employed (which makes the banks very comfortable) to owning a business or being self-employed (which the bankers view with extreme caution).

Their willingness to loan you money is related to:
- The state of the economy
- The business' track record with the bank
- Your experience in operating successful businesses
- The overall availability of money
- How competitive the banking business is at that time
- The bank's loan portfolio history
- Its interest in developing new business

Bankers simply want to be assured that they will be repaid all of the moneys that they lend. Sounds rather elementary, doesn't it? Well, it's not quite that simple.

Through the mid-90s, with the Federal Reserve Board trying to stimulate growth in the economy, interest rates have dropped as banks attempted to attract new commercial and consumer business and maintain their competitiveness and revenues. This provided a good climate for business owners to secure business loans and start-up capital for their ventures. One thing to remember is that you must be prepared to sell yourself to your banker to get a loan. The banker will be interested in your expertise, financial strength, ability to repay the loan, and whether you can qualify for assistance under a U.S. Small Business Administration program to reduce their risk of lending to you.

At the same time, bankers relish being in on the ground floor of a new idea, a new trend, a new concept. But, they feel comfortable only when the idea, concept, or trend proves to be a real winner. That's not so elementary. Here's how banks seem to operate:

1) Put up *your own* money first, Mr. Entrepreneur. Banks do not like to finance 100% of any venture. They like the borrower to have at least 20%-30% of his own money at risk. So try to line up additional "votes of confidence" (in the form of funds) from family, friends and associates. Bankers like to see successful people (particularly those with accounts in the same bank) among your list of advisors and investors.

2) If your new venture produces a positive cash flow, the bank will lend you more and more. Yes, banks will even solicit you with offers of additional funds. As long as you are successful and as long as you are making payments on time, you'll be a valuable customer to them.

3) When applying for loans and financing, have a financial statement available. A word of caution: Some small businessmen, too eager for funds, have resorted to distorting their records. Intentionally misrepresenting information in order to secure a loan is considered fraud. It is subject to both federal and state statutes, and can result in imprisonment or fines.

4) Bankers will require you to provide proof of income. This is particularly difficult, if not altogether impossible, for you to do after you leave a corporate job. This is why you must set up a "war chest" prior to leaving a job. You should be aware that, as proof of income, bankers will require the last three years of personal tax returns as well as pay stubs. Much of this required documentation is governed by banking regulations, and the bank must comply.

5) Banks like to "sink their teeth" into equity, particularly real estate, unless, of course, you have a very strong financial statement or a high credit rating. Generally, they like to have some tangible property they can hold on to as a guarantee that they'll get something of value back for their money, in the event of a default.

6) You should be aware that lending decisions by banks are under increasingly close scrutiny by the banks' auditors, which means that cases cannot be treated on a personal basis like they once were. It's important to note however, that your personal reputation, integrity and previous history are still very important in supporting any lending decision.

Relationships with Bankers

If you're considering using loan expediters who promise to prepare a winning loan application for a fee, beware! You should not believe anyone who promises to get you a loan. As a business owner, your personal involvement and efforts will in most cases be much more beneficial. Ask yourself the following questions:

- Have I developed a good relationship with my banker?
- Does my banker know my business?
- Do I have a good accountant who can assist in the preparation of the loan application?
- Do I look at the actual preparation of a business plan as an extremely worthwhile exercise?

A long-term relationship with a banker provides the most favorable conditions for them to help you. Establish a relationship with a bank and the manager before you need the money. But which bank do you cultivate a relationship with? A 1995 Federal Reserve study concluded that branch banks, smaller banks owned by multi-bank holding companies and banks owned by out-of-state companies tend to lend small businesses a smaller share of their funds than in-state independent banks. Conversely, while small banks have greater local autonomy, multi-branched banks have less flexibility to make small loans. This may be a signal that further growth in multi-office and interstate banking may create funding voids for small businesses.

IT'S GOOD TO MAINTAIN A PERSONAL RELATIONSHIP WITH YOUR BANKER

In the old days, a banker was characterized as an elderly, resolute man sitting behind a big mahogany desk. Times have changed. The account manager or loan officer now spends 25% - 50% of his time visiting prospective customers, to develop new relationships and to better understand the business of his existing customers. Today's bank officers want to know your business. And, today's banks are competing aggressively for the valuable, profitable, small to medium-sized business accounts and loans.

The "relationships" referred to are business relationships built on person-to-person as well as company-to-company connections. If they were only between companies, changes in personnel would have no effect on deals. Therefore, it is critical to know your officer, and his or her boss. Banks are notorious for their officer turnover. So you should develop secondary or "back-up" relationships. If your banker changes banks to advance his career and your relationship was particularly good with him, you might consider moving your account to the new bank. But don't act too hastily. Let your officer settle in at the new bank. Let him establish a relationship with his new loan committee on other deals first. Then, you might consider changing bank affiliations.

There is another factor frequently overlooked by entrepreneurs: Invite your banker to visit your place of business. Take him on a tour of your facility, and introduce him to your employees. Show him the systems you have in place, and how the "numbers" are generated. The best time to do this is when you are NOT asking for a loan. But, after receiving a loan for a new piece of machinery, invite your loan officer back to see the new machinery in operation and what impact it is having on your business. After receiving a large order from a customer, call your banker. Let him hear the enthusiasm in your voice. He will be flattered that you included him on your call list. The message here is "communicate, communicate, communicate!"

Credit Cards

Should you not be successful with bank credit, you may periodically receive "pre-approved" credit offers in the mail along with other enticements for consumer borrowing. Cash advance features are prevalent and make new credit card offerings attractive; but the interest rate on unpaid credit card debt is very high. As well, some states require credit card issuers to specify that personal credit cards be used only for personal expenses. However, enforcement is rare, as lenders and credit card companies who issue these cards are indifferent to how and when you use your cards.

Credit card borrowing is not something we recommend. It is "financing of the last resort," and is accompanied with a high degree of risk. By stringing together several credit card loans, which often carry low introductory interest rates (as low as 6.9% in 1995), borrowers are able to gain access to an unsecured loan for a limited period of time. When the time period for the introductory period – typically six to twelve months, comes to an end, these borrowers simply transfer the balances to new low interest cards. Note that a great risk occurs should a new low interest card not be available. This forces the borrower to repay the loan or secure a much more expensive loan to pay off the low interest credit card debt. This predicament would be a sure sign of trouble, both for you as an individual and for the business.

Suppliers

Credit from suppliers is a very popular source of financing startups. A poll of 300 business owners found that 65% depend on credit from suppliers, 40% use credit cards and 35% rely on commercial bank loans for funding. Note that these statistics can vary among minority and non-minority owned businesses, as well as among firms who have been in business for more than five years. The criteria used by suppliers to extend credit purchase terms varies. Your credit record, and your ability to negotiate favorable terms play key roles in supplier financing.

Customers

Alternatively, if your business will be a valuable supplier to a larger corporation, you might want to approach this large customer for funds. As large companies streamline their operations, it may be in their interest to ensure that their suppliers stay healthy and provide them with a reliable and trouble-free source of product and service supply. If your business is in such a position, then your customers might well be a source of capital to you.

Small Business Administration Loans

Programs of the SBA have been instrumental in the growth of small business in the country. Since its inception in 1953, the SBA has guaranteed more than 480,000 loans totaling in excess of $60 billion. Under the guaranty program, a bank extends the loan and the SBA guarantees repayment of a percentage (typically 75% to 90%) of the principal amount. The SBA program offers three key advantages:

1) Repayment terms are generally more favorable than for conventional commercial financing. (Note that an SBA program guarantees your loan with the bank. It reduces a bank's risk of lending money to you by guaranteeing a large portion of the loan. Your bank provides the borrowed funds, and you make repayments to the bank).

2) There is no minimum dollar amount for an SBA loan, although local banks may have their own minimums.

3) There are fees involved, but the cost of financing is relatively low.

About 25% of all SBA loans are extended to start-up companies, which are generally shunned by conventional commercial banks. Because the SBA assumes most of the financial exposure, commercial banks generally are more willing to consider relatively risky deals.

Equity Financing

Struggling small companies who have difficulty attracting conventional financing often turn to riskier sources. Some entrepreneurs' excessive ambitions blind them to whom they should trust. Dealing with very small brokerage investment houses with questionable track records or carelessly agreeing to other sources of capital investment without carefully researching their merits can be quite costly. It may result in high brokerage fees, giving up large stakes in ownership or control, or even losing the company where conditions of non-performance arise.

In searching for sources of capital, one thing is sure: Without the right amount of capital, it is difficult to be successful. But what about the funding source? It is important to match your needs and objectives with those of the capital provider. If you plan to expand the business slowly, it may not be prudent to entertain a willing source of funds if it expects a much faster rate of growth.

A May, 1995 *Wall Street Journal* article suggests that by taking the time to qualify sources of capital thoroughly, you'll be much more likely to find one that can also be a strong business ally. In addition to supplying capital, the source might be able to assist you with introductions to potential partners, buyers and customers, and help you inject the financial discipline that your company might need. Over time, as the face of your business and your needs change, it follows that new sources and providers of capital can bring a new perspective and some needed positive changes to your company.

Growing Pains

When a venture will reach critical mass is another important component to consider if you're thinking about going into business for yourself. We can define critical mass as reaching that critical level of business activity, sales and cash flow that will in all probability be maintained consistently. It is the point at which the business will comfortably support the costs of doing business and provide a reasonable level of profit to its owners, and allow them to think about reaching the next plateau in the growth of the business.

A factor that will affect cash flow and critical mass for a company are the tax costs or benefits that may be derived from running one's own business. Many people going into business are under the mistaken notion that there are numerous tax benefits that will accrue to them. This is a fallacy. Suffice it to say that generally, deductions are allowed for tax purposes for incurring costs that provide a reasonable likelihood of generating revenues. These may vary depending on the type, size and legal structure of the business and the expenses incurred. The deduction of expenses incurred for a small office/home office (e.g., mortgage interest, use of personal automobile, depreciation for capital equipment purchased), is often dependent on the circumstances of the business. A good place to begin your research on starting your own company is to check with your accountant or financial advisor about which tax benefits and deductions are available to you, and how they might affect the financial well-being of your company and your individual tax situation. Tax planning has become as important as sales and expense planning.

Size Isn't Everything

The question of business size is not thought of very seriously when a business is first started. When will I know that I'm a big company? Some people view "big" as having one employee to delegate to. Others see it as building annual revenues of $5 million or $10 million, or having more than 50 or 100 employees. Depending on the type of product or service your company offers, the level of revenues will be limited by the physical limitations and technical capabilities of your staff and employees, and the level of automation and technology applied by the business. As a business owner, stay with what you are comfortable managing, be it one or two employees, or thirty employees, and stay with what makes sense for the business. Many entrepreneurs that we interviewed expressed uneasiness that the growth of their companies has distanced them from what they enjoy the most. Instead of creating new products and formulating marketing plans, they are forced to deal with personnel problems, operational miscues and the like. There is no rule that says one size fits all.

Today, technology can help your fledgling business give the perception of bigness to outsiders while improving your work efficiency inside. The use of personal computers and modems, fax and answering machines encourage the growth of small office, home office operations, and allow you to be very competitive in the marketplace.

With intelligent switches, one phone line can direct call traffic to the phone, the answering machine, the fax machine or the computer modem. As well, there are software solutions for message center, voice mail capabilities, and fax communications (both receiving and sending faxes directly from the computer). You can stay in touch with your office and clients using pagers and cellular phones. With the continued growth of online bulletin boards and the Internet, you now have convenient access to a wealth of research for your company, market, products and services. With the availability of highly sophisticated technology, your only limitation is your ability to use it.

A second priority for you is to gain access to a pool of resources, consultants or contractors with specialized capabilities who can help your business grow and support the needs of your operations.

Choosing a Name for Your Business

The name you choose for your business can affect how your customers and market react to you, and whether you will experience growth in sales or loss in business. Choosing the right name is often taken quite lightly, with many stories of people arriving at what they believe to be a catchy name in the shower or at a dinner party.

Be wary of names which carry a hidden meaning or double-entendre, or have a meaning to you personally which may not be apparent to others. This may be a sign of problems to come. Basic, understandable names are more likely to work in your favor. Draft a list of names that are:
- Short, strong or solid
- Related to the business you're in without being overly technical
- Understandable even to people not from your area of specialty or expertise; one that has wide acceptance and appeal.
- Distinguishes your business from your competitors
- Not offensive when translated to other languages and cultures

A name, chosen correctly and responsibly, can go a long way in adding value and drawing attention to what your business is selling.

Blind Spots and Failures

Most entrepreneurs will tell you the same thing: Everyone underestimates the costs associated with a sustained marketing effort or the expenses required to continue operating a business until it achieves its sales goals or breaks even. While it is a great feeling to know that the business is all yours, *all yours* includes a huge overhead that can keep you awake at nights. For example, it is not surprising that business owners sometimes struggle to pay their rent or meet their payroll, or stretch their suppliers when bills become due, because they are waiting for funds to arrive from their customers so that they can make their payments. The need for cash will always be cause for insomnia.

Entrepreneurial blind spots — those aspects of the business owners often overlook, forget to consider, or neglect to plan for — are numerous:

1) Sales will not grow as quickly as you predicted.

2) Miscalculations are usually made in what it costs to sell, including everything from salaries for sales people to projected travel expenses to the cost of developing new business.

3) Most small companies pursue too many kinds of customers or too large a geographic territory, or introduce too many products, given their limited resources. Remember that it is always better to stay focused and do a few things well than many things poorly.

4) People with experience that is key to the success of the company ought to be given stock or some other incentive to keep them fully involved, but too often are not involved.

5) It's easy to let operating costs and overhead slide up, and too often that's what happens.

6) Selling someone once doesn't make that customer a loyal buyer.

7) Some business owners may not have what it takes to diligently collect accounts receivable, or to afford an employee to do it. They are embarrassed to be both sellers and bill collectors.

8) When you're eager to start your own business, you're more susceptible to making an emotional decision and being caught off guard by a scam. Don't be "sucked in" by someone offering you a business opportunity that sounds too attractive to let go. This is a time to keep your wits about you and balance logic with intuition. Don't be rushed into a quick decision that may come back to haunt you. When in doubt, check it out.

About Con-Artists and Scams

Today's world can accommodate a variety of small businesses and home-based businesses. Early retirees, ex-employees with hefty severance packages, and other displaced workers seek economic independence through businesses of their own. It is these groups who have been victimized by telemarketing scams, phony franchise offerings, and supposed new technologies.

To avoid being taken advantage of, here are some basic pointers:

1) Don't be so eager to believe that others really want to help set you up a business, particularly when you are extremely excited to get something "up and running."

2) Call your local Better Business Bureau to see if any complaints have been lodged about the group that has solicited your investment.

3) Always reject an all-expense paid visit to the company's headquarters.

4) Don't give away "non-refundable deposits" for an opportunity that sounds too good to be true.

5) Before making any investment, ask to see the disclosure documents that are required to be filed with regulatory authorities.

6) Personally meet the company's references, including current clients, and see how they work. Be careful, scam artists sometimes steer potential clients to people who have been paid to lie about a deal's attractiveness.

7) Consider retaining the services of a lawyer or accountant to review the company's financial statements and state of affairs.

8) Be skeptical of earnings claims that are too good to be true. Always question any fact that seems too good to be true.

9) Confirm with your state attorney general that the business has complied with state registration laws.

10) Resist high-pressure sales tactics. Legitimate ventures usually don't require a snap decision.

11) Play the advocate's role. If the venture is so darn good, ask "Why me? Why isn't their whole family in it? Why are they being so generous to a stranger like me?"

The bottom line: If it just doesn't feel right to you, or the people don't impress you, trust your instincts and don't go any further.

Other Considerations

Make no mistake that planning the business is an important first step. There are thousands of books available on how to write a business plan, how to forecast expenses, and how to do sales planning. Yet, almost every one of those books will tell you that you will never ever think of everything. An experienced quarterback can fade back to make a pass just as he has done hundreds and hundreds of times, only to be tackled by an opposing player he never saw coming. There will surely be something that you won't have anticipated.

A May 22, 1995 *Wall Street Journal* article, "All the Wrong Moves," stated that a major cause of failure is in not getting out and talking with potential customers. By finding out what they want and why they would buy your product or service, you have a better chance of relating your product or idea to their needs. So often, new business owners forget the customer and focus on developing and getting a product out quicker, only to find that customers are not interested in buying it.

Today's products tend to have a shorter product life cycle because new, improved versions are being developed constantly, and replacing and competing with products with better technologies, improved features or lower prices. By not considering the impact of technology or the potential for competitors to introduce better products, the risk of failure will increase for your business.

An often fatal flaw of new and small business owners is poor time management. Time and cash flow are two of the most important factors impacting success. If time is not managed well to address the priorities of vital importance to the business, then unnecessary cash drain will usually result as the entrepreneur tries to stay or get back on track.

Finally, because there is never enough cash available, entrepreneurs may have the tendency to not get the appropriate help for their businesses. A strong product will not survive if other aspects of your business are weak. You can increase your chances of success by choosing and relying on advisors whom you can count on to give you good advice. It is always better to start off on the right foot or do things right the first time than to have to go back and correct mistakes, or worse yet, to lose your business because of a mistake you know you could have prevented.

Are You Up to It?

Lawyers and ex-Wall Street employees, among many others, start their own businesses to recover from burn out. They are stressed out from the long and tiring hours of deal-making, having to be "on" day and night, and being consumed by their responsibilities at work. They come to the realization that there are other important things in life, and job demands have prevented them from enjoying life. Nonetheless, Wall Streeters, as an example, often have a difficult time making the switch because of their focus on the transaction of getting a deal done. Their managerial skills, so important in running a company, were generally not needed or tested in their work experience. Running a company demands a broader, long-term outlook.

If your reasons for going into business for yourself are to get rich, to become famous, or to prove something to an ex-employer and/or your friends, please re-think your motivation and ideas. Much of owning your own business is in the passion for an idea, for independence, or for control. While making a living in your own business is a fine objective, getting rich or famous are goals which may bring disappointing results and take your eye off what's important to make the business a success.

Starting your own business brings a number of psychological effects that you may be aware of, but whose impact you may not have fully considered:

   1) No feedback loop. No one to talk to or pat you on the back. Your efforts may not get recognized.

2) Risk of personal embarrassment if you fail. This is in addition to financial risk. For a perfectionist and those who fear failure, this can be devastating.
3) Loneliness and/or loss of identity. Lack of affiliation with a large organization creates a void. No more "I'm with Procter & Gamble." Prepare yourself for the isolation.

In buying or starting your own business, not only will you be your own boss, you will take the responsibilities of a CEO. In addition to being chief technologist, strategist or salesperson, the role will include interior decorator, human-resource director, and office manager too. One hurdle that often trips up start-up owners is the amount of time that must be invested in a start-up before realizing any payback, whether financial or emotional.

Beyond the operational aspects of running a business, new companies usually start with the founder's vision. However, once the business is established, that original vision can be difficult to maintain. When a company is new and small, founders can stay close to their employees and their customers. As it grows, new demands can overwhelm the founder's vision. It sometimes gets to the point where owners ask themselves, "Am I running the business or is it running me?" Then, they start to think that the frustrations they once faced working for a large company have surfaced again in their very own company.

The very strengths that the entrepreneur marshals to achieve initial success — tunnel vision, specialization, a passion for control — become liabilities that can undermine attempts to expand the company. Those that succeed seem able to augment their start-up strengths with a new set of skills. They figure out what they do best, and hand over the rest of the chores to associates or to new hires from outside. Ego takes a back seat and they realize that their way isn't the only way. No more "my way or the highway." Not surprisingly, those who don't wish to relinquish control or face the thought of building a large company are content to remain one-man bands in small office, home office businesses.

Are You a Fast Starter?

"Corporate refugees" are bringing additional financial discipline and operating sophistication to small businesses. They tend to have more capital because of hefty severance packages, or, they know how to raise capital. They often start bigger businesses or invest larger amounts of capital when purchasing existing businesses. Many of these new entrepreneurs have spouses with outside salaries and benefits that help to reduce the risk and rate of failure for their businesses. The reason is that they can often take that additional action that will help them turn the corner to success and leave failure behind.

There have been several good success stories of start-ups which began in the middle of a recession. In addition to the investment of severance packages and business acumen, three other factors have been effective in starting successful businesses:

1) Experienced managers in small businesses know that suppliers, in a rut themselves, are willing to extend themselves more and help new customers.

2) Some businesses, like used clothing, video rentals, reconditioned furniture, to mention a few, actually may thrive in recessionary times.

3) Businesses which are struggling and find themselves on the verge of bankruptcy or liquidation with any downward turn in the economy might be good candidates for acquisition.

Astute entrepreneurs and experienced managers can take advantage of these factors to create successful small businesses.

Women, Minorities and Others

Women, minorities and other groups have over the years not gotten the attention and support in a white-male dominated business world. While many government programs have attempted to even the playing field, there is strong sentiment that obstacles continue to exist to prevent these groups from carrying out business on an equal footing. The proportion of women college graduates, business owners and entrepreneurs continues to grow. Yet, while we'd like to believe that women will be provided all the same opportunities to find financing, sources of components, or access to the market, they still face many prejudices and disadvantages that come from competing in the male-dominated business world. Men who deal with women-owned companies must recognize that they are dealing with a vital part of the economy, and not participating in a social revolution.

Minorities and immigrant groups have had a great influence on the growth of American business. The U.S. Census Bureau and William O'Hare of the University of Louisville compile statistics on minority entrepreneurs. This 1987 ranking, published in *The Wall Street Journal* on August 8, 1991, showed the following ranking of minorities in business:

1. Korean
2. Asian Indian
3. Chinese
4. Cuban
5. Vietnamese
6. Filipino
7. Other Hispanic
8. Hawaiian
9. Mexican
10. Black
11. Puerto Rican

This appears to be consistent with what we see today.

Business owners and entrepreneurs will continue to come from all walks of life, reflecting the increasingly diverse base of business in the United States and internationally. This is a sure sign that the number of minority entrepreneurs will continue to grow well into the 21st century. This will provide new opportunities for others to follow, as well as niches to offer specifically targeted products and services.

Additional Advice

To maintain focus and provide you with some experienced guidance for your business, it is a good idea to assemble a group of advisors for your business. These advisors are much like a board of directors, but can be less formal. Retired, successful executives, marketing specialists, bankers, etc. are good candidates. Proven executives are better than professionals, particularly lawyers. They can be excellent in settling disputes in family owned businesses, and very objective and practical in defusing tensions over succession in family companies. And where unfortunate circumstances occur, they can advise the surviving spouse and help him/her to arrive at the appropriate resolutions for their future participation in the business.

As a small business, you might consider taking a disciplined approach in the operations of the company by:

- Engaging a group of advisors similar to a Board of Directors.
- Operating as if you were a public company facing the scrutiny of the public eye.
- Becoming disciplined in the preparation of a report to investors and other interested parties, and meeting many of the legal requirements for full disclosure as if you were a public company.

This will demonstrate a willingness to accept advice from others. It is a sign of maturity to recognize that you don't know all the answers. Outside investors or lenders will respect and admire the professional approach you've taken toward your business.

Location, Location, Location

Geography sometimes plays a role in the success of start-ups. A good example of this is the proliferation of high tech companies in Silicon Valley, California and Austin, Texas. This concentration of companies and technologies provides a great opportunity for networking, and access to a great pool of experienced talent. An important added advantage is that lending institutions in areas like these tend to understand the nuances of an industry better.

Business magazines including *Success*, *Fortune*, and *Inc*. provide periodic surveys of the best cities, towns and locations for doing business in the country, including the type of business, available resources and facilities, relocation and employment incentives, costs of living and doing business, etc. However, one consideration is to start the business in a location that you're comfortable and familiar with, assuming that the market is ready for what you have to offer. It is always better to maintain some constant factors in your business and personal lives so that the level of stress in starting a new business is reduced.

> **I CAN DO IT ON A SHOESTRING
> AND OTHER MYTHS ABOUT STARTING A BUSINESS**
> (*The Wall Street Journal*, 1993)
>
> **Myth #1:** I'm smart - I can just wing it.
> **Myth #2:** I can do it on a shoestring.
> **Myth #3:** No sweat; I have a great idea.
> **Myth #4:** I've got nothing better to do.
> **Myth #5:** Maybe starting a business will help our marriage.
> **Myth #6:** With all my experience, starting a business should be easy.
> **Myth #7:** A bad economy will mean fewer competitors.
> **Myth #8:** I'm mad as hell and I'm not going to take it anymore.
> **Myth #9:** If I can't think of anything else, I'll open a bar.

What You Must Have and What You Must Do

As you look at the option of being in business for yourself, a big part of your success will be in your passion for your product or service. Chapter 9 raises issues to help you to get the right advice at the right time and avoid the minefields that stand in the way of your success.

A business requires tremendous focus and commitment, both in emotion and time. Here are some pointers that will assist you in preparing you for success in your own business.

What to Have:

- Self-confidence
- Adequate capital
- Emphasis on good service
- Full time devotion to the business
- Knowledge of the product or service
- Working hard but knowing when to stop

How to Do It:
- Keep overhead low
- Start a business you enjoy
- Prepare to fill several business roles
- Start a business in an area you know something about

Start your business with a strong foundation based on early and good preparation given your unique circumstances.

You've Come a Long Way

You have determined what your strengths and interests are, and what businesses might be suitable for you.

1) You reviewed some of the challenges and opportunities for starting or buying a business, or purchasing a franchise.

2) You have an appreciation of some of the considerations relative to available financing sources, cash flow, size of business, and operating a business. You can interpret them to apply to your own business concept and circumstances.

3) You have a good idea of what business you are going to start, and the products or services that you hope to offer.

4) You are realistic about the capital and cash flow that will be necessary to operate and build the business. You understand what your personal budget needs are.

5) You have decided whether or not you want a partner. If there will be more than one owner-manager in the business, be clear about the roles and the talents each of you brings to the venture.

6) There is no such thing as too much preparation.

7) While it is hard work, you've chosen this path for all the right reasons.

Chapter 9 Checkpoint

There are some basic, yet important considerations that will take advantage of your skills and capabilities, point your business in the right direction, and help you to avoid pitfalls that can easily drain you of your time and money when you go out on your own.

✎ Whether you want to start your own business, or buy an existing business or franchise, there are some fundamental questions you'll want to investigate thoroughly beforehand, so that you don't invest your life savings in an idea that is not fully developed.

✎ Other considerations, such as working out of your home, working with family members or partners, getting the most out of your banking relationships, or finding help for the potential challenges that may arise, are equally important to making your venture a success.

Careful planning and research will help you to confidently navigate the minefields and get your business off on the right track.

Chapter 10

PERSONAL STUFF:
The Spouse, The Kids, The Mortgage

How does America define success? Each of us has our own meaning and definition, regardless of the similarity of the words we use. Nevertheless, we all talk about it, dream about it, and hope one day to achieve more of it. Some years ago, a survey of what Americans believe that success is, produced these top four answers:

> *Being a good parent*
> *Having a happy marriage*
> *Having a good relationship with another person*
> *Having friends who respect you*

Note that the answers are related to family, children and friends. NOT listed at the top were work, salaries or big titles; yet many of us place a great emphasis and weight on corporate stature as a measure of success and achievement. After all is said and done, each of us will be remembered for the type of person we were to others, not that we earned a big salary or had an impressive title. We'll be remembered for the difference we made in others' lives.

So often, thinking about changing jobs or starting a business of our own is met by the challenge of our families and financial resources.

Having gone through the previous chapters, and researched the information sources, you should have a clearer understanding of which fork in the road you wish to take.

The main challenge facing you now is "the personal stuff." This will include your spouse, the kids, and level of comfort you have about your financial resources and expenses — your mortgage, the cost of education, health care, etc. These are the things that have caused you to stop or think about "If only…" in the past. So often, we tend to forget that our personal, family, financial, and emotional states play a key part of the decisions we make. It's no different in this case. In order to be happy with your business or career decision, you need the support of the facts, your intuition, and your family. Without them, your future will be as insecure as the present.

Get an Annual Fiscal Examination

Regardless of whether you are reading this book out of fear, boredom, desperation, or ambition, an important aspect of life planning involves taking a detailed look at your financial commitments and condition. It's a good idea to update your records regularly, even if you're not applying for a home mortgage, car loan, or credit card. Taking a hard look at your finances as part of the decision-making process is critical to help you manage your expenses, re-evaluate your budget and spending, and understand how your financial reserves and condition might impact your business decisions and long-range plans. This chapter's exercises help you look at how your career decisions will impact your finances.

As an aside, once you're through this round of decision-making, we advise you to review your net worth every year. This might take one or two short hours each time to do, but it will buy you some peace of mind. You may not have an abundance of wealth, but at least you know what you have and what you're doing with it.

Organize Your Expenses

Let's begin. Start by dividing your expenses into those that are fixed and those that are discretionary.

A fixed expense is just that. It is a "must" payment that you make regularly, whether each month or each year. Fixed expenses include your mortgage, property taxes and anticipated income taxes, medical bills, utilities, automobile loans, college tuition and the cost of food.

Discretionary expenses are those than you can revise upward and downward according to what you can or want to spend on clothing, eating out at restaurants, and for entertainment and leisure-time activities.

Make two separate lists of all your monthly expenses – a list of fixed expenses and a list of discretionary expenses. Generally, the fixed list is your "no frills" set of living expenses. Regardless of what you do, these are the costs that must be spent on a monthly basis. Your discretionary list is your "would be nice to have" set of expenses. They are expenses you can do without if you have to cut costs. Look critically at your non-essential or discretionary expenditures. Can you cut back on toys and games, purchases of music discs, videos or clothing you can do without?

Doing this exercise will produce a bottom-line cash figure required for ordinary living expenses in your current circumstances. It can often help you see how much you've been spending on discretionary expenses, and what you are able to cut back on comfortably to pay for other essentials, or build your savings or rainy day account.

By comparing your ordinary expenses to your family income, not only with the paychecks you've been receiving, but with what you might realistically anticipate monthly over the next one to three years, you'll be able to evaluate your comfort level with the list of ordinary living expenses. This might include some actions you would consider if the expenses will present a financial struggle for your family.

As we mentioned earlier in the book, it is always best to plan ahead while you're still employed and receiving a paycheck. This is especially true if your financial condition will require refinancing of your home mortgage loan, getting an equity line of credit or applying for any other form of credit. You'll at least have current pay stubs, or be able to get a verification or letter of employment to support a credit or loan application.

Organize Your Income

There are two ways you should look at your income – what you understand to be your monthly salary or pay, and what you get in cash. For example, if you are earning a base salary of $60,000 a year, your monthly salary is $5,000, but what you get in cash after all the withheld taxes and deductions might be $3,657.23 per month. It is the $3,657.23 that you have available to cover your ordinary expenses, not the $5,000. So be careful so that you don't budget to spend more than you have in hand.

A regular paycheck will stop if and when you leave your job, and are not employed. You may receive a severance package ranging from a few weeks to a few months depending on your circumstances and ability to negotiate, along with any amount owed to you for unused vacation time earned. The severance pay might be given to you at the time you leave the company's employ, or be given to you (like a regular or periodic paycheck) over a period of time in some form of a salary continuation plan.

Include in your listing of income your severance pay, proceeds from a company savings plan, interest income, rental income if you own income-producing property and dividends that you receive from any stocks you might own. Be sure to distinguish whether each of these payments is a regular monthly amount, or a one-time receipt. This will give you some assurance so that you don't budget to spend more than you have. For example, proceeds from a company savings plan might be given to you in one lump sum should you no longer be an employee of the company, while rental income might be paid to you monthly.

From your list of income sources, the total monthly income received in cash will generally be what you have available to pay for at least your ordinary expenses. A word of warning, just because it looks like you can comfortably pay for your ordinary expenses should not encourage you to increase spending on items on your list of discretionary expenses. Use your best judgment in an uncertain environment. It's generally not easy to find a good job or new career, and it is certainly not very easy to earn a good living in your own business. Know what your cash flow will be and budget accordingly.

In Chapter 4, we spoke about having cash reserves equivalent to at least six to nine months of your monthly paychecks. This will help you to cover your monthly expenses for that period of time, and allow you to weather financial difficulties, and get yourself started in a new job. We noted that this amount will be larger if you are considering starting and running your own business. As well, depending on the state of the business economy, the amount of your cash reserve will vary. A difficult job market would suggest holding a larger reserve so that you can weather the risk of not having a steady paycheck or income for that period of time. Needless, to say, it will in all cases be better to have a larger cash reserve.

Organize Your Insurance

Insurance provides a form of future security for you and your family. Take the time to review each policy that you have in terms of its necessity, cost and benefits. If possible, try to categorize them into life insurance, health and disability insurance, homeowners and auto insurance, and other, based on their importance to you.

Often we continue to pay insurance premiums each year without taking the time to discuss the policies with our insurance agents or brokers. Given that situations change, it is always wise to review your situation with your agent periodically, every three to five years. You want to ensure that you have the appropriate coverage, and as important, that you aren't paying premiums unnecessarily for coverage that is duplicated or not needed.

List each life insurance policy with the following information:
- Type of coverage (e.g., $100,000 of life insurance)
- Cash value, if applicable
- Premiums, and when paid (remember to include each of these in your list of fixed expenses)

List Your Assets

Your assets are the things you own. They are what a bank or lending institution would consider valuable and available to pay back any loan or credit line. You may look at your assets as all your worldly possessions that contribute to determining your wealth. In general, the value of your assets is the value in cash should they be sold on the market, whether it is today, in six months, or sometime in the future.

Make a list of your assets as follows (note that you may hold assets that may not be included in the categories below):
- Cash balance in your bank and trust accounts
- Cash balance in other financial institutions such as credit unions
- Marketable securities, including stocks, bonds and mutual funds
- Non-marketable securities (unlisted and private issues)
- Loans owed to you (are they covered by a promissory note?)
- Cash surrender value of life insurance policies
- Personal residence (current market value, not the purchase price)
- Other real estate owned (summer homes, rental properties)
- Investments in partnerships (what the current value is, not the original investment)
- IRA, Keogh, profit sharing, and pension fund accounts (vested amounts)
- Deferred income

- Automobiles (realistic market value, e.g., the *Kelly Blue Book* value which an auto dealer might have; or what similar makes and models are being sold for at used car dealers or in the classified ads)
- Boats and airplanes (similar to automobiles)
- Jewelry
- Collectibles and antiques (appraised values)
- Household effects (note that many of these have a greater value to you than what they might be sold for in the market)

Try and list them in order of liquidity; that is, your ability to convert them into cash. The faster and easier the asset can be converted to cash, the more liquid it is.

To improve your liquidity, take a realistic look at the assets you own. Do you have more automobiles than you need? For instance, do you have a recreational vehicle that may be expendable? Think about converting some of these assets to cash while you're employed. You will be in a better position since you can hold firm on your asking price when negotiating with buyers. By converting some assets to cash, you will improve your liquidity and be able to reduce some ongoing liabilities and obligations.

List Your Liabilities

Your liabilities include amounts that you owe to a bank or other financial institution, a lender or other business or person who has extended you credit in the purchase of goods and services. Some of these are secured (where your home, automobile or other asset is the collateral for the loan), while others are unsecured (lines of credit, credit card purchases).

Make a detailed list of your outstanding liabilities, indicating whether they are secured or unsecured, and noting the asset which is the security for the loan or liability. Your liabilities might include:

- Loans payable to bank (for home mortgage, outstanding credit lines)
- Loans payable to others
- Automobile loans (itemize your list if you have more than one vehicle)
- Margin accounts held with stockbrokers on which there is a balance owing
- Life insurance loans
- Taxes payable (property, income and other)
- Credit card debts
- Other moneys owed

List the liabilities as either short term (due and payable in the next year) or long-term, and show the amounts owed and payable on a monthly basis.

List Your Contingent Liabilities

Contingent liabilities are those that may happen, but are not likely. They might be a concern to you if you are a guarantor, co-maker, or endorser for any debt to an individual, corporation or partnership.

Are there any law suits filed against you? This is important when determining contingent liabilities. If any of these law suits eventually result in a judgment against you, it may have a significant effect on your financial condition and subsequent credit worthiness.

If you are not sure about whether you might be affected by a contingent liability, check with your accountant or lawyer.

Create a Personal Financial Statement

Your financial statements should include at the minimum, a balance sheet and an income statement. Your personal balance sheet is a snapshot

Personal Stuff 241

of your financial condition or state at a particular moment in time. It summarizes your assets, liabilities, and net worth. Your income statement shows your revenues (or income) and expenses over a set period of time.

Most financial statements are prepared at year end. This provides a clear comparison with the statement prepared at the previous year end. You will want to prepare a balance sheet to represent a true picture of your financial condition and net worth on a specific date, perhaps on your first day after leaving a corporate job.

By providing as much detail as possible when making the entries under assets and liabilities, you will gain a good understanding of what you are capable of financially. Investors, bankers and anyone who will potentially lend you money or participate in a venture with you will require that you give them this information. By doing this exercise, you'll be ready.

Your net worth is determined by subtracting your liabilities from your assets. This figure provides a quick look at your financial strength.

How Do I Create a Personal Balance Sheet?

To create your personal balance sheet, start by first organizing your assets and liabilities as we described above.

Let's use the following basic example, for an imaginary person, Bill, who supplies the following information to us in mid-July, 1996:

1. Bill has a bank checking account with First National Bank, and receives a bank statement monthly. On his June 30th bank statement, his checking account balance is $2,674.

2. He also has a savings account at the bank, with a balance on June 30th of $9,635.

3. Bill has an investment brokerage account with Golden Financial, and holds a securities portfolio composed of the following:
    - 200 shares Ford Motor Company which he bought at $26 per share, but which were trading at $32.75 per share on June 30th

242 Entrepreneur Or Employee?

- 50 shares IBM which he bought at $87 per share, but which were trading at $100 per share on June 30th
- A $500 investment in GT Global Fund, which is composed of 8.33 shares with a net asset value of $60. As of June 30th, the fund had a net asset value of $69 (each share has a value of $69)

4. Bill has loaned his brother Bob $2,500, for which his brother has signed a promissory note.

5. His wife, Janet, is the beneficiary of his $100,000 life insurance policy, which has a cash surrender value of $7,500 if Bill should cancel coverage today.

6. Bill and Janet own a house, which they bought in 1992 for $350,000. The real estate agent says the house has a current market value of $250,000.

7. Bill has an IRA account, to which he has contributed $3,500 in total over the last few years. With interest, the IRA has a current balance of $4,236.

8. Bill and Janet both own cars. Bill drives a domestic mid-sized sedan, which currently has a blue book value of $12,050, and Janet drives a sports utility van, with a blue book value of $16,500.

9. Together, Bill and Janet have household effects valued at $27,000 for insurance purposes.

10. Bill and Janet have a mortgage outstanding with the bank, and owe approximately $207,010. Bill has a Ford Motor Credit auto loan, with an outstanding balance of $7,600.

11. Bill has borrowed money from his mother and father at various times for the house, and for his car, and currently owes them $26,350.

12. A credit card user, Bill has a VISA credit card balance outstanding of $3,500, and an American Express credit card balance owing of $1,200.

To create Bill's personal balance sheet as of June 30th, we're going to make two basic assumptions about Bill's financial situation:
   a) Bill and Janet each own 50% of the house and household effects.
   b) No significant changes in market value or outstanding balances have occurred between June 30th and the time that Bill supplied the information.

1. The cash balance is a total of the checking and savings accounts, $12,309 ($2,674 + $9,635).

2. The Investment brokerage account is calculated at market value: The Ford Motor Company shares are valued at $6,550 (200 shares @ $32.75), IBM shares at $5,000 (50 shares @ $100), and GT Global Fund shares at $574.77 (8.33 shares @ $69), for a total of $12,124.77, let's say $12,125.

3. The house and household effects are jointly owned, so Bill can show 50% of the value of the house, or $125,000 (50% of $250,000), and 50% of the personal effects, or $13,500.

Bill's Balance Sheet
as of June 30, 1996

Assets		Liabilities	
Cash in Bank	$ 12,309	Bank Loans	
Money Market Accounts		Car Loans	7,600
Amounts Owed to Me	2,500	Mortgages	103,505
Marketable Securities (Stocks and Bonds)	12,125	Other Loans Owing	26,350
Other Investments		Lines of Credit	
Life Insurance Cash Surrender Value	7,500	Credit Card Balances	4,700
IRA, Keogh and Other Retirement Accounts	4,236	Taxes Owed - Income	
Real Estate - Home	125,000	- Property Taxes	
- Other		- Other	
Personal Property		Other Liabilities	
Car	12,050		
Household Effects	13,500		
Total Assets	**$ 189,220**	**Total Liabilities**	**$ 142,155**
		Net Worth	**$ 47,065**

Format taken from *The Wall Street Journal's Guide to Understanding Personal Finance*.

When listing your assets, you should identify the "liquid assets" and separate them from "non-liquid assets." Liquid assets are those easily convertible to cash, and include securities listed on the major stock exchanges. Examples of non-liquid assets include household effects such as your furniture, clothing or appliances. Similarly, separate your liabilities into short term and long-term liabilities as we defined earlier.

Investing in Unlisted Stocks

If you think that you may be leaving your job within the next few years, it would be very wise not to purchase stocks in closely held companies, or those not listed on the major stock exchanges. Not only is there no ready market for these types of securities, they don't pay dividends either. Unlisted stocks and shares of privately held companies are difficult to convert to cash as the market for them is much smaller than publicly traded or listed securities. Listed securities can be sold, and cash can be received in three to five business days given their wide exposure and ease of conversion to cash by stockbrokers.

Borrowing and Credit

One thing we've learned about lenders is they do not like surprises. They can always handle adverse news; they're used to that. What they don't like is not to hear from you. They do like good, constant communications, especially when initiated by the borrower. Earlier in the book, we talked about visiting your banker periodically, and in particular, when you're doing well. Borrowing money is more than the strength of your financial condition. It includes the relationship you have with your banker.

Sometimes, the most innocent action can cause you unneeded frustration in your credit rating. For example, you may have withheld payment from someone years ago while a defective product was replaced; another time, your mortgage payment may have been received a day late. These late payments may still appear on your credit report and may affect your current rating.

Dealing with an impersonal credit reporting service usually is a long and annoying experience. Our advice is that it's never too early to start to clean up your personal credit report. If you've been denied credit, you are entitled to a free report from the reporting agency.

Ask for a credit report on yourself. A good place to start is with TRW, Equifax or another major consumer credit reporting service. Review it carefully and try to clear up any negative comments and entries, both recent and old.

If you have outstanding balances on your bank credit cards, try your best to reduce them as the interest charged to you is among the highest of all consumer debt. If reducing all of them is not possible, reduce at least the balances outstanding that carry the highest charges for interest. You will want to clear as many outstanding balances as you can without significantly affecting your cash flow. This will give you more capacity for revolving credit on credit cards should you one day own your own business and not be able to secure cash from any other lending source.

Your financial condition will always be a very important factor to weigh in your career, business and family decisions. By taking the time to carefully evaluate your situation, you'll gain the confidence of at least knowing and having control over your situation. It will help you to do some personal and family financial planning, and at least leave you with a plan of action and a time frame that will suit you best.

What About the Family?

Previously, we mentioned the importance of remaining the strong leader to your family. Make sure that you demonstrate just how important your family is to you. You can never verbalize your love for them too often.

Another thing we think you should know is that it's better to **discuss** what happened and what is going to happen with your family than to **tell** them about the events and thoughts you're experiencing. Now is the time to include, rather than exclude, them. Discuss the fact that you may not have as much leisure time to spend with them because you have to focus your energy and efforts on a new career or business. Spouses and children can become jealous of the attention you are giving elsewhere, and can feel somewhat cheated.

Don't ignore their feelings because you're "doing all of this for them." Regardless of the great bond that exists among family members, way down deep, we're all somewhat selfish and look out for our own interests. Your spouse and children may be asking, "How's all this going to affect me?" It's your job to level with them. Let them know what's in store for everyone. For instance, "We may have to be more cost-conscious. We have to stretch our food budget." Take your family into your confidence and have a frank discussion with them about keeping expenses down and doing without personal indulgences and a few conveniences for now. Then, continue to update your family on your activities and progress. Remember to celebrate the upside and share the downside with them.

What Do I Tell the Kids?

What do you tell the children and how will they react? The manner in which you handle the discussion with your children depends, of course, on their ages. Most children are more adaptable to change than parents give them credit for. You must demonstrate your continued love and commitment to them. Be honest and frank with them. If you don't tell them, they'll know something is wrong, and may assume a situation is worse than it is.

You can help your children with what to say to their friends when they ask why you're home all day and similar questions. Youngsters can be very nosy, very candid and very cruel. Reassure your family that things will be okay, and these problems are only temporary. Provide the caring and leadership they need to work through the issues they're dealing with. Practice what they can say when people ask them questions or make comments about what you're doing. Remember, children don't have the social skills that adults have. They can be hurt easily, and feel alone or ostracized. With or without a job, you're still their mother or father. Don't get so absorbed in your own concerns that you jeopardize this very important relationship. Use the strength of your love and commitment as a balancing point. When family, spiritual, friends, health, and intellectual areas of your life are stable, you have more resources for bringing the work and financial areas into alignment. Keep your perspective. Don't let a couple of troublesome aspects of your life sabotage the functioning portions.

What Do I Tell My Spouse?

During your years as an employee and the time that you've given serious thought to making a career move, how much have you confided in your spouse? If you have done a rather poor job of communicating your true feelings about your career, now's the time to change things. In a setting free of interruptions, have a good, open discussion with your mate.

This is the point where good marriages get stronger, or where weak marriages can easily fall apart. During this period, a spouse may grow more distant and intimacy may suffer. Statistics show that many separations and divorces have their gestation period during times of stress and uncertainty. However, most marriages, reacting to a need for mutual support, actually are strengthened during a critical time like this.

Ask your spouse to evaluate your strengths and weaknesses. After all, who knows your personality quirks, interests and latent skills any better than she does? Based on her insight, what does she recommend that you do? This can be some of the best advice you'll ever receive. If you love your spouse; if you value your relationship with her, you'd better have her on your side. Take the time to nurture the relationship to a new level.

You and your spouse should also explore her income potential. Which of her skills are marketable? If your spouse has been out of the work force for some time, how does she feel about re-entering the job market? Because you may need some extra family income, this should be discussed very candidly.

If you are seriously contemplating your own business, will you and your partner be able to handle the change from your previously structured corporate work week? Can the two of you adapt from a 9 to 5 work week to a "whatever it takes" regimen of seven days a week? Do you both understand and accept the hard road that will be in store for both of you? Take the time to discuss this and other issues that include giving up old corporate friends, a change in lifestyle, the absence of a guaranteed paycheck, and explanations to family, neighbors and friends.

Open up this new world to your companion who may have never thought of various career opportunities before:
- Visit business opportunity shows together.
- Two of you should go to franchise-offering presentations.
- Share the information you've gathered on new business and career opportunities.
- Visit accountants or lawyers together to go over your finances.
- Make your helpmate part of the new venture planning process.

The more you include your family in your thought process, the stronger the outcome.

Facing the Skeletons in Your Closet

Don't forget the most important person in the decision-making process – YOU. After all, you'll be the one who has to live with the decisions you make for some time to come. From a personal perspective, now is a good time to deal with some of the things that might come back to haunt you, or might affect your thinking if they are not taken care of now.

Office Romances

If you have been engaged in a clandestine office romance or other inappropriate personal relationships, you had better cut this off as soon as you have concluded that you will be leaving your job. As tough as you think you are, the accompanying anxiety and stress will only add to your additional burdens – both financial and emotional, during a time when you will be undergoing some other stresses that are beyond your control.

Escapes

Don't resort to alcohol, an affair, or a spending spree as a remedy to your situation. "Drowning your sorrows" doesn't even work well in the movies. If you think you can numb yourself against reality to relieve the pressure of losing a job or starting a new business, think again. Be assured that the opposite will happen. Make sure to eliminate distractions from your life. For instance, if you have an alcohol or drug dependency problem, you'd better start by getting help before adding other problems and uncertainties to your life.

Anger

Become very aware of where you are placing your anger. Don't take it out on those who had nothing to do with your situation. Your best support group has probably been your family and close friends. During this period of anger, frustration, stress and uncertainty in your life, be careful not to alienate the group that has been, and will be, there for you. However strong, invincible and independent you may think you are, you'll need support from others now more than ever.

Lead the Way

Until this point, you have been the strong one. Don't change now. You must maintain a facade of strength, and a stiff upper lip. You must demonstrate your leadership through this difficult time, both for yourself and your family. An old proverb comes to mind: "When the going gets tough, the tough get going." If you're not confident about anything else, be confident that you will take the steps to be strong and resolute in your decision.

Single Mothers

As a single mother, you may face additional issues when embarking on a progressive career or new business life. Juggling a career with child-rearing responsibilities brings different twists and turns for single moms.

1) That old nemesis, guilt, will continue to rear its ugly head, particularly because you have competing priorities in customers, employer and family. "Am I ignoring a customer because I must be at my child's school conference?" "Am I spending too much time on my business?" "Who is going to watch my son play his first baseball game; I have to be out of town?"

2) Friends, neighbors and even ex-husbands can add tremendous pressures to your life when you least expect them. As a cruel example, during the 1995 O.J. Simpson trial, the husband of the lead prosecutor launched a custody battle for their children, claiming they were not receiving sufficient attention from their mother.

As always, finding common ground and communicating with your customers, employers, family and friends about your responsibilities, priorities and time constraints will be helpful.

On a positive note, children of mothers who are dedicated and happy with their work become more self-sufficient. These children tend to mature quicker, and go on to careers that they did not think possible. This in many cases is a result of the positive role models provided by their mothers.

Friends and Neighbors

Friends and neighbors will be uncomfortable in your presence because you are out of work. One thing to remember is that being out of work can carry with it a stigma. Many people have the perception that it just isn't "normal" (whatever that means) to not go to work daily like you have been doing. Your friends and neighbors may suddenly not know what to talk to you about. You may feel just fine, but they don't know what's appropriate for them to feel — disdain, pity, or envy.

While you may not be confident about your predicament, you can demonstrate optimism and resolve by taking the initiative to talk about your situation. Talk about what happened to you and what your plans are now. This approach will go a long way to put everyone at ease.

By spending some time and energy at the very beginning to talk honestly to friends, family, neighbors or business acquaintances, the rewards can be enormous. You'll feel better yourself and you'll invite ideas, feedback, referrals, and other forms of support from all of those around you.

The Nitty-Gritty of Dealing with Personal Issues

You should now be ready to complete the decision-making process at the fork in the road. Are you a *Type E^M* or *Type E^N*? Will you continue along the path of employment, or strike out in a business of your own?

1) You have discussed the concerns you have about the future of your corporate job with your loved ones.

2) You've had some serious discussions with your spouse, children, and/or confidantes about the decision you are facing. They are now solidly behind you, and together, you now share a consistent view of your expectations for yourself and your family.

3) You've taken an objective and realistic view of your financial condition. You've addressed some of the concerns you have about money and available resources. You have a clearer picture of what you can do economically today, and the capital you plan to have in place given your income, expenses and net worth.

4) You've taken an honest look at the emotional hooks that still tie you to your current corporate job. You've taken steps to let go and resolve these feelings so that they don't cloud or diminish your decision-making ability.

5) If there are still outstanding concerns about your personal issues, then you are not ready to move forward. Go back and try to resolve those concerns that are causing you discomfort.

You are confident that you've done a thorough job in collecting the information you need to make an informative decision. You've satisfied yourself that you've dealt with the personal issues, and feel comfortable and confident that you are ready to make your decision. You are ready to begin confidently taking steps in the direction of your chosen path.

Chapter 10 Checkpoint

Spouses, children and family finances are important factors to consider in any decision to start a business or to stay employed.

- ✎ An annual review of your personal and family finances, including a careful review of your borrowing, credit and cash flow, can help you to organize and plan your savings and spending.

- ✎ Taking the time to discuss your employment situation and business plans with your spouse and children will be helpful in maintaining their confidence and support, gaining their input and ideas, and creating a stronger decision and outcome.

Consideration of your finances and family will add confidence to your decision to get out or stay in your current job.

Chapter 11

MAKING THE DECISION

Harry Truman, the venerable and often-quoted 33rd President of the United States, had a sign on his desk that could easily sit on yours at this moment: "The Buck Stops Here"

It is a great accomplishment to use all the tools at your disposal, if you use them productively. In reading through the book, you've reflected upon and analyzed your skills, capabilities and tendencies, and considered some of the challenges and obstacles you face in your next career or business choice. You see yourself more clearly now than you did before you journeyed through this book with us.

What Have You Done to Get to this Point?

Many of the findings and conclusions you have arrived at about yourself may have come naturally to you. You may even have thought about acting on your intuition many times before. You have achieved more than just uncovering your likes, dislikes and interests. You have now gained a deeper appreciation for your *Type E^N* (entrepreneurial) or *Type E^M* (employee) tendencies. In fact, deep down, you should have a pretty good idea if you are a *Type E^N* or *Type E^M*. You've even come to recognize some of the challenges and obstacles that you have to overcome in order to take charge of your career. Hopefully, you have developed a greater sense of confidence in your ability to make the right choice between a job and a business.

Are You Ready to Make a Decision?

Let's look at the information you've collected over the course of reading and working through this book, and how you can best apply its insights and strategies.

In Chapter 2, you prepared nine lists and a summary about yourself. These lists served as points of reference for decision-making. You then compared how your answers matched the jobs and careers you've had. This helped to point out those facets of your working life you want to hold on to, and others you want to let go. We hope you discussed your lists with a close friend. A confidante can give you valuable input through their perceptions of your strengths and weaknesses. From your lists and feedback, you should have a summary that captures your profile accurately.

In Chapters 3 and 4, you reviewed your *Type E^N* and *Type E^M* characteristics, along with the choices to get out of, or stay in, the corporate world.

Chapters 5 to 7 provided you with various sources of information to thoroughly research and prepare for your decision. You also received some pointers for coping with termination and job loss if this is the situation you find yourself in. These chapters directed you to available information about your employer, information sources such as the library, online services and the Internet, consumer and trade publications, and other organizations. We suggested a number of ways to get your personal finances and banking relationship in order.

If you are a *Type E^M*, Chapter 8 showcased several career options in today's dynamic economy. We pointed out the skills which will be in demand in the 21st century. For *Type E^N* individuals, Chapter 9 alerted you to some pitfalls of going into a business of your own.

Whether you've considered remaining an employee or starting out in a new business venture, Chapter 10 helped you through some personal considerations affecting your decision. These included your spouse, the kids, and your financial resources.

Having read and worked through this book, and researched and discussed your findings with others, you know what you want and need to do. You should now be able to answer five defining questions:

1) What are the key findings you made about yourself? That is, what hot buttons were pushed as you read the early chapters and made those lists?
2) What would you really like to do?
3) What are you really good at?
4) What is going on inside your head that may not be all that apparent to those around you?
5) Should you get out or stay in your current job?

There is no one who can do this for you. The buck *does stop with you*. Change, particularly where it affects our own careers and lives, can bring discomfort if the unknown factors are not at least considered. Now that you have done all the exercises and researched a number of the resources, you have taken a major step towards casting those uncertainties and your fears aside. Will you stay in your corporate job? Will you strike out on your own?

Whatever decision you make will be a powerful one. Have confidence in your decision. Believe that you are heading in the right direction in your career or business choice.

Do You Need a Little Extra Help?

Having been there, we can honestly tell you that this is one of the most fearful and most exhilarating processes you can go through and survive. You are applying your decision-making and reasoning skills from the workplace in a decision about yourself. Just in case you need a little extra help, we offer the following final thoughts and tips:

1) Intuition is sometimes an intangible thing. What does your intuition tell you? Have you validated your intuition? This book has helped you through an analysis of your skills in writing. Knowing your real capabilities and true motivations will point you in the direction of continued employment, or towards striking out in your own business. Our hope is that the facts will clearly support or refute your gut feelings and point you on your way.

2) Do you have enough information to support the decision that you are about to make? Is this information reliable, credible and current?

3) Can you support your decision to others? Finish this sentence: I am going to _____ because _____.

4) Make a timeline with a set of due dates for specific actions you're going to take. For each of the due dates, make two columns – 1) FOR - List the conditions and traits that are moving you towards your goals; 2) AGAINST - List the conditions and traits that are keeping you from attaining your goals. Then develop strategies to overcome the challenges in the AGAINST column, and put those positive actions into column one. Remember, the dates you select are yours. They can be next month, next year or 5 to 10 years from now.

Scheduling deadlines for performance goals (including decision-making), improves your chances of following through with actions that will move you toward the life you want.

What If You are Not Ready to Make a Decision?

One of the goals of this book is to enlighten you. If, after reading the book and exploring "getting out or staying in," you haven't arrived at a decision, or you've decided to do nothing, that's fine. After spending all this time on the subject, you owe it to yourself to list the reasons why. Is it because you don't have the necessary information to make an intelligent, rational decision? Or is it just a matter of time, like waiting for the kids to get out of college and be on their own? Are you afraid to make a decision, or simply don't want to make the effort?

If you feel compelled to postpone a decision or action, write down the reasons for doing so. Try to arrive at some conclusions based on your reasons. If it is a lack of information, pinpoint where the deficiencies are, and continue to search for the needed information to eliminate these deficiencies. If it is related to a skill or capability that you are lacking, look for courses or other ways of upgrading or gaining the skills you need. Whatever the reason, create a set of actions or commitments to help yourself address them. Then put a date on your notes and file them away. You'll probably revisit these ruminations and conclusions again at a later date. Be proactive, not passive. This is your life, and your family's future!

Sometimes, another set of events in your life takes precedence over making any changes. We know of many executives who gave up the so-called "good life" because they weren't significantly involved in their children's lives as the children were growing up. They missed out on so much that they wanted to improve their quality of life. They walked away from the corporate world and set up a business at home to avoid the travel and time away from family.

Perhaps your decisions and actions revolve around your health and that of your family. A serious illness or disability may force you to make a decision long before you planned to do so. If this is the case, then after reading our book, you should put a plan together that prepares you for this contingency.

There are people who start a part-time business with the intention to test a new concept, market a new invention, or turn a hobby into a business. Some have discovered that it could not support them as a full-time endeavor. These folks at least "gave it a shot" and got it out of their system. They concluded that the corporate world was better for them after all. Today, they are happy and contented employees. Passion is great, but horse sense helps, too!

If you have been forced out or terminated from your job, you'll have to take a measured look at your options. You may not have the luxury of time for a broad self-analysis, but the exercises and considerations in this book apply equally to you.

What Have Others Done?

You can learn a lot from those who have gone through this decision-making process before you. In general, the fact that a person stays with the same company for twenty years may indicate that he is not a good candidate for an entrepreneurial adventure. On the other hand, many who find happiness in small businesses were the ones eager to accept transfers and job changes during their employment. They learned every step in how to adapt to each new situation, and how to be self-directed. When they were finally ready, they made the big leap from employee to entrepreneur.

We know of one highly paid purchasing agent of an automotive firm who bought a muffler franchise. He went into business for himself after he lost his job of many years. He thought his investment would rid him of corporate pressures forever. He thought he was putting his automotive knowledge to good use. Yet, he did not know how to handle personnel problems, general management, cash flow, advertising or even keeping the shop clean. After having spent half his severance pay on the muffler venture, the would-be entrepreneur took another job as a corporate purchasing agent and abandoned all thoughts of being a business owner. The lists and notes you've made about yourself over the course of this book bring an axiom to mind: Know Thyself!

For *Type E^N* individuals, a history of experience in line jobs is more promising than a series of narrow staff jobs. One former division head went into business mainly because he wanted equity in whatever business he was involved in. He now enjoys the myriad of tasks a small business owner does for himself. He types some of his own letters, and rolls up his sleeves to do whatever has to be done. He finds the diversity of the daily activities very stimulating.

Newly self-employed people find that it helps to have managed a troubled operation at some point in their careers, even if the troubles weren't successfully resolved. If you are a *Type E^M*, however, you may have a terrible time operating your own business. No matter what numbers you put down on paper, the business is too much of a risk for your logic. No business will ever be perfect enough! And, there isn't any backup. You are it. Sink or swim.

There have been numerous instant millionaires, and even newly-minted billionaires, as a result of the phenomenal success of high tech companies. While these extraordinary fortunes make front page stories, little is heard about the less glamorous failures and devastated lives of would-be high-flyers.

New opportunities abound every day. The market's insatiable appetite for new products has lured many "corporate refugees" to new and rewarding careers with upstarts and new ventures. This offers an opportunity to chase the dream of riches, or perhaps more importantly, to gain control of their own careers.

Once-in-a-lifetime opportunities can develop at any time, and may prompt you to make a quick decision. They can be triggered by a large lump-sum payout, generous early retirement programs, and the tremendous market changes caused by burgeoning technologies such as the

Internet. Whether you decide to continue your job in a corporation, to join a company that strongly supports intrapreneuring, or to be a full-fledged entrepreneur, the dynamic marketplace and emerging technologies of the nineties and the next millennium provide tremendous promise unsurpassed over the last fifty years.

What's Your Decision?

The Thesaurus provides the following *synonyms* and *antonyms* for the word "decision":

Synonyms: settling, determination, choice, judgment, election, guess, conclusion, resolution, preference

Antonyms: vacillation, wavering, waffling, indecision

Remember, not making a decision is the same as making the decision not to decide. Whether you decide to stay in your present job for another year or for a longer time, or to pursue a new job or a business of your own, we hope this book has helped you to make a more informed choice.

What's Next?

If you are still employed, use your time wisely while you still have the comfort of a steady paycheck. If you have made up your mind to start an entrepreneurial venture, now is the time to map out the activities that will get you closer to your goal. As you gain confidence and rally support behind your direction, you can begin to organize your "work day" and let your family know what your schedule and priorities are. This will help you to gradually focus on the actions that you will need to take in the direction you've decided to pursue.

By developing priority lists and making sure you are productive each day, you will stay organized, gain more confidence in your decisions and actions, and maintain the support of those around you.

> *Far better it is to dare mighty things, to win glorious triumphs, even though checkered by failure, than to take rank with those poor spirits who neither enjoy much nor suffer much, because they live in the gray twilight that knows not victory nor defeat.*
>
> *- Theodore Roosevelt*

You Can Do It!

In this chapter, you have brought all your insights and discoveries from the previous chapters to make your decision and confirm your new direction.

1) You have had an opportunity to go back and summarize your capabilities, strengths and weaknesses, and gained comfort with your *Type E^N* or *Type E^M* tendencies.

2) You have allowed your intuition to help you reach your decision, and your intuition fully supports what you have found out about yourself in reading and working through this book.

3) Based on the above, you are now able to make a choice about the direction of your career or work. You feel in control over your decision to stay in, or get out of, the corporate world.

4) You have arrived at a decision, and will begin to map out the activities that will make your decision a successful one.

264 Entrepreneur Or Employee?

5) You have arrived at one of four choices in making your decision:
- You will stay in the corporate world, whether with your present employer, or with a different employer, and focus on your current career.
- You will engage in an entrepreneurial venture of your own to take advantage of a market opportunity by applying your talents and tendencies.
- You will wait for an event to occur (whether in your family, career or financial situation) before making a change.
- You will make no decision about your career or work at this time. However, you will commit to specific actions to gain greater confidence about your strengths and weaknesses, *Type E^N* or *Type E^M* tendencies, and the choices open to you at the fork in the road.

Chapter 11 Checkpoint

Making the decision to go out on your own or to stay employed is exhilarating when you have the right tools, and address considerations and challenges that can affect the success of your career or business choice.

✎ This book has brought you greater clarity about who you are and the options available to you, and more confidence in what information to look for and where to find it.

✎ Your choice and decision will carefully weigh the considerations that are unique to you, your career and your family.

Making the *Entrepreneur or Employee?* decision represents a new beginning. Now it's time to plan and follow-through on the activities that will make your decision a successful one.

SOME CONCLUSIONS YOU MAY HAVE REACHED

1. The book's self-assessment sections were very revealing. I now have a better understanding of who I am, and what my strengths and weaknesses are.

2. This is the first real insight (no holds barred, stripped of glamour) that I've ever had into the world of entrepreneuring. Now I know it's not for me OR now I understand why it frustrates me to work for someone else.

3. Time spent with my family, hobbies, and interests are more important to me than I thought. The best vehicle to enhance these is through a corporate job.

4. The practical drills regarding my personal finances were very beneficial. As a result of knowing my limitations as well as analyzing how rewarding my employer's compensation package is, the best place is for me to remain in my corporate job.

5. I had become complacent. This book alerted me to the enormous changes that are happening everywhere. Until now I didn't think that I was affected. I will need to retrain myself and gain a broader set of skills before I strike out in my own business.

6. I need to be more communicative and assertive in dealing with other managers. If I can improve in these areas, I will gain self-confidence, become a more productive employee, and find my work more satisfying.

7. The facts regarding downsizing, terminations, employee dislocations have opened my eyes. Job security is not what it's cracked up to be. As a result, I feel I'll be in greater control by going out on my own.

8. I've been dreaming of owning a business for a long time. The idea that I had just doesn't hold up to the scrutiny that you discuss in the book. Now that I understand more about it, I realize that it was just a dream, and it's going to stay that way.

9. Just by taking a step back and reviewing my industry, my company, my department, and myself, I have become more realistic in my expectations of the corporate world, and my capabilities to start my own business. I now know the decision to make.

10. I know what's realistic given my present situation. I will stay in the corporate job for now, but will use the time to good advantage - assembling information on my company, its competitors, my industry and the like. Then, when I'm ready to leave, I'll be much better informed.

The Future Looks Brighter When You Are in Control

Chapter 12

BACK IN CONTROL AGAIN

"People are always blaming their circumstances for what they are. I don't believe in circumstances. The people who get on in this world are the people who get up and look for the circumstances they want, and if they can't find them, make them." — George Bernard Shaw, 1893

You have made the decision to stay in the corporate world or decided to leave and go into your own business. This will rank among the big moments of your life, like moving to a new house, graduating from a college or technical school, getting married, or becoming a parent.

Major events like these do not occur very often. When you consider that today's workers spend about half their lives, and about three quarters of their waking days at work, you realize the far-reaching aspects of your choice. What you do for a living should not be taken lightly.

Once you select the road you're going to travel, a new phase of your career begins. With a clear view of where you're going, you can apply the best of your talents to fulfill your aspirations.

The Right Job

A strong and loyal employee is one who adds value to the employer's business, products, or services. As a *Type E^M*, your contribution to your employer will be in a well-defined area that you and your employer agree is where you can be most valuable.

So often, we find examples of employees who are highly competent in many areas of a business. While they may perform well in each distinct area, they spread themselves too thin by taking on more responsibilities than they are able to handle in the available time. Their efforts are diluted, and their performance significantly declines.

There are also examples of employers and employees who conspire to make the Peter Principle a reality. Lawrence Peter developed the concept to describe how employees rise to their level of incompetence through ill-conceived promotions. An employer promotes a well-performing employee out of his area of strength and beyond his limitations because he has done well at his job. When an individual's limitations or weaknesses are not addressed, or his strengths are not appropriately applied, a promotion can lead to dissatisfaction, stress, burnout, and even incompetence. Under these circumstances — a mis-match between an employee and his job — a valuable company worker has been rendered useless. He becomes dispensable.

Today's super employee is not one who is involved in so many work responsibilities that it takes away from his productivity. He is focused on those specific areas where he can best apply his skills to provide the largest positive impact for the company. It is a win-win situation.

In order to stay in demand as an employee, you must become your own best sales representative. That is, let people know what you're doing, what your competencies are, and what you do for the growth and strength of the company. In any business, your success is predicated upon how well you operate within the system and how creative you are in thinking through and solving problems. Network throughout the company, learn who does what and how to get things done. Get to know your local business, trade, or professional groups. Make new business connections for your company and create future career contacts for you.

Five years ago, you rarely met unemployed people who did what you do. These days, you often meet them. As we said earlier, of all the skills for which demand is disappearing, management is the one losing ground the quickest. Why? General management skills are becoming archaic. However, good managers with strong technical skills, or who contribute to producing the end-product, will experience continued high demand.

The Right Employer

If your employer does not provide the right setting for you, then you are the one who has to find the right environment. A "new lease on life" can start with a change from one company to another, or from a job in a large corporation to one in a small company. Patti Lewis held high profile marketing jobs at Proctor & Gamble, Mattel and Tonka Toys. She experienced great success in well-paying jobs at outstanding companies. Patti was recruited to a job as senior vice president of marketing, design, and strategic planning for Alexander Doll Co. She left the comfort of a position at a well-known company to join the much smaller boutique company that produces high-priced, hand crafted collector dolls.

The Alexander Doll Co. faced two major challenges: Each doll sold for as much as $600 in an age of mass marketing and low priced, foreign made goods, and the company was under-capitalized and on the road to bankruptcy. Ms. Lewis was very comfortable with the toy business, and recognized the opportunity. She took the risk of leaving a very safe and comfortable corporate womb, and helped Alexander Dolls through a classic turnaround. Later, she became its CEO.

Your experience as a manager in a particular industry provides you with a strong base from which to act. Her experience and instinct helped

Patti Lewis to decide that Alexander Dolls was the right opportunity for her.

> *I know of no more encouraging fact than the unquestionable ability of man to elevate his life by a conscious endeavor.*
>
> - Henry David Thoreau, 1854

Sensing an Opportunity

How often do you think of or get excited about the possibilities of an idea and then do nothing more about it? How often do you read about someone else successfully turning your thoughts into a profitable business?

It happens over and over again. In thousands of cases, people like yourself, with no particular notoriety, secure their new lease on life by taking command of a situation and doing something about it. Take the case of someone, we'll call him Mike Brown, who worked for twelve years as a Prudential insurance agent. He was a financially successful, high performer who sold life insurance to executives.

Mike is a *Type E^N* who had known all along that he wanted to go into business for himself. While his fellow Prudential agents were busy buying exotic sports cars and expensive watches, Mike lived frugally, building a war chest for himself. He wanted to accumulate enough cash to support his plans and advance his objective. Eventually, Mike started and developed his own niche insurance agency. He is very successful at providing customized policies for buy-sell agreements, key man insurance, and estate planning for specialized situations and high income clients. Mike was determined to find a new lease on life. He got it!

Whether it is a career with a company, a business opportunity that you see, or an idea that you have, our point is that if you want to start a fire, you first have to light a match.

> *If you think you can, you can. If you think you can't, you're right.*
>
> - Mary Kay Ash, *Mary Kay Cosmetics*

Bouncing Back

If you have been forced out or terminated from your job, or feel that you may be laid-off soon, we have helped you to take a measured look at your strengths and weaknesses, behaviors, values, beliefs, and options. Once you have done this, you will find that there are countless opportunities worthy of your effort. If you know what you are capable of and what you are looking for, you'll know which opportunities to focus on and pursue. They won't come to you; you'll have to look for them. The only prerequisites are resiliency and determination, which are illustrated well by the following:

> *He had little formal schooling. His family had no wealth. He had no administrative experience. He served a single, uneventful two year term in the U.S. House of Representatives. He never served as a Mayor. He never served as a Governor. For the prior ten years, he held no public office. He was elected President of the United States. His name was Abraham Lincoln.*

There are many instances of managers and coaches of professional teams who are fired as a result of their or their team's poor performance. These managers and coaches are re-hired again and again by other teams, hoping to find the right "chemistry" for their talents to flourish. Some have been fortunate enough to rebound from losing seasons and the loss of their jobs to make it to the World Series or Super Bowl as champions.

Lee Iococca played a key role in the successful introduction of the Ford Mustang. Yet, he suffered public humiliation when he was fired from the Ford Motor Company by Henry Ford II. Iococca's people skills, creative talents, financial know-how, and manufacturing and marketing experience were of great value to the automotive industry. He leveraged them in the legendary recovery of an ailing Chrysler Corporation from the brink of bankruptcy.

> *A man is not finished when he is defeated. He is finished when he quits.*
>
> *- Richard Nixon, 1978*

If you are in the right work environment, have the right teams of people and motivation, then you are lucky. Stay focused on your strengths, minimize your weaknesses, and continuously improve your performance to add value to your employer's company.

The Harder You Work, the Luckier You Get

Some people will always be envious of others who have succeeded. Don't be one of them. Get off the sidelines and into the game. Learn what they do right, and emulate them. Find a role model or mentor and promise yourself that you will help someone else when you get to the top. You've heard the expression, "Luck is what happens when preparation meets perspiration." Somehow, luck seems to be linked with focus and hard work. The more focused you are, and the harder you work, the more "luck" you make for yourself.

Steve and Lori Leveen found themselves out of work in 1987. Steve looks back at the event as a real blessing in disguise. He'll be the first to say, "I'll forever be in debt to my old employer. It's easier if someone gives you the boot."

Steve was laid off from a software design firm while his wife was on maternity leave from IBM. The Leveens decided to go into the mail order business. They found a niche in the market selling hundreds of accessories and gift items to "serious readers." The business grew from scratch to $60 million dollars in revenue, and continues to grow at a rapid rate.

The Leveens' primary motivation was to "find something to do." They also had a desire to be involved in a business that sold products they felt good about. Their mission was to help people read. While they don't sell books, they sell just about everything else that a "serious book reader" would want. Their line of products includes lamps, tables, foot rests, bookcases, magnifying glasses and a myriad of other products that you won't find anywhere else.

Their business has outgrown its facilities several times, and now occupies a state-of-the-art facility of approximately 225,000 square feet in Delray Beach, Florida. Their catalogs are extremely well done and have won many awards in the direct marketing industry. You may even have received one of their outstanding Levenger catalogs. After all, they mail over twenty-five million of them each year.

You have to do lots of research and then go with your gut instinct. There's a point at which you have enough information to act. And if you wait to get everything, you may be too late. The Leveens struck while the opportunity was great. Opportunity is a time-sensitive issue. The difference between a good and bad situation can be a narrow window of favorable interest rates, access to scarce supplies, or the availability of key people. Applying planning and instinct, the Leveens made a choice and stuck with it. It's your turn.

> *Whenever you see a successful business, someone once made a courageous decision.*
>
> *- Peter F. Drucker, 1985*

It Doesn't End Here

Inevitably, the marketplace and technologies will continue to change. To stay competitive, businesses will have to stay abreast of and apply appropriate new technologies, continue to develop new products, and find new markets. By the same token, workers and managers will find success through an ongoing process of continual learning and professional growth. They will continue updating and reinventing their skills to avoid obsolescence and redundancy. You need to continuously assess whether your job skills are becoming outmoded or your potential job targets are shrinking. Organizations place increasing value on working with computer and communications technologies, collaborative work teams, and efficiencies. How you are connected and whom you are allied with make a difference for employees as well as entrepreneurs. You must develop and sustain working relationships with co-workers, customers, vendors, suppliers and other strategic partners.

This will probably not be the last career choice you will ever make. While you may not face the same dilemma again, you will remain the chief decision-maker every mile down the road. As your career and life circumstances change, or your perspective on career and work changes, you will want to revisit the thoughts, notes, and decision that you have so painstakingly pursued in reading this book. The same practical approach that you have learned in going through this process can help you again sometime in the future.

Chapter 12 Checkpoint

Having a clear view of where you're going will allow you to apply the best of your skills, talents and strengths to be successful.

✎ Your career choices and decisions will depend on your tendencies to be a *Type E^N* or *Type E^M*, your skills, capabilities, strengths and weaknesses, and the circumstances surrounding your family, finances and stage in life.

✎ As your life or career circumstances change, you can again rely on our practical approach, along with your intuition, to uncover those options and opportunities for which you are best suited.

Knowing you have choices, and that you have taken control over your life, will help you to gain peace of mind and greater satisfaction in your career or work.

Seeking Your New Lease on Life

Whether you stay in your current job, switch to another company, or go into business for yourself, a new lease on life can be yours. But, it usually doesn't come and seek you out; you must get yourself ready, have a well thought-out plan and go for it. Millions before you have faced disruptions in their careers and their lives. Those very same millions are enjoying their new lease on life. While it won't be a bed of roses, you can plant the seeds of satisfaction and fulfillment.

Success in uncovering opportunities for your career growth comes from the ability to balance an objective view of yourself with a bit of intuition to arrive at the right choices. Intelligent choices come when you have the tools or framework to help you to decide whether going out on your own, or working for someone else's company, is right for you.

We have provided you with a practical approach to make intelligent choices about whether or not to leave the corporate world. We have helped you to gather the right types of data to arrive at an informed decision and set of choices.

If you have decided to stay in your present job for another year or longer, then this book has performed a great service in helping you determine that staying the course as an employee is the right choice. If you are convinced that you will pursue a new job or a business of your own, then this book has helped you become better informed about your decision. Regardless of your decision, we hope that you now feel confident to follow the direction that you have chosen.

We are certain that you will find success and happiness in whichever fork in the road you have chosen. We wish you well and hope to hear of your successes and experiences as you become the steward of your dreams. We wish you good fortune.

Additional Resources
Recommended Reading

There is an enormous selection of books available to help you in your career or business. Once you've made the decision about whether you want to stay in or leave your corporate job, these books may be helpful to you.

Rather than provide an exhaustive listing of books for our readers, we have assembled a compendium of books that are written from a practical perspective. They offer a "street-smart" approach to the subject matter.

The entrepreneurial *Type E^N* may find the following books helpful in starting and operating a successful business:

Your First Business Plan, By Joseph Cavello and Brian Hazelgren

Guerrilla Marketing Excellence: The Fifty Golden Rules For Small Business Success, By Jay Conrad Levinson

Guerrilla Marketing Online: The Entrepreneur's Guide To Earning Profits On The Internet, By Jay Conrad Levinson and Charles Rubin

How To Buy A Business: Entrepreneurship Through Acquisition, By Richard A. Joseph, Anna M. Nekoranec and Carl H. Steffens

Focus: The Future Of Your Company Depends On It, By Al Ries

Winning The Entrepreneur's Game: How To Start, Operate And Be Successful In A New Or Growing Business, By David E. Rye

Entrepreneurs Are Made, Not Born: Secrets From 200 Successful Entrepreneurs, By Lloyd E. Shefsky

Streetfighter Marketing, By Jeff Slutsky

The *Type E^M* company person will find the following books helpful in building and ensuring a successful career with a company:

The Three Boxes Of Life, By Richard N. Bolles

Your Career: Choices, Chances, Changes, By David C. Borchard, John J. Kelly, and Nancy Weaver

Fired For Success, How To Turn Losing Your Job Into The Opportunity Of A Lifetime, By Judith Dubin and Melanie Keveles

How To Find A Job When Jobs Are Hard To Find, By Donald R. German and Joan W. German

Moving On: A Guide For Career And Life Planning, By Peggy Greiner

Shifting Gears, By Carole Hyatt

Change Your Job, Change Your Life: High Impact Strategies For Finding Great Jobs In The '90s, By Ronald L. Krannich

The 1996 National Job Hotline Directory, By Marcia P. Williams and Sue A. Cubbage

About The Authors

For over twelve years, Ken Chane and Glenn Poy have researched and collected data on the subject of terminations, career transition, starting successful entrepreneurial businesses and their effect on employees and their families. During the course of their research, they identified the unique characteristics of both an entrepreneur (which they classify as a *Type E^N*) and an employee (a *Type E^M*).

Ken Chane has been a speaker to numerous business organizations and has been interviewed on several radio and television shows. He wrote a personalized monthly "how-to" business column for Hearst Publications entitled, *Mind Your Business*. He contributed to the 1979 premiere issue of *Inc.* Magazine. A booklet, *How to Develop a Contingency Plan For a Major Disaster* was published as a result of the New York World Trade Center disaster of 1993.

Over the span of 25 years, Ken held senior management positions including President, Sun Drug Stores, Vice President, General Nutrition Corporation, and Vice President, Carnation Company, now a subsidiary of Nestle. Since leaving the corporate world, he has owned and operated a direct marketing business.

A graduate of Temple University in Philadelphia, Pennsylvania, Ken has additional training in Journalism, Finance, Data Processing, Marketing and Advertising.

He lives in a suburb of Los Angeles, is an avid reader of business and history books, a long-time automobile enthusiast, and an ardent collector of antique toys.

Glenn Poy has been a guest speaker to a number of business organizations on subjects including *Strategy and Leadership*, *Lessons from Sports Coaches*, and *The Asian American Entrepreneur*. He has also written and published a series of articles on leadership and corporate planning.

Glenn's career positions have included President, JPS Microsystems, Inc.; Managing Director, Designworks/USA; and Director of Finance, Advanced Programs at Magna International, Inc. Today, his consulting firm, Inside Leadership, Inc. uniquely applies coaching principles from sports to assist businesses in implementing performance management systems, process improvement and organizational planning to ensure profitability and effective operation.

Glenn holds a Master of Business Administration degree, specializing in Strategies for Organizational Change and Information Systems, from Heriot-Watt University, Edinburgh, Scotland, a Bachelor's degree in Accounting and Finance from McMaster University, Hamilton, Canada, and the designation of Certified Management Accountant (CMA).

Formerly from Toronto, Canada, he now lives just outside of Los Angeles, and enjoys tennis and walking. His expertise in tennis has taken him around the world to coach corporate leaders, and celebrities including Dick Cavett, David Frost and Victoria Principal.

Today, Ken Chane and Glenn Poy are engaged in projects related to defining and addressing *Entrepreneur or Employee?* issues. Their international projects include a *CareerSmarts*™ column, audio tapes, seminars and workshops, and an Internet outreach program.

How to Reach The Authors

Ken Chane and Glenn Poy plan revised editions and additional products to assist you. They are interested in hearing from you. How did you like this book? How did it assist you? What suggestions do you have for improvement? Are there additional topics you would like covered in future editions? As a result of reading this book, what course of action did you take?

Let us know of your interest in attending a seminar in your area or purchasing audio tapes. To be on our mailing list, please fill out the registration form at the back of the book.

When writing, be sure to include your street address, city, zip code and e-mail address.

THE VANALDEN PRESS
9755 Independence Avenue
Chatsworth, CA 91311-4318

FAX: (818) 407-0850

e-mail: kschane@msn.com

Visit our web site on the Internet at:
http://www.vanaldenpress.com

Quantity Purchases and Special Programs

Entrepreneur or Employee? is available at special discounts for quantity purchases for sales promotions, premiums, career management and counseling, personnel and outplacement programs, client recommendations or educational use.

For details, write, fax or e-mail to:

>Director of Special Programs
>THE VANALDEN PRESS
>9755 Independence Avenue
>Chatsworth, CA 91311-4318
>
>FAX: (818) 407-0850
>e-mail: kschane@msn.com

A "Street-Smart" Index

This index has been arranged to enable you to quickly find information relevant to the situation you find yourself in.

A "Street-Smart" Index

Age and new career options 155-157, 164
Age as a factor in termination 124
Alcoholism following termination 250
Anger following termination 126, 250-251
Attorneys: When to see them 129-130
Bankers: Dealing with them 210-213
Business incubators to help new businesses 107
Buying an Existing Business 197-200
    Information-gathering
        Current business owners: Things you should know 99
        Competition: Who will your competition be? 100-101
        Sellers of companies: What to ask them 106-107
Career Options
    Capitalize on your strengths 178
    Career choices: Finding the right path for you 41-42
    Consultants: Can you make it as one? 176
    Contract assignments for those with specialty skills 174
    Hobbies as a primary business 176-177
    Impact of the information age on jobs 164-166
    Innovative career options: Some examples 179
    International career options 174
    Internet: Help-wanted 171
    Inventors: Inventions as a business 181-182
    Jobs of the future 166-168
    Jobs on the extinct list 164-166
    Large company to small company: transition problems 183-184
    Pearls of wisdom to manage your career 196
    Personnel placement firms 171-172
    Preparing for the jobs of the future 166-168
    Reinvent yourself: How to do it 169-170
    Search firms 171-172
    Skills: How to capitalize on them 169-170
Changing jobs: Doing it the right way 96-97
Children: Communications with 247-248
Computers and career options 171, 172-173
Con-artists and new businesses 228-229
Consolidation: Its impact on jobs 117-118
Contract employees 174
Credit cards: A source of financing 111-112
Credit lines: A source of financing 110
Decision-Making 17-19
    Are you ready? 256-257

Index 285

    How to make decisions 17-19
    Learning from others 260-261
    Some conclusions you may reach 265
    Timing in decision-making 259-260
    What if you're not ready? 259-260
    Your decision-making style 18-19
Dissatisfaction with your job: Some signs 65-66
E^M, *Type* mindset 42-43, 48-49
Emotional distress after termination 126-127, 147-150
Employers: Dealing with them in termination 93-94
E^N, *Type* mindset 43-45
Emotions, keeping in check 126-127, 130
Employee
    Are You a *Type* E^M? 42-43
    Company culture: Effect on job satisfaction 51-52
    Cross-over mistakes 43-45
    Diversity as a consideration in job satisfaction 60
    Enjoying your job: Factors that will help you 59-60
    Finding your place in the corporate world 59
    Four basic options to stay employed 54-58
        Stay with current job/stay with current employer 54
        Join a new department/stay with current employer 55
        Perform the same job/join a new employer 56
        Find a new position/join a new employer 58
    Influences of your past on your career 52
    Influences of your education on your career 52
    Intrapreneuring in corporations 58
    Job dissatisfaction, causes of 65-67, 160-161
    Jobs opportunities of the future 162-164, 166-168
    Mindset of an employee 42-43
    Opportunities: How to sense them and act on them 272-274
    Preparing to leave while you're still employed 73-74
    Reasons to leave your job 66-67
    Reasons to stay in your job 64
    Skills to sharpen 161-162, 169-170
    Staying in demand 162-163, 169-170
    The right employer 59-60
    The right job: Finding a good fit 268-269
    Traits that define an employee 48-49
Employee leasing: A means to find out what you like 171
Employment contracts: Do you have one? 127-128
Entrepreneur
    Are you a *Type* E^N? 42-45, 67-69
    Basic considerations of going into your own business 222-224
    Cross-over mistakes 43-45
    Do you have what it takes? 73-74
    Executives moving from large to small companies 67-68, 69-70, 182-184
    Is it right for you? 73-74
    Mindset of an entrepreneur 43, 68-69, 72
    Preparing yourself while you are still employed 76-77, 92

286 Index

    Rewards of being an entrepreneur 67-69
    Traits that define an entrepreneur 68-69
    What it would be like to be your own boss 67-68, 88-90, 222-224
    What's stopping you from going out on your own? 78-79
Evaluating yourself: Job skills and preferences 25-33
Failure rates of new businesses 67
Family, Dealing with 246-249
    Friends and neighbors 252
    Remaining the strong leader 251
    Single mothers 251
    What to tell the kids? 247-248
    What to tell the spouse? 248-249
Family businesses 206-207
Finances (see Personal Finances)
Financial statement, personal 241-245
Forced retirement: Finding new career options 155-156
Franchises: A closer look 201-204
Friends and neighbors: How to deal with them 252
Hobby-based businesses 176-177
Home equity: A source of financing 109-110
Home-based businesses 79
Incubators, business: To help new businesses 107
Influences of your past on your career 52
Influences of your education on your career 52
Information-gathering (see Researching your Options)
Internet 102-103, 173
    Finding a job 171
    Finding financing 103, 209
Inventors as entrepreneurs 181-182
Investing in stocks 245
Job loss (see Termination) 119-127
Job opportunities of the future 162-163, 166-168
Jobs on the extinct list 164-166
Knowing Who You Are
    Influences of your past: Shaking them 36-37
    Personal profile, creating a 33-34
    Self-assessment 24-25, 33-34
    Who makes decisions for you? 69, 92
Job dissatisfaction, reasons for 49-51, 59-60
Job loss: Effects on the individual 126-127, 146-150
Job security, lack of 1-2
Lawsuits after termination 127-128
Lawyers: When you should see one 129-130
Leaving Your Job Voluntarily
    Company property: Respect for 98
    Non-compete agreements 138-139, 184-185
    Preparing by gathering information about:
        Current employer 93-97
        Finances 108-112
        Industry 107-108

Index   287

    Potential competitors 100-101
    Preparing while you still have a job 76-77, 92
    Timing 92-93
Loans: A source of financing 109
Locations: Finding the right site 228
Losing your job: Danger signals 65-66, 119-120, 122-125
Managers
    Learning new skills 162-164, 249
    Transferable skills 34, 161-162
    What skills are needed in the future? 162-164
Mergers: Impact on jobs 117-119
Minorities in business 226
Mortgage: A source of financing 109-110
Money (See Personal Finances)
    Where will the money come from? (see Owning a Business)
Office Romances 250
Owning a Business
    Angel financing 209
    Attributes of a business owner 229-230
    Bankers, dealing with 210-213
    Blind spots 219-220
    Board of Advisors 227
    Buying an existing business 197-200
        Due diligence 198-199
    Capital: How much is needed? 192-193
    Capitalize on your strengths 178
    Cash flow 193-194
    Competing against your former employer 184-185
    Defining the right business for you 189-191
    Executives from large companies, problems with 182-183
    Failure rates 67
    Family businesses 206-207
    Financing
        Customers as sources 215
        Equity Financing 216
        Suppliers as sources 214
    Franchises 201-204
    Hobby-based businesses 176-177
    Home-based businesses 79
    Ideas for businesses: Will yours work? 190-191
    Innovative career options 179
    Invention-based businesses 181-182
    Is your business idea or concept viable? 189-191
    Location: Finding the right site 228
    Minorities 226
    Myths of owning a business 229
    Naming a business 218-219
    Partnerships 208-209, 223-224
    Pitfalls of business ownership 219-220
        Blind-spots and failures 219-220

288 Index

        Con-artists 220-221
        Scams 220-221
        Unplanned events 191-192
    Psychological effects 223-224
    Resiliency: How to bounce back 271
    Retail businesses 205-206
    Size of business 217-218
    Small Office, Home Office (SOHO) 205
    Starting your own business 194-196
    Timing: When to strike out on your own 90-91
    Valuing a business 198-199
    Venture capital 107
    What business are you in? 188-189
    What it would be like? 88-90, 194-196, 223-225
    Women 226
Partnerships 208-209
Personal Finances
    Annual fiscal exam 234
    Assets, list of 238-239
    Automobiles 110-111
    Balance sheet 240-245
    Borrowing and credit 245-246
    Credit cards 111, 246
    Credit lines 110
    Credit reports 246
    Expenses: How to organize 235-236
    Home equity 109-110
    Income: How to organize 236-237
    Insurance: How to organize 237-238
    Investing in stocks 245
    Liabilities, list of 239-240
    Lifestyle 112
    Loans 109
    Loans, secured 109
    Loans, unsecured 111
    Mortgage 109-110
    Personal financial statement: How to create one 241-245
Personal financial statement 241-245
Personal profile 33
Personnel placement firms 171-172
Peter Principle 268
Planning, the importance of 225
Physical distress 126, 147-149
Psychological problems of job loss 147-149
Researching Your Options 121
    Information from sellers of companies 106-107
    Information, where to get it
        Business incubators 107
        Internet 102-103
        Library 101-102, 103-104

Index   **289**

    Newspapers 104-105
    Online 102-103
    Periodicals 103-104
    Sellers of companies 106-107
    Trade publications 105-106
    What can you learn about your employer? 93-96
Retail businesses 205-206
Retirement, forced: Finding new career options 155-157
Retraining yourself 52-53, 163-164, 169-170
Scams 220-221
Search firms 171-172
Self-assessment   25-33
Self-Engineering
    Are you a *Type E^M*? 42-43
    Are you a *Type E^N*? 42-43
    Creating your summary profile 33
    Evaluating who you are 25-33
    Shaking your past influences 36-37
Senior citizens 155-157
Severance benefits: Getting a better package 131-133
Single mothers 251-252
Skills upgrading (see Retraining yourself)
Skills, transferable 33-34, 161-162
Small Business Administration 67, 197, 215
Small Office, Home Office (SOHO) 205
Spending sprees after termination 250
Spouse, dealing with 248-249
Stress, dealing with 126, 146-149
Takeovers: Its impact on jobs 138
Termination
    Anger 126, 250-251
    Company property 98
    Danger signals 119-120
    Do's and don'ts 128-129
    Employment contracts 127-128
    Hush-hush reasons for termination 123-124
    Hush money 135
    Is your job a candidate for termination? 120-121
    Is your job safe? 120-121
    Job loss: Effects on the individual 126-127
    Lawsuits 127-128
    Lawyers: Should you see one? 129-130
    Leaving voluntarily (See Leaving Voluntarily)
    Negotiation pointers 136-137
    Non-compete agreements 138-139
    Preparing for termination 138-140
    Questions to ask 128-129
    Reasons for termination 122-124
    Settlements 131-133, 134
    Severance benefits: Getting a better package 94-96, 96-97, 131-133

Takeovers: Its impact on jobs 138
Timing 94-96
Warning signals 119-120
What employers may not do 127-128
What to do before your last day 116, 140-141
What you're entitled to 131-133, 135
When to see a lawyer 129-130
Wrongful termination 134-135

Termination, Day After
Becoming an outsider 146
Do's and don'ts 150-153
Early retirement 155-156
Feelings: Are they normal? 146-147, 151-153
Forced retirement 155-156
Getting started again 153-154
Over 55 155-156
Physical and emotional distress 147-149, 250
Planning your time 154-155
Stress, tension and distress 147-149
Typical reactions 146-147
What to do? 150-153, 153-154

Timing of terminations 94-96
Type E^M (see E^M) 42-43
Type E^N (see E^N) 43-45
Vengeance following termination 153
Whistleblowers 137-138
Women 226
    As entrepreneurs 73-74
    Single mothers 251-252
    Termination issues 250
Wrongful termination 134-135

REGISTRATION FORM

Make a copy of this page, complete it and mail or fax to us at:
The Vanalden Press
9755 Independence Avenue
Chatsworth, CA 91311-4318

Fax: (818) 407-0850

Or visit our web site at **http://www.vanaldenpress.com**

Register with us and you will be on our mailing list to receive information about our projects dealing with *Entrepreneur or Employee?* issues.

_____
Name

_____   _____
Street Address   P.O. Box No.

_____

_____
City, State, Zip

_____
Phone

_____   _____
Fax   e-mail address

If you have friends, relatives or co-workers who would benefit from learning about our projects, please pass along their names to us.

_____   _____
Name/Title   Name/Title

_____ _____   _____ _____
Street Address   P.O. Box No.   Street Address   P.O. Box No.

_____   _____

_____   _____
City, State, Zip   City, State, Zip

_____   _____
Phone   Phone

_____   _____
Fax   Fax

_____   _____
e-mail address   e-mail address

IT'S EASY TO ORDER...
For Friends, Associates, Clients, Co-workers and for Gift-Giving

CALL 1-800-552-0899
8 A.M. - 4 P.M. Pacific Time
Monday - Friday
Have your credit card ready
Outside U.S. & Canada, call (818) 885-6636

FAX (818) 407-0850
24 Hours a Day
Make a photocopy of this page and complete the order form below

MAIL TO:
The Vanalden Press
9755 Independence Avenue
Chatsworth, CA 91311-4318
U.S.A.

INTERNET:
http://www.vanaldenpress.com

1. ORDERED BY (Please Print)

Name/Title

Company Name

Street Address   P.O. Box No.

City, State, Zip

Phone

Fax   e-mail address

2. SHIP TO (Please Print)

Name/Title

Company Name

Street Address   P.O. Box No.

City, State, Zip

Phone

Fax   e-mail address

3. PAYMENT INFORMATION

☐ Check or money order enclosed (Make payable in U.S. Funds to: **The Vanalden Press**)
☐ VISA   ☐ MasterCard   ☐ Discover   ☐ American Express

1	2	3	4	5	6	7	8	9	10	11	12	13	14	15	16	Month	Year

Expiration Date

Signature

Name as it appears on credit card

Address where you receive your credit card statements

City, State, Zip

4. YOUR ORDER

QUANTITY		PRICE EACH	TOTAL AMOUNT
	ENTREPRENEUR OR EMPLOYEE? Should You Get Out Or Stay In Your Current Job?	$23.95 U.S.	
		Merchandise Total	
		California shipments add $1.98 sales tax per book	
		Shipping & Handling (See chart at left)	
		TOTAL	

SHIPPING & HANDLING
U.S. - $4.95 per book
Canada - $7.95 per book
All other countries - Call or fax for rates